BIG CITY ELECTIONS IN

MW01516412

Edited by Jack Lucas and R. Michael McGregor

Local elections are an increasingly popular area of research among scholars of Canadian political behaviour, offering invaluable insights into the attitudes and motivations of Canadian electors. The Canadian Municipal Election Study (CMES) has collected unparalleled individual-level survey data in eight major Canadian municipal elections: Vancouver, Calgary, Winnipeg, London, Mississauga, Toronto, Montreal, and Quebec City. These elections, which took place in 2017 and 2018, were high-profile, contentious, and often surprising, featuring mayoral defeats, record-breaking turnouts, provincial-municipal tensions, and the first ranked-ballot election in Canada in decades.

Combining unprecedented individual-level survey data from the CMES with local expertise from political scientists across Canada, *Big City Elections in Canada* provides a data-driven overview of each election, while also highlighting the more general lessons the elections teach us about municipal politics and voting behaviour. The chapters in this book make substantial empirical and theoretical contributions to the voting behaviour and urban political science subfields and will appeal to students, journalists, and engaged citizens who are interested in learning more about municipal elections in their cities.

JACK LUCAS is an associate professor in the Department of Political Science at the University of Calgary.

R. MICHAEL McGREGOR is an associate professor in the Department of Politics and Public Administration at Ryerson University.

Big City Elections in Canada

**EDITED BY JACK LUCAS
AND R. MICHAEL McGREGOR**

UNIVERSITY OF TORONTO PRESS
Toronto Buffalo London

© University of Toronto Press 2021
Toronto Buffalo London
utorontopress.com
Printed in the U.S.A.

ISBN 978-1-4875-2855-3 (cloth)   ISBN 978-1-4875-2858-4 (EPUB)
ISBN 978-1-4875-2856-0 (paper)   ISBN 978-1-4875-2857-7 (PDF)

_____

Library and Archives Canada Cataloguing in Publication

Title: Big city elections in Canada / edited by Jack Lucas and
    R. Michael McGregor.
Names: Lucas, Jack, 1982–, editor. | McGregor, R. Michael, editor.
Description: Includes bibliographical references and index.
Identifiers: Canadiana (print) 20210233036 | Canadiana (ebook) 20210233249 |
    ISBN 9781487528553 (cloth) | ISBN 9781487528560 (paper) |
    ISBN 9781487528584 (EPUB) | ISBN 9781487528577 (PDF)
Subjects: LCSH: Local elections – Canada. | LCSH: Municipal government –
    Canada. | LCSH: Voting – Canada. | LCSH: Voting research – Canada.
Classification: LCC JS1718.3 .B54 2021 | DDC 324.971 – dc23

_____

This book has been published with the help of a grant from the Federation
for the Humanities and Social Sciences, through the Awards to Scholarly
Publications Program, using funds provided by the Social Sciences and
Humanities Research Council of Canada.

University of Toronto Press acknowledges the financial assistance to its
publishing program of the Canada Council for the Arts and the Ontario Arts
Council, an agency of the Government of Ontario.

ONTARIO ARTS COUNCIL
CONSEIL DES ARTS DE L'ONTARIO
an Ontario government agency
un organisme du gouvernement de l'Ontario

Canada Council   Conseil des Arts
for the Arts   du Canada

Funded by the   Financé par le
Government   gouvernement
of Canada   du Canada

Canada

To our favourite future big city electors: Hannah, Zoe, Maddy, Margot, and Marion.

Contents

Figures

Tables

Acknowledgments

From the beginning, the Canadian Municipal Election Study has been a team effort. We are grateful to our CMES colleagues (Cameron Anderson, Eric Bélanger, Sandra Breux, Scott Matthews, Anne Mévellec, Aaron Moore, Scott Pruysers, Laura Stephenson, and Erin Tolley) for their contributions to all aspects of the project, including the chapters in this volume. We are also indebted to Helen Hayes and Eric Lum for their outstanding research assistance with this project.

The CMES, and this volume, would not have been possible were it not for generous financial support from the Social Sciences and Humanities Research Council (Insight Grant number 435-2017-0993) and the Government of Ontario (Early Research Award number: ER17-13-035).

We are also extremely thankful for the meticulous and gracious work of this volume's reviewers, and of our editor at the University of Toronto Press, Daniel Quinlan.

Finally, we are grateful to the more than 14,000 residents of eight of Canada's largest cities, who took the time to answer our questions.

BIG CITY ELECTIONS IN CANADA

1 Local Elections in Canada

JACK LUCAS AND R. MICHAEL McGREGOR

Contrary to what the famous catechism suggests, Canadians live in more than two "political worlds." Besides participating in federal and provincial contests, Canadians vote in countless *local* elections: for mayor or reeve, city council, borough mayor and council, regional chair and council, school board, and park board, as well as referendums and ballot initiatives on issues ranging from local land-use planning to nuclear disarmament.[1] Canadians thus make more voting decisions locally than they do at any other level. This is a "political world" different from any other we inhabit.

The world of local elections deserves our attention for several reasons. First, as we will explain below, local elections are remarkably different from their federal and provincial counterparts. Second, cities are valuable laboratories for academic learning, allowing us to explore how Canadian voters make important political decisions under highly variable institutional and electoral circumstances. Finally, and most simply, the vast majority of elections in Canada are held at the local level; even if we exclude school boards and other local special-purpose bodies, municipalities account for 99.6% of all governments and 95.8% of all politicians in Canada.[2] The study of local elections and electors is vital for understanding how Canadian voters think and behave.

Unlike federal and provincial elections, local elections in Canada require voters to make several decisions – mayor, councillor, school board trustee, and so on – all at the same time. This is not the only respect in which local elections are distinctive. The issues, institutions, and political personalities that shape individual attitudes and behaviour at the municipal level are also distinct. In contrast to federal and provincial elections, most local elections are non-partisan, incumbency rates are significantly higher, and non-traditional electoral systems (at-large districts, ranked ballot elections) and voting methods (internet and telephone) are common. Many important research questions can therefore only be studied by looking locally.

There is also evidence that Canadians themselves view local elections differently than provincial or federal elections. Data from the Canadian Municipal Election Study (CMES) – our core data source for this book, which we will describe in more detail below – suggest that Canadians themselves think differently about local elections. When we asked respondents how interested they were in municipal politics on a scale from 0 (low) to 10 (high), the average value was 6.22. When asked about federal and provincial politics, their average responses were 7.3 and 7.03, respectively.[3] We also asked respondents how much of an impact the three levels of government had upon their lives; 87.4% said that the municipal had either "a lot" or "some" effect (as compared to "not very much" or "none"). While this figure is high, it is lower than the corresponding values for the provincial (93.1%) and federal (89.3%) governments.[4] Our respondents were also less likely to believe that participating in local elections is a democratic duty, as opposed to a choice: 70.8% of CMES participants viewed municipal voting as a duty, compared to 80.2% at the federal level and 77.8% provincially.[5] Most respondents were therefore less interested in local politics, believed it affected them less, and were less likely to feel duty-bound to participate in local elections.

These differences across levels of government are substantively important and valuable for academic research. Differences *between* municipalities, however, may be even more revealing. Cities vary from one another in countless ways: turnout rates, electoral systems, governance structures, socio-demographic diversity, economic conditions, and the presence or absence of local political parties. This variation provides an opportunity to explore the effects of a variety of institutional and contextual factors on the Canadian elector. Municipalities serve as important laboratories for the field of political behaviour, providing an opportunity to consider questions that would not be possible to answer using federal or provincial data.

Fortunately, then, the study of municipal political behaviour is enjoying somewhat of a *naissance* within academia, and Canadian researchers are at the forefront of this growing subfield. Rapid advances in data collection and dissemination mean that scholars are now able to ask and answer important new questions about local voters and elections, and as a result, as we discuss below, the literature on the subject is evolving quickly.

The purpose of this volume is to work toward closing the long-standing gap between research on municipal elections and their provincial and federal "cousins" (Cutler and Matthews, 2005), leveraging data from eight very different Canadian cities to provide insights into how Canadian electors reason and behave politically. We use data from the Canadian Municipal Election Study (CMES), which collected survey responses from nearly 15,000 urban residents in eight of Canada's largest cities during municipal elections in 2017 and 2018. Our goal is to provide both breadth and depth: breadth of comparative analysis across all eight city elections, alongside more focused and in-depth analyses of the distinctive features of each city in the CMES study.

The State and Direction of the Literature

For years, the opening sentences in studies of Canadian local elections and voting behaviour were filled with lamentation. Kushner et al.'s (1997, p. 539) claim that "students of Canadian voting behaviour traditionally have directed most of their attention toward elections at federal and provincial levels" is a characteristic observation, as is Cutler and Matthews's (2005, p. 359) description of municipal elections as "poor cousins" in the field of political behaviour. Hannah Stanwick lamented that studies of mayoral elections are "virtually non-existent" (2000, p. 549). More generally, Taylor and Eidelman (2010, p. 305) followed American policy scholars in referring to the field of Canadian urban politics as a "black hole"; Andrew Sancton once called it an "academic ghetto" (Sancton 1983, p. 310). Writing a dozen years after Kushner and colleagues' study, Dostie-Goulet et al. (2012, p. 909) noted that "les choses n'ont pas beaucoup change depuis" – things haven't changed much since then.

There are several reasons why local elections have received little attention compared to provincial and federal contests. The first, and perhaps most obvious, is simply that municipal contests are local and generally lower-profile affairs, attracting less attention from citizens and scholars alike. While many political scientists and engaged citizens pay attention to federal elections, and a substantial number pay attention to provincial elections outside their province, attention to municipal elections outside one's own city is rare. Second, researchers may be hesitant to study local elections due to concerns about the generalizability of their research. Research on federal or provincial elections often involves findings that apply to tens of millions of eligible voters. Given the significant variation across Canada's municipalities, results from single-city studies may not travel as well. Though some scholars see great value in careful examinations of single cities, others may worry that concerns of generalizability will limit the reach and interest of their findings.

A third explanation for the relative scarcity of studies of local elections, which we expect has had the greatest effect, has to do with the availability of the individual-level data necessary to confidently draw conclusions about electors. Canadian Election Study (CES) data, which have formed the basis of hundreds of articles and books since the 1960s, are collected by a team of experienced researchers who make their data publicly available for use by others. Until recently, the costs involved in undertaking similar studies at the municipal level – which traditionally involved extremely expensive face-to-face and telephone interviews – made similar municipal election studies prohibitively expensive. In the past few years, however, it has become much easier to conduct surveys via the internet, and to do so in a way that is both cost effective and rigorous.

Recently, then, things *have* begun to change. In the pages that follow, we explain how the literature in the field of Canadian local elections research has evolved in recent years along four dimensions: (1) quantity, (2) content, (3) data and methods, and (4) geography. In doing so, we suggest that the words of Kushner and colleagues (and their successors) are no longer as true as they once were.

The most obvious advance in the field is simply the *volume* of research on Canadian municipal elections that has appeared in recent years. A survey of articles published since 2000 in the *Canadian Journal of Political Science* (CJPS) provides a simple indicator of the relative popularity of work in the fields of federal, provincial, and municipal voting behaviour.[6] This analysis suggests that municipal elections do receive less attention from scholars, but also that the gap between municipal and other elections is closing. Between 2000 and 2019, the *CJPS* published a total of 96 articles on the subject of Canadian voting behaviour; most examined a single level (federal, provincial, or municipal), though some addressed multiple levels of government. Of the 96 works published in this period, 69 focused on the federal level,[7] 30 on the provinces[8], and 17 on municipal elections and/or voters.[9] Only 11 articles were focused exclusively on the municipal level. However, while Dostie-Goulet et al. (2012) are correct that the literature on municipal political behaviour remains more modest than for federal and provincial elections, the frequency of studies on local elections is increasing. Six CJPS articles were published on municipal elections and voting between 2000 and 2009, but 11 were produced between 2010 to 2019. Though municipal elections still receive less attention than provincial or federal elections, the gap appears to be closing.

The field of Canadian municipal voting behaviour is also expanding in terms of content. Early studies concentrated largely on two subjects: the characteristics of successful candidates, and the role of gender in local electoral success. Thus much of the earliest work focused on the features that were associated with candidate success – such as incumbency, gender, spending, and electoral district types (Kushner et al., 1997;Kushner et al., 2001).

Gender has long been a topic of special interest at the local level, motivated by claims that "local government has traditionally been considered more accessible to women" (Gidengil and Vengross, 1997, p. 514). There are several reasons for this claim; for instance, local positions are often part-time and do not involve relocating, which may make local elected positions compatible with familial responsibilities, of which women still bear a disproportionate share. It has also been thought that the nonpartisan character of local elections, and their minimal barriers to entry, may encourage women to participate. Nevertheless, the most recent research finds that women remain underrepresented at the local level (Lucas et al. 2021, Tolley, 2011), except in the case of school boards, where they slightly outperform their share of the population (Davidson et al., 2020).

Though these topics are certainly important and worthy of continued study (see Spicer et al., 2017; Breux et al., 2019), scholars of municipal political behaviour have broadened their focus dramatically. Much of the early work in the field focused on City Council candidates, but mayoral elections have drawn increasing attention (Cutler and Matthews, 2005; McGregor et al., 2016; McGregor et al., 2021), as have school boards (McGregor and Lucas, 2019). Studies of turnout (McGregor, 2016; Breux et al., 2017) and vote choice (Cutler and Matthews, 2005; McGregor et al., 2016; Taylor et al., 2017) are increasingly common – the questions of why electors choose to vote (or not) and why they choose a particular candidate are two fundamental puzzles of political behaviour. In this respect, the literature on local elections is becoming more similar to work on federal and provincial elections.

Many recent studies also focus on the unique features of local elections within the Canadian system. The special power of incumbency at the local level has been a subject of repeated investigation (Moore et al., 2017; Taylor and McEleney, 2017; Lucas, 2020a), as have the effects of the absence of party cues on the role played by other informational shortcuts such as gender, ethnicity, incumbency, and familial ties (see Bird et al., 2016; McGregor et al., 2017; Stephenson et al., 2018). Only at the local level are multiple elections held concurrently in Canada, and researchers have begun to explore how Canadians make decisions in this distinctive context (McGregor, 2016; McGregor and Lucas, 2020; Anderson and McGregor, forthcoming; Tessier and McGregor, forthcoming). Researchers have also explored the consequences of distinctive electoral systems at the municipal level in Canada, including at-large and ward elections (Spicer et al., 2017) and the history of electoral reform in

Canadian cities (Lucas, 2020b). Finally, hundreds of Canadian municipalities employ internet voting, and the topic has received a great deal of attention, particularly as it pertains to effects upon voter participation (Goodman, 2014; Goodman et al., 2018; Goodman and Stokes, 2020).

Scholars have been able to study these various topics in part due to advances in the quality and availability of data – a third respect in which the literature in the municipal elections subfield has changed in recent years. An important component of this evolution has been a new focus on individual-level data from voters themselves. While aggregate election results and candidate-level data continue to be used in studies of municipal political careers (Lucas and Sayers, 2018), voting behaviour (Couture et al., 2014; Siemiatycki and Marshall, 2014; Breux et al., 2017), and incumbency advantage (Lucas, 2020a), the availability of survey research on municipal attitudes and behaviour has clearly led to a marked shift in the data sources that political scientists are using to understand Canadian municipal elections.

Election studies typically rely on individual-level data, collected via surveys like the Canadian Election Study, which has been conducted in nearly every federal election since the 1960s. At the provincial level, studies such as the Comparative Provincial Election Project and the Making Electoral Democracy Work Project have included large-scale surveys of electors. Until recently, however, such studies have not existed at the local level. Cutler and Matthews were the first to conduct a Canadian municipal election survey, in Vancouver in 2002.[10] The 2014 Toronto election was the subject of multiple large surveys (see Schatten et al., 2015; McGregor et al., 2016; Kiss et al., 2020), and tens of thousands of online voters in Ontario participated in an online survey in 2014 about their attitudes toward internet voting in local elections (see Goodman et al., 2018). The Canadian Municipal Election Study is the largest study of voters and non-voters yet, but it is one that builds upon and has been inspired by a number of previous Canadian studies.

Finally, the subfield of Canadian municipal elections and behaviour is growing geographically. Municipalities in Quebec have long been well-represented, due in part to readily available municipal election data through Élections Québec, but also due to the existence of a devoted group of political scientists who have worked diligently to understand the dynamics and idiosyncrasies of municipal elections in that province. In other provinces, municipal clerks are responsible for maintaining election data, and researchers must rely on archival sources or direct contact with clerks to obtain election results and other information. This paucity of data is beginning to come to an end, as local election data are being posted in accessible formats online, aggregated by organizations such as the Association of Municipalities of Ontario, and collected and disseminated by research projects such as the Canadian Municipal Barometer. Quebec remains a significant focus of scholars in this subfield (see, for instance, Breux and Bherer, 2011; Dostie-Goulet et al., 2012; Chisson and Mévellec, 2014; Breux et al., 2016; Bélanger et al., forthcoming; along with an entire special issue of the *Canadian Journal of Urban Research* in 2014 on municipal elections in Quebec).

At the same time, cities in other provinces are increasingly well-represented in the field. Outside of Quebec, Ontario has traditionally received the most attention; in addition to earlier works on Ontario cities by Kushner et al. (1997) and Stanwick (2000), a number of researchers have more recently published papers about political attitudes and behaviour in Ontario cities (McGregor & Spicer, 2016; Goodman and Lucas, 2016; Spicer et al., 2017; Goodman et al., 2018). The 2010 and 2014 Toronto elections also received considerable research attention (see Schatten et al., 2015; Silver et al., 2020; Kiss et al., 2020; and a number of pieces from the Toronto Election Study, including McGregor et al., 2016; Bird et al., 2016; Anderson et al., 2017; and Caruana et al., 2018). Outside of Quebec and Ontario, Western Canadian cities have received increasing attention since Cutler and Matthews's (2005) foundational study (Lucas 2020a, 2020b). Finally, the Canadian Municipal Election Study, described in more detail below, considers eight large cities, six of them outside Quebec. With the noteworthy and unfortunate exception of cities in the Atlantic provinces, the recent geographic growth of the municipal elections subfield has been substantial.

While no longer in its infancy, the literature on local political behaviour in Canada remains in its adolescence. Canadian researchers are paying more attention to local elections, studying new topics, using more sophisticated data, and exploring an ever-increasing number of cities. Still, the fact remains that there is markedly less academic research on elections and voters at the local level than on the other political "worlds" we inhabit. We see this as an opportunity rather than a cause for concern. Given the number and variety of cases available to researchers, the local level is, without a doubt, the most fertile ground for Canadian political behaviour researchers. The chapters in this volume take advantage of this opportunity and represent important contributions to this growing field.

The Canadian Municipal Election Study

Each of the chapters in this book is based primarily on data from the Canadian Municipal Election Study, the largest individual-level academic study of municipal elections ever undertaken anywhere in the world. The purpose of the CMES is to generate the individual-level data required to study a wide variety of questions about local electors in Canada. The cornerstone of the project is a survey of eligible voters in eight Canadian cities that held elections in 2017 and 2018: Calgary, Montreal, Quebec City, Vancouver, London, Mississauga, Toronto, and Winnipeg.[11] In each city, the CMES research team collected data in a two-stage panel, with one questionnaire before Election Day and one questionnaire shortly after Election Day. The total N for the pre-election survey was 14,458, while 9,409 respondents completed the post-election questionnaire.[12] Data were primarily collected for academic use, though there were some limited data releases to media during elections in Calgary (Fletcher, 2017), Toronto (Ogilvie, 2018), and Winnipeg (Santin, 2018).

CMES surveys were modelled on previous federal and provincial election studies, while also taking into consideration the distinctive characteristics of municipal government in our eight case cities. Thus while standard questions on attitudes toward candidates, orientations toward politics, and the socio-demographic characteristics of candidates themselves are included, so too are questions about council, borough, and school board elections, local issues and media consumption, and measures of attachment to one's city. Some questions with particular relevance to one city were included only in that city's survey, but most questions were included in multiple surveys to allow for comparison across cases. Appendix I contains a complete list of the CMES survey questions that we draw on in this book.

CMES survey participants completed their surveys online. Participants were recruited in two ways. Most respondents (roughly 75%) were recruited via random digit dialing (RDD) by telephone and then connected to an operator, who, after confirming survey eligibility, collected an email address to which a survey link was sent. In some cities, pressures of time and cost meant that the RDD sample was supplemented by an additional pool of respondents from an existing online panel.[13] Recruiting new respondents via telephone was a necessity, since, with the exception of the very largest cities in the study, data providers are unable to access the number of respondents required for an election survey of this type – they simply do not have enough existing panelists to do so. Forum Research Incorporated was responsible for the recruitment of respondents and the administration of the surveys.

Canada's Big Cities

Of the thousands of municipalities in Canada, this volume focuses on the eight cities included in the Canadian Municipal Election Study, each of which held a municipal election in 2017 or 2018: Calgary, Montreal, Quebec City, Vancouver, London, Mississauga, Toronto, and Winnipeg. These cities are among the largest in the country, containing nearly one quarter (24.6%) of the Canadian population. A staggering 2.4 million votes were cast in the eight elections in this study, and together, the winning mayoral candidates received 1.3 million votes: more than the total number of votes received by the winning party in the most recent provincial elections in British Columbia, Alberta, Saskatchewan, and Manitoba – and four times more votes than all of the winning parties in the Maritime provinces combined. The mayors of these eight cities represent some of the largest constituencies in the country; Toronto and Montreal each have larger populations than six Canadian provinces. With 479,659 ballots cast in his favour in 2018, Toronto mayor John Tory received more votes than any single candidate in Canadian history at any level of government. Tory also received more votes than did any party's candidates in Toronto's ridings in the 2018 provincial election: he was elected by more voters in Toronto than Doug Ford's Conservatives (363,337 votes), Andrea Horwath's NDP (400,846 votes), or Kathleen Wynne's Liberals (287,129 votes). These may be *different* worlds than the ones we commonly study in the political science of elections and voting, but they are certainly not small ones.

Though these cities are among Canada's largest, population was not the only factor that led to their inclusion in the CMES. Besides providing analytically useful variation across a number of dimensions, each city is worthy of study for its own sake, and each provides an opportunity to explore questions about Canadian voting behaviour that can really only be answered at the local level. Though each chapter's authors provide a vivid description of their case city, we see value in providing readers here with a glimpse of what makes each city's election distinctive.

Calgary was the first major city in North America to elect a Muslim mayor, Naheed Nenshi. Nenshi's surprising victory in 2010 was remarkable, as has been his dominance since then (he has now been elected three times). Facing difficult economic headwinds in 2018, he was able to retain his office despite facing off against a well-funded conservative challenger – Bill Smith, former president of the Progressive Conservative Party of Alberta. The 2018 election saw the highest voter turnout in Calgary since the Second World War.

Montreal similarly saw an incumbent mayor, Denis Coderre, seeking re-election in 2017. In Montreal, however, the mayor lost his position. Valérie Plante, a one-term city councillor representing a left-wing party, Projét Montréal, accomplished a rare feat in the world of municipal politics by unseating the incumbent. Montreal's election was one of the three in this volume where municipal political parties were present. Montreal is also noteworthy for the complex structure of its city government, which includes not only city mayor and council, but also analogous positions for the city's many boroughs (or *arrondissements*). Plante's party took control of City Council as well as most boroughs.

The story in nearby Quebec City was altogether different. Here, incumbent Régis Labeaume won his fourth election, besting his nearest competitor by nearly 28 points. "King Régis," as he is occasionally called, also saw his party win 17 of 21 seats on council. Surprisingly, given this uncompetitive victory, turnout in the Quebec City election was the second highest of any in the CMES, at nearly 51%. Elections and government in Quebec City are structured by parties, but the city does not share Montreal's complex borough structure.

The first CMES city to hold its election in 2018 was Vancouver. Though that city has a well-established party system, two of the top three mayoral candidates, including winner Kennedy Stewart, chose to run as independents. After 10 years in office, incumbent Gregor Robertson from Vision Vancouver had chosen not to seek re-election. Stewart, a former NDP MP, won by a hair (just 0.6 points) over Ken Sim of the right-wing Non-Partisan Association. Vancouver's local elections are unique within the CMES in that city councillors are elected at-large rather than in wards, meaning that the mayor and councillors represent the same city-wide constituency.

With a population of less than 400,000, London is the smallest city in the CMES and only the 15th-largest in the country. The "Forest City" is noteworthy for the fact that in 2018, London was the first Canadian city in many decades to employ a ranked ballot electoral system.[14] The mayoral election did not have an incumbent: Mayor Matt Brown had chosen not to run again following an extra-marital affair with councillor and former deputy mayor Maureen Cassidy. This open mayoral race, which attracted a number of noteworthy candidates, was won by former Conservative MP Ed Holder on the 14th round of counting.

Just down Highway 401 in Toronto, another former Conservative politician, John Tory, was handily re-elected as mayor of the country's largest city. Tory was first elected in 2014, a year he faced strong candidates to his right (Doug Ford) and his left (Olivia Chow). In 2018, only one noteworthy challenger emerged – former chief city planner Jennifer Keesmaat. Keesmaat had registered as a candidate on the nomination deadline in response to dramatic and last-minute changes imposed on the city by Doug Ford's Conservative provincial government. Tory won handily, increasing his margin of victory from less than 7 points in 2014 to nearly 40 in 2018.

Next to Toronto is Mississauga, the country's sixth most populous city. Mississauga's elections are perhaps best-known for the 36-year tenure of popular former mayor Hazel McCallion. "Hurricane Hazel" resigned prior to the 2014 election, in which she endorsed eventual winner Bonnie Crombie. In 2018, Crombie faced no significant challengers and was re-elected by an overwhelming margin of victory of more than 63 points. Mississauga's 2018 municipal election also featured an abysmally low rate of voter turnout, at 27.4% – unsurprising perhaps, given the uncompetitive election, but still notable in one of Canada's largest cities.

Winnipeg is the eighth and final city included in the CMES. The city's 2018 election was a rather unremarkable affair, with middling turnout. Incumbent mayor Brian Bowman was returned to office following a convincing win over a right-wing challenger, Jenny Motkaluk. The case is notable, however, because of a plebiscite that was held concurrently with the municipal elections. Winnipeggers were asked whether one of Canada's most famous intersections, Portage Avenue and Main Street, should be opened to street-level pedestrian crossing. Voters soundly rejected the change, even though Bowman has been a long-time supporter of pedestrian access.

Our eight cities also have other features worthy of attention. Table 1.1 includes some addition contextual data on each of our cases. The table includes information on the winner of the 2017–18 election, whether an incumbent mayor contested the race (and if so, whether that person won), and whether parties were present or not. It also provides information on the competitive dynamics of the race, such as the effective number of mayoral candidates (Laakso and Taagepera, 1979), the margin of victory, and voter turnout rate.[15]

Structure and Organization

This volume is structured by city: each chapter focuses on a single election and is written by experts on the city under discussion. This allows the authors to provide rich detail and context on their respective elections and to focus their attention on research questions that are especially well-suited to their case city. Chapters are organized chronologically by election date.

A principal goal for this book was to enable our authors to undertake a detailed analysis of their case cities while also enabling readers to see important points of similarity and difference across the eight cities. To this end, each chapter's authors have divided their chapters into three consistent sections: an election narrative, a mayoral vote choice analysis, and a more focused thematic analysis.

Table 1.1. City characteristics

City	Winner	Incumbent present/ victorious?	Parties present?	Effective number of mayoral candidates	Margin of victory (percentage points)	Voter turnout (%)
Calgary	Naheed Nenshi	Yes/Yes	No	2.2	7.7	58.1
Montreal*	Valérie Plante	Yes/No	Yes	2.1	5.8	42.3
Quebec	Régis Labeaume	Yes/Yes	Yes	2.5	27.6	50.9
Vancouver†	Kennedy Stewart	No	Yes	4.7	0.6	39.4
London‡	Ed Holder	No	No	4.1	17.6	40.0
Mississauga	Bonnie Crombie	Yes/Yes	No	1.6	63.2	27.4
Toronto	John Tory	Yes/Yes	No	2.2	39.9	40.9
Winnipeg§	Brian Bowman	Yes/Yes	No	2.4	17.6	42.3

* Borough council elections held concurrently.

† At-large council elections.

‡ Ranked ballots.

§ Plebiscite held concurrently.

In the first section of each chapter – the election narrative – our authors provide a data-driven overview of the election in their case cities, including information on the major candidates and issues in the election – we compare the importance of a number of issues across all cities, but also consider some city-specific issues.[16] Each chapter provides a detailed overview of the election outcome in both the mayoral and the council/borough elections, as well as a map of the winning mayoral candidate's vote share across the city. The authors use CMES data, along with media accounts, public opinion polls, and their own observations to provide a rich summary of what happened in the election in their case city.

In the second section of each chapter, our authors examine the correlates of mayoral vote choice in their case cities. In each chapter, the variable of interest in this second section is the respondent's mayoral vote, with a consistent set of predictor variables in every chapter to allow for easy comparison. These predictors fall into four types. The first are sociodemographic characteristics, which are often associated with individual vote choice across levels of government in Canada (Blais et al., 2002; Gidengil et al., 2012). Second, to understand the role of ideology in local vote choice, we include indices of social and economic ideology.[17] These variables provide valuable insight into long-standing debates about the role of ideology in local elections Bherer, 2006; Belley and Lavigne, 2008, McGregor et al., 2016). Next, we include a measure of retrospective economic evaluations. Prior research has shown that, even at the

Table 1.2. Topics in final "focused analysis" section of each chapter

Chapter	City	Authors	Topic
2	Calgary	Lucas and Santos	The role of partisanship in non-partisan elections
3	Montreal	Bélanger and Daoust	How prospective voting shapes mayoral votes
4	Quebec	Couture and Breux	Third-party emergence in municipal politics
5	Vancouver	De Rooij et al.	Social pressure and attitudes toward housing
6	London	Anderson and Stephenson	The effects of ranked ballots
7	Mississauga	Tolley and Rayment	Diversity and representation
8	Toronto	McGregor and Pruysers	Coalitions of mayoral support, 2014–18
9	Winnipeg	Moore	Local plebiscites and municipal voter turnout

municipal level, where mayors might be thought to have relatively few economic levers, economic evaluations can influence decisions regarding whether to punish or reward incumbent candidates (Anderson et al., 2017; Bélanger and Tessier, forthcoming). Finally, because issues have been found to influence local vote choice (Cutler and Matthews, 2005; McGregor et al., 2016), we include a battery of issue importance variables (allowing for some variation to account for contextual differences between cities). A series of four models are included for each city, with variables being added in a step-wise fashion, in order to develop a thorough understanding of the relationship between each variable and mayoral vote choice. Note that we present full model results in Appendix II. This consistency across cities allows for useful insights within each case city while also allowing us to identify the variables that predict vote choice consistently across cities. We return to a detailed discussion of this analysis in our concluding chapter.

In the third and final section of each chapter, our authors pursue research questions that take advantage of distinctive characteristics of their case cities to provide broader lessons for scholars of urban politics and political behaviour. These analyses allow us to better understand each individual case, while also providing general insights into the attitudes and behaviour of the Canadian municipal voter. We have provided a list of the themes of these focused final sections in Table 1.2.

Preview of Coming Attractions

In chapter 2, Jack Lucas and John Santos explore the surprisingly competitive re-election of Mayor Naheed Nenshi in Calgary. The challenger in that election, Bill Smith, was a former president of the Progressive Conservative Party of Alberta, and the authors conclude their chapter with an analysis of how perceptions of the provincial partisanship of mayoral candidates bled into voters' calculus. They suggest that despite the officially non-partisan character of local politics in Calgary, the city's mayoral election retained "a considerable partisan flavor."

In chapter 3, Éric Bélanger and Jean-François Daoust describe the fascinating case of Montreal, which has a complex system of concurrent elections for both city and borough councils. The Montreal election is also noteworthy for being the only one in this volume in which the incumbent mayor was defeated. Bélanger and Daoust conclude the chapter with an analysis of the role of prospective voting – expectations about who might win the election – on Valérie Plante's success in unseating Denis Coderre.

In chapter 4, Jérôme Couture and Sandra Breux examine Régis Labeaume's commanding mayoral victory in Quebec City. That race also saw the rise of a new party, Québec 21. Couture and Breux assess the relevance of Maurice Pinard's (1971, 1973) famous theory of third-party emergence for understanding Québec 21's success – that party was founded just months prior to the 2017 election, yet it finished second in both the mayoral and council races. The authors find the election results to be largely congruent with Pinard's theory. First, the mayoral race was extremely uncompetitive – the incumbent, Régis Labeaume, won by nearly 28 points – which is one of Pinard's criteria for the rise of a third party. The other criterion, dissatisfaction among the population, was also present. Still, these conditions were not strong enough to see Québec 21 surpass Démocratie Québec to become the strongest opponent to Labeaume and his party.

In chapter 5, we move from 2017 to 2018, with Eline de Rooij, Scott Matthews, and Mark Pickup's analysis of the municipal election in Vancouver. Given that they face the most expensive housing market in Canada, it is unsurprising that, according to CMES data, Vancouverites rank affordability as the most important election issue. De Rooij and colleagues conducted a unique survey experiment designed to uncover the effects of the affordability issue on attitudes and behaviour. They report that Vancouverites responded to social pressure to conform to perceived norms among those with the same political identity as themselves. This provides insight into a mechanism through which attitudes on this important issue are manifested.

In chapter 6, which focuses on London, Ontario, Cameron Anderson and Laura Stephenson discuss a mayoral race that included four major candidates. As noted earlier, London is currently the only city in Canada with a ranked ballot electoral system, which it used for the first time in 2018. The authors consider how the election might have turned out under the previous, single-member plurality electoral system. They also consider how the electoral reform affected perceptions of the election outcome.

In chapter 7, Erin Tolley and Erica Rayment examine Mississauga, one of Canada's most important "majority-minority" cities (half of the city's population is "racialized"). The authors discuss the extremely uncompetitive mayoral race, in which incumbent Bonnie Crombie faced no real opposition, and note that 2018 was the first time that a non-white councillor was ever elected in Mississauga. They consider the disconnect between the city's diverse population and the distinct lack of diversity on City Council.

In chapter 8, which turns to neighbouring Toronto, Michael McGregor and Scott Pruysers focus on the 2018 mayoral contest between incumbent John Tory and former chief city planner Jennifer Keesmaat. Noting that Tory faced very different opponents in 2014 and 2018, the authors consider his bases of support across the two elections. They show that despite his dominant performance in both years, Tory won with coalitions of support from very different segments of the population in each of the two elections.

In chapter 9, Aaron Moore considers Winnipeg, our final case city. Winnipeg's mayoral race saw incumbent Brian Bowman convincingly fend off Jenny Motkaluk, a challenger to his right, in a race that saw substantially reduced turnout in comparison to the previous election. Winnipeg held a plebiscite concurrently with the election, where voters voiced their opinions regarding whether a busy intersection (Portage Avenue and Main Street) should be opened to street-level foot traffic. Moore finds that interest in the plebiscite was low and that the plebiscite failed to boost voter turnout more generally.

The city-specific analyses in these chapters fall into three broad categories. The first two consider the two key variables in the field of political behaviour: vote choice and voter turnout. The chapters on Calgary, Montreal, Quebec, and Toronto all consider questions about how voters form attitudes toward candidates, while the chapter on Winnipeg considers turnout. The third set of chapters – on Vancouver, London, and

Mississauga – speak to questions that are more specific to the cities at hand but that nevertheless have relevance in other contexts. The effects of social pressure (Vancouver), ballot structure (London), and the diversity of the electorate (Mississauga) are important to understand at the local level, as elsewhere. In all instances, our understanding of the topics under study is made richer by answering these questions using data from the local level.

In our concluding chapter, we step back to consider all eight cities together, contemplating the lessons learned from the careful analyses in each of the eight contributions. We focus especially on what the vote choice models tell us about the correlates of voting behaviour across big-city elections in Canada, and we discuss the relevance of these lessons for long-standing debates about the distinctiveness of the municipal political "world."

More than fifty years ago, in one of the first survey-based studies of individual voting behaviour in Canada, political scientist John Meisel acknowledged the enormity of the "gaps in knowledge" that remained for scholars of Canadian elections and voting to explore in the years to come. Those gaps in knowledge would be filled, Meisel wrote, only when studies of elections and voting behaviour in Canada were undertaken "not only nationally, but also at the regional, provincial, and local levels" (Meisel, 1964, p. 288). We agree. We hope that readers will find that important questions are answered, and new ones raised, in each of the chapters to come – questions about each of the eight case cities, about big city elections in Canada more generally, and about all that we can learn from rigorous analysis of elections and voting behaviour in the diverse and vibrant world of Canadian municipal electoral politics.

NOTES

1 Not all Canadians cast ballots for all of these offices, of course. For instance, park board elections take place only in Vancouver, and regional council/ chair elections take place only in some parts of Ontario.
2 For information on the number of elections see Quesnel (2007) and Sancton (2015). Information on the number of elected official in municipalities is from Federation of Canadian Municipalities (2013).
3 N = 13,878. This difference is statistically significant (p < 0.001).
4 N = 13,612. This difference is also statistically significant (p < 0.001).
5 This difference is statistically significant (p < 0.001).
6 There are certainly other outlets we might have included, but the CJPS remains a leading outlet for scholars in the field of Canadian politics generally and voting behaviour more specifically.

7 Studlar, 2001; Lublin and Voss, 2002; Cutler, 2002; Jenkins, 2002; Blais et al.,
   2002; Godbout and Bélanger, 2002; Carbert, 2003; Bélanger, 2003; Gidengil
   and Everitt, 2003; Blais et al., 2003; Trimble and Sampert, 2004; Eagles,
   2004; Bélanger, 2004; Perrella, 2005; Walks, 2005; Blais, 2005; Gidengil
   et al., 2006; Martinez and Gill, 2006; Nakhaie, 2006; Bélanger and Eagles,
   2006; Tellier, 2006; Small, 2007; Anderson, 2008; Cutler, 2008; Merolla
   et al., 2008; Anderson and Goodyear-Grant, 2008; Nakhaie, 2008; Rekkas,
   2008; Roy, 2009; Raney and Berdahl, 2009; Loewen and Bastien, 2010;
   Loewen, 2010; Esselment, 2010; Anderson and Stephenson, 2011; Cross and
   Young, 2011; Goodman et al., 2011; Perrella et al., 2012; Matthews et al.,
   2012; Marcotte and Bastien, 2012; Mahéo et al., 2012; Dostie-Goulet et al.,
   2012; Pétry and Bastien, 2013; Bodet, 2013; Fournier et al., 2013; Silver
   and Miller, 2014; Lindgren, 2014; McGregor and Anderson, 2014; Caruana
   et al., 2015; Ruderman and Nevitte, 2015; Gauvin et al., 2016; Wilkins-
   Laflamme, 2016; Cross, 2016; Harell, 2017; Breton et al., 2017; Cutler, 2017;
   Blais and Daoust, 2017; Belfry Monroe and Monroe, 2018; Snagovsky and
   Kerby, 2018; Daoust and Dassonneville, 2018; Galais, 2018; Sevi et al., 2018;
   Anderson and Stephenson, 2018; Dabin et al., 2019; Stevens et al., 2019;
   Mongrain, 2019; Sevi et al., 2019; Matthews and Pickup, 2019; Johnston,
   2019; Schimpf, 2019.
8 Studlar, 2001; Lavoie and Serré, 2002; Carbert, 2003; Carty and Eagles,
   2003; Mendelsohn, 2003; Haddow and Klassen, 2004; Jansen, 2004;
   Nakhaie, 2006; Tellier, 2006; Brown et al., 2006; Anderson, 2008; Cutler,
   2008; Anderson and Goodyear-Grant, 2008; Loewen et al., 2008; Raney and
   Berdahl, 2009; Esselment, 2010, Brown et al., 2010; Bélanger and Gelineau,
   2011; Tolley, 2011; Mahéo et al., 2012; Dostie-Goulet et al., 2012; Harell,
   2017; Cutler, 2017; Roy and Esselment, 2016; Chouinard, 2017; Blais-
   Lacombe and Bodet, 2017; Galais, 2018; Tessier and Blanchet, 2018; Mahéo
   and Belanger, 2018; Giasson et al., 2019.
9 Bédard and Tremblay, 2000; Stanwick, 2000; Kushner and Siegel, 2003; Cutler
   and Matthews, 2005; Nakhaie, 2006; Raney and Berdahl, 2009; Tolley, 2011;
   Dostie-Goulet et al., 2012; Couture et al., 2014; Harell, 2017; McGregor et al.,
   2017; Bird et al., 2017; Koop and Kraemer, 2017; Breux et al., 2017; Tessier
   and Blanchet, 2018; Breux et al., 2019; McGregor and Lucas, 2019.
10 Another early study worthy of mention is the work of Kushner and Siegel
    (2003), who conducted a phone survey of several thousand residents in
    several small and medium-sized Ontario cities. Their study was about
    attitudes toward municipal amalgamations, rather than attitudes more
    directly related to local elections.
11 Aside from the theoretical considerations discussed below, financial,
    logistical, and timing limitations factored into case selection. The study
    therefore excludes some of Canada's largest cities (including Edmonton

and Ottawa), small and medium-sized cities, and cities in the Atlantic provinces. We agree with Marschall et al.'s (2011, p. 97) assessment that the possibilities for research on municipalities are "practically limitless," and expect that future research will emerge that considers these other contexts.

12 Surveys were fielded on the following dates:

Calgary: Pre-election: 29 September to 15 October 2017, post-election: 17 October to 6 November 2017.

Québec and Montreal: Pre-election: 20 October to 4 November 2017, post-election: 6 to 29 November 2017.

Vancouver: Pre-election: 28 September to 19 October 2018, post-election: 21 October to 21 November 2018.

London, Mississauga, Toronto: 24 September to 21 October 2018, post-election: 23 October to 22 November 2018.

Winnipeg: 28 September to 23 October 2018, post-election: 21 October to 15 November 2018.

13 No recruitment quotas were used for the telephone respondents (given that calls were sent randomly). Quotas for age and gender were applied to the panel respondents, according to the most recent census data.

14 Many Western Canadian cities experimented with ranked ballot electoral systems in the first half of the twentieth century, but very few kept the system for more than a few years. Calgary and Winnipeg notably retained STV for council elections, and an alternative vote for mayoral elections, until after the Second World War.

15 These latter two factors have a strongly negative correlation (Pearson = −0.575).

16 Four issues are considered for all cities: transit, property taxes, traffic and congestion, and economic development.

17 The social conservativism index includes measures of attitudes toward sexual minorities, immigrants, and traditional gender roles. The economic conservatism index includes questions about government intervention in the job market, maintaining a minimum standard of living, and wealth inequality.

REFERENCES

Allen Stevens, B., Islam, M., De Geus, R., Goldberg, J., McAndrews, J., Mierke-Zatwarnicki, A., & Rubenson, D. (2019). Local candidate effects in Canadian elections. *Canadian Journal of Political Science, 52*(1), 83–96. https://doi.org/10.1017/S0008423918000367

Anderson, C. (2008). Economic voting, multilevel governance and information in Canada. *Canadian Journal of Political Science, 41*(2), 329–354. https://doi.org/10.1017/S0008423908080414

Anderson, C., & Goodyear-Grant, E. (2008). Youth turnout: Adolescents' attitudes in Ontario. *Canadian Journal of Political Science, 41*(3), 697–718. https://doi.org/10.1017/S0008423908080773

Anderson, C., McGregor, R.M., Moore, A., & Stephenson, L. (2017). Economic voting and multi-level governance: The case of Toronto. *Urban Affairs Review, 53*(1), 71–101. https://doi.org/10.1177/1078087415617302

Anderson, C., & Stephenson, L. (2011). Environmentalism and party support in Canada: Recent trends outside Quebec. *Canadian Journal of Political Science, 44*(2), 341–366. https://doi.org/10.1017/S0008423911000138

Anderson, C., & Stephenson, L. (2018). Mobilizing the young: The role of social networks. *Canadian Journal of Political Science, 51*(4), 861–880. https://doi.org/10.1017/S0008423918000161

Bédard, G., & Tremblay, M. (2000). La perception du rôle des femmes en politique au Canada: Le cas des conseillères municipales au Québec en 1997. *Canadian Journal of Political Science, 33*(1), 101–131.

Bélanger, É. (2003). Issue ownership by Canadian political parties 1953–2001. *Canadian Journal of Political Science, 36*(3), 539–558. https://doi.org/10.1017/S0008423903778755

Bélanger, É. (2004). The rise of third Pprties in the 1993 Canadian federal election: Pinard revisited. *Canadian Journal of Political Science, 37*(3), 581–594. https://doi.org/10.1017/S0008423904020554

Bélanger É., Anderson C., & McGregor R.M. (Forthcoming). *Voting in Quebec municipal elections: A tale of two cities*. University of Toronto Press.

Bélanger, É., & Gélineau, F. (2011). Le vote eonomique en contexte de crise financiere: L'election provinciale de 2008 au Quebec. *Canadian Journal of Political Science, 44*(3), 529–551. https://doi.org/10.1017/S0008423911000461

Bélanger É., & Tessier, C. (Forthcoming). Economic voting in the 2017 Montréal and Québec municipal elections. In E. Bélanger, C. Anderson, & R. M. McGregor (Eds.), *Voting in Quebec municipal elections: A tale of two cities*. University of Toronto Press.

Bélanger, P., & Eagles, M. (2006). The geography of class and religion in Canadian elections revisited. *Canadian Journal of Political Science, 39*(3), 591–609. https://doi.org/10.1017/S0008423906060227

Belfry Munroe, K., & Munroe, H. (2018). Constituency campaigning in the age of data. *Canadian Journal of Political Science, 51*(1), 135–154. https://doi.org/10.1017/S0008423917001135

Belley, S., and Lavigne, M.-A. (2008). Apolitisme, partis politiques et prégnance des institutions: le cas de l'élection municipale de 2005 à Québec. *Recherches Sociographiques, 49*(1), 47–68. https://doi.org/10.7202/018193ar

Bherer, L. (2006). Le cheminement du projet de conseils de quartier à Québec (1965–2006): un outil pour contrer l'apolitisme municipal? *Politique et Sociétés, 25*(1), 31–56. https://doi.org/10.7202/013514ar

Bird, K., Jackson, S., McGregor, R.M., Moore, A., & Stephenson, L. (2016). Sex (and ethnicity) in the city: Affinity voting in the 2014 Toronto mayoral election. *Canadian Journal of Political Science, 49*(2), 359–383. https://doi.org/10.1017/S0008423916000536

Blais, A. (2005). Accounting for the electoral success of the Liberal Party in Canada: Presidential address to the Canadian Political Science Association, London, Ontario, June 3, 2005. *Canadian Journal of Political Science, 38*(4), 821–840. https://doi.org/10.1017/S0008423905050304

Blais, A., & Daoust, J. (2017). What do voters do when they like a local candidate from another party? *Canadian Journal of Political Science, 50*(4): 1103–1109.

Blais, A., Gidengil, E., Dobrzynska, A., Nevitte, N., & Adeau, R. (2003). Does the local candidate matter? Candidate effects in the Canadian election of 2000. *Canadian Journal of Political Science, 36*(3), 657–664. https://doi.org /10.1017/S0008423903778810

Blais, A., Gidengil, E., Nadeau, R., & Nevitte, N. (2002). *Anatomy of a Liberal victory: Making sense of the vote in the 2000 Canadian election.* Broadview Press.

Blais, A., Nadeau, R., Gidengil, E., & Nevitte, N. (2002). The impact of issues and the economy in the 1997 Canadian federal election. *Canadian Journal of Political Science, 35*(2), 409–421.

Blais-Lacombe, A., & Bodet, M. (2017). Les députés et les partis politiques sortants profitent-ils d'un avantage électoral? Une analyse des résultats électoraux au Québec. *Canadian Journal of Political Science, 50*(3), 723–746. https://doi.org/10.1017/S0008423917000464

Bodet, M.A. (2013). Strongholds and battlegrounds: Measuring party support stability in Canada. *Canadian Journal of Political Science, 46*(3), 575–596. https://www.jstor.org/stable/43298204

Breton, C., Cutler, F., Lachance, S., & Mierke-Zatwarnicki, A. (2017). Telephone versus online survey modes for election studies: Comparing Canadian public opinion and vote choice in the 2015 federal election. *Canadian Journal of Political Science, 50*(4), 1005–1036. https://doi.org/10.1017/S0008423917000610

Breux, S., & L. Bherer (dir.). (2011). *Les élections municipales au Québec: Enjeux et perspectives.* Presses de l'Université Laval.

Breux, S., Couture, J., & Goodman, N. (2017). Fewer voters higher stakes? The applicability of rational choice for voter turnout in Quebec municipalities. *Environment and Planning C: Politics and Space, 35*(6) 990–1009. https://doi.org/10.1177/0263774X16676272

Breux, S., Couture, J., & Koop, R. (2017). Turnout in local elections: Evidence from Canadian cities, 2004–2014. *Canadian Journal of Political Science, 50*(3), 699–722. https://doi.org/10.1017/S000842391700018X

Breux, S., Couture, J., & Koop, R. (2019). Influences on the number and gender of candidates in Canadian local elections. *Canadian Journal of Political Science, 52*(1), 163–181. https://doi.org/10.1017/S0008423918000483

Brown, S. D., Docherty, D., Henderson, A., Kay, B., & Ellis-hale, K. (2006). Exit polling in Canada: An experiment. *Canadian Journal of Political Science, 39*(4), 919.

Brown, S. D., Perrella, A. M. L., & Kay, B. J. (2010). Revisiting local campaign effects: An experiment involving literature mail drops in the 2007 Ontario election. *Canadian Journal of Political Science, 43*(1), 49–67. https://doi.org/10.1017/S0008423909990758

Carbert, L. (2003). Above the fray: Rural women leaders on regional development and electoral democracy in Atlantic Canada. *Canadian Journal of Political Science, 36*(1), 159–183.

Carty, R. K., & Eagles, M. (2003). Party activity across electoral cycles: The New Brunswick party system, 1979–1994. *Canadian Journal of Political Science, 36*(2), 381–399.

Caruana, N. J., McGregor, R. M., & Stephenson, L. B. (2015). The power of the dark side: Negative partisanship and political behaviour in Canada. *Canadian Journal of Political Science, 48*(4), 771–789. https://doi.org/10.1017/S0008423914000882

Chisson, G., & Mévellec, A. (2014). The 2013 Quebec municipal elections: What is specific to Quebec? *Canadian Journal of Urban Research, 23*(2), 1–8.

Chouinard, S. (2017). Les études électorales au Québec depuis 1970 ou l'analyse de l'exceptionnalisme Québécois aux urnes. *Canadian Journal of Political Science, 50*(1), 369–376. https://doi.org/10.7202/1053488ar

Couture, J., Breux, S., & Bherer, L. (2014). Analyse écologique des déterminants de la participation électorale municipale au Québec. *Canadian Journal of Political Science, 47*(4), 787–812. https://doi.org/10.1017/S0008423914001152

Cross, W. (2016). The importance of local party activity in understanding Canadian politics: Winning from the ground up in the 2015 federal election: Presidential address to the Canadian Political Science Association, Calgary, 31 May 2016. *Canadian Journal of Political Science, 49*(4), 601–620. https://doi.org/10.1017/S0008423916000962

Cross, W., & Young, L. (2011). Explaining local campaign intensity: The Canadian general election of 2008. *Canadian Journal of Political Science, 44*(3), 553–571. https://doi.org/10.1017/S0008432911000497

Cutler, F. (2002). Local economies, local policy impacts and federal electoral behaviour in Canada. *Canadian Journal of Political Science, 35*(2), 347–382.

Cutler, F. (2008). Whodunnit? Voters and responsibility in Canadian federalism. Canadian Journal of Political Science, *41*(3), 627–654. https://doi.org/10.1017/S0008423908080761

Cutler, F. (2017). Political conditions for electoral accountability in federalism. *Canadian Journal of Political Science, 50*(4), 1037–1059. https://doi.org/10.1017/S0008423917000282

Cutler, F., & Matthews, J. S. (2005). The challenge of municipal voting: Vancouver 2002. *Canadian Journal of Political Science, 38*(2), 359–382. https://doi.org/10.1017/S0008423905040151

Dabin, S., Daoust, J., & Papillon, M. (2019). Indigenous peoples and affinity voting in Canada. *Canadian Journal of Political Science, 52*(1), 39–53. https://doi.org/10.1017/S0008423918000574

Daoust, J., & Dassonneville, R. (2018). Beyond nationalism and regionalism: The stability of economic voting in Canada. *Canadian Journal of Political Science, 51*(3), 553–571. https://doi.org/10.1017/S000842391800001X

Davidson, A., McGregor, R. M, & Siemiatycki, M. (2020). Gender, race, and political ambition: The case of Ontario school board elections. *Canadian Journal of Political Science, 53*(2): 461–475.

Dostie-Goulet, E., Blais, A., Fournier, P., & Gidengil, E. (2012). L'abstention sélective, ou pourquoi certains jeunes qui votent au fédéral boudent les élections municipales. *Canadian Journal of Political Science, 45*(4), 909–927. https://doi.org/10.1017/S0008423912001084

Eagles, M. (2004). The effectiveness of local campaign spending in the 1993 and 1997 federal elections in Canada. *Canadian Journal of Political Science, 37*(1), 117–136.

Esselment, A. L. (2010). Fighting elections: Cross-level political party integration in Ontario. *Canadian Journal of Political Science, 43*(4), 871–892. https://doi.org/10.1017/S0008423910000727

Federation of Canadian Municipalities (FCM). (2013). *2013 – Municipal statistics: Elected officials gender statistics.* http://www.fcm.ca/Documents/reports/Women/2013_municipal_statistics_elected_official_gender_EN.pdf

Fletcher, R. (2017). Nenshi has big lead over closest contender in Calgary's mayoral race, new Forum poll suggests. 13 October. *CBC News Online.* https://www.cbc.ca/news/canada/calgary/nenshi-poll-forum-research-1.4354390

Fournier, P., Cutler, F., Soroka, S., Stolle, D., & Bélanger, É. (2013). Riding the orange wave: Leadership, values, issues, and the 2011

Canadian election. *Canadian Journal of Political Science, 46*(4), 863–897. https://doi.org/10.1017/S0008423913000875

Galais, C. (2018). How to make dutiful citizens and influence turnout: The effects of family and school dynamics on the duty to vote. *Canadian Journal of Political Science, 51*(3), 599–617. https://doi.org/10.1017/S0008423918000021

Gauvin, J., Chhim, C., & Medeiros, M. (2016). Did they mind the gap? Voter/party ideological proximity between the BQ, the NDP, and Quebec voters, 2006–2011. *Canadian Journal of Political Science, 49*(2), 289–310. https://doi.org/10.1017/S000842391600038X

Giasson, T., Le Bars, G., & Dubois, P. (2019). Is social media transforming Canadian electioneering? Hybridity and online partisan strategies in the 2012 Quebec election. *Canadian Journal of Political Science, 52*(2), 323–341. https://doi.org/10.1017/S0008423918000902

Gidengil, E., Blais, A., Everitt, J., Fournier, P., & Nevitte, N. (2006). Back to the future? Making sense of the 2004 Canadian election outside Quebec. *Canadian Journal of Political Science, 39*(1), 1–25. https://doi.org/10.1017/S0008423906060069

Gidengil, E., & Everitt, J. (2003). Conventional coverage/unconventional politicians: Gender and media coverage of Canadian laders' debates, 1993, 1997, 2000. *Canadian Journal of Political Science, 36*(3), 559–577.

Gidengil, E., Nevitte, N., Blais, A., Everitt, J., & Fournier, P. (2012). *Dominance and decline: Making sense of recent Canadian elections.* University of Toronto Press.

Gidengil, E., & Vengross, R. (1997). Representative bureaucracy, tokenism, and the glass ceiling: The case of women in Quebec municipal administration. *Canadian Public Administration, 40*(3), 457–480. https://doi.org/10.1111/j.1754-7121.1997.tb01519.x

Godbout, J., & Bélanger, É. (2002). La dimension regionale du vote économique canadien aux élections fédérales de 1988 à 2000. *Canadian Journal of Political Science, 35*(3), 567–588.

Goodman, N. (2014). Internet voting in a local election in Canada. In B. Grofman, A. Trechsel, & M. Franklin (Eds.), *The internet and democracy in global perspective: Voters, candidates, parties, and social movements.* Springer.

Goodman, N., Bastedo, H., LeDuc, L., & Pammett, J. H. (2011). Young Canadians in the 2008 federal election campaign: Using Facebook to probe perceptions of citizenship and participation. *Canadian Journal of Political Science, 44*(4), 859–881. https://doi.org/10.1017/S0008423911000783

Goodman, N., & Lucas, J. (2016). Policy priorities of municipal candidates in the 2014 local Ontario elections. *Canadian Journal of Urban Research, 25*(2), 35–47.

Goodman, N., McGregor, R. M., Couture, J., & Breux, S. (2018). Another digital divide? Evidence that elimination of paper voting could lead to digital disenfranchisement. *Policy and Internet, 10*(2), 164–184. https://doi.org/10.1002/poi3.168

Goodman, N., & Stokes, L. (2020). Reducing the cost of voting: An empirical evaluation of internet voting's effect on local elections. *British Journal of Political Science, 50*(3): 1155–1167.

Haddow, R., & Klassen, T. R. (2004). Partisanship, institutions, and public policy: The case of labour market policy in Ontario, 1990–2000. *Canadian Journal of Political Science, 37*(1), 137–160.

Harell, A. (2017). Intersectionality and gendered political behaviour in a multicultural Canada. *Canadian Journal of Political Science, 50*(2), 495–514. https://doi.org/10.1017/S000842391700021X

Jansen, H. J. (2004). The political consequences of the alternative vote: Lessons from Western Canada. *Canadian Journal of Political Science, 37*(3), 647–669. https://doi.org/10.1017/S0008423904030227

Jenkins, R. (2002). How campaigns matter in Canada: Priming and learning as explanations for the Reform Party's 1993 campaign success. *Canadian Journal of Political Science, 35*(2), 383–408.

Johnston, R. (2019). Liberal leaders and liberal success: The impact of alternation. *Canadian Journal of Political Science, 52*(3), 423–442.

Kiss, S., Perrella, A., & Spicer Z. (2020). Right-wing populism in a metropolis: Personal financial stress, conservative attitudes, and Rob Ford's Toronto. *Journal of Urban Affairs, 42*(7): 1028–1046.

Koop, R., & Kraemer, J. (2016). Wards, at-large systems, and the focus of representation in Canadian cities. *Canadian Journal of Political Science, 49*(3), 433–448. https://doi.org/10.1017/S0008423916000512

Kushner, J., & Siegel, D. (2003a). Effect of municipal amalgamations in Ontario on political representation and accessibility. *Canadian Journal of Political Science, 36*(5), 1035–1051. https://doi.org/10.1017/S0008423903778950

Kushner, J., & Siegel, D. (2003b). Citizens' attitudes toward municipal amalgamation in three Ontario municipalities. *Canadian Journal of Regional Science, 26*(1), 49–59.

Kushner, J., Siegel, D., & Stanwick, H. (1997). Ontario Municipal elections: Voting trends and determinants of electoral success in a Canadian Province. *Canadian Journal of Political Science, 30*(3), 539–553.

Kushner, J., Siegel, D, & Stanwick, H. (2001). Canadian mayors: A profile and determinants of electoral success. *Canadian Journal of Urban Research, 10*(1), 5–22.

Laakso, M., & Taagepera, R. (1979). "Effective" number of parties: A measure with application to West Europe. *Comparative Political Studies, 12*(1), 3–27. https://doi.org/10.1177/001041407901200101

Lavoie, N., & Serré, P. (2002). Du vote Bloc au vote social: Le cas des citoyens issus de l'immigration de Montréal, 1995–1996. *Canadian Journal of Political Science, 35*(1), 49–74.

Lindgren, A. (2014). Toronto-area ethnic newspapers and Canada's 2011 federal election, an investigation of content, focus, and partisanship. *Canadian Journal of Political Science, 47*(4), 667–696. https://doi.org/10.1017 /S0008423914000912

Loewen, P. J. (2010). Affinity, antipathy, and political participation: How our concern for others makes us vote. *Canadian Journal of Political Science, 43*(3), 661–687. https://doi.org/10.1017/S000842391000065X

Loewen, P. J., & Bastien, F. (2010). (In)significant elections? Federal by-elections in Canada, 1963–2008. *Canadian Journal of Political Science, 43*(1), 87–105. https://doi.org/10.1017/S000842390999076X

Loewen, P. J., Milner, H., & Hicks, B. M. (2008). Does compulsory voting lead to more informed and engaged citizens? An experimental test. *Canadian Journal of Political Science, 41*(3), 655–672. https://doi.org/10.1017 /S000842390808075X

Lublin, D., & Voss, D. S. (2002). Context and francophone support for the sovereignty of Quebec: An ecological analysis. *Canadian Journal of Political Science, 35*(1), 75–101. https://doi.org/10.1017/S0008423902778189

Lucas, J. (2020a). The size and sources of municipal incumbency advantage in Canada. *Urban Affairs Review.* https://doi.org/10.1177 /1078087419879234

Lucas, J. (2020b). Reaction or reform? Subnational evidence on P.R. adoption from Canadian cities. *Representation, 56*(1), 89–109. https://doi.org/10.1080/00344893.2019.1700154

Lucas, J., & Sayers, A. (2018). Responsiveness, accountability, and the long-term development of local political careers in Calgary and Edmonton. In S. Breux & J. Couture (Eds.), *Accountability and responsiveness at the municipal level: Views from Canada* (pp. 107–131). McGill–Queen's University Press.

Mahéo, V., & Bélanger, É. (2018). Is the Parti Québécois bound to disappear? A study of the current generational dynamics of electoral behaviour in Quebec. *Canadian Journal of Political Science, 51*(2), 335–356. https://doi.org/10.1017/S0008423917001147

Mahéo, V., Dejaeghere, Y., & Stolle, D. (2012). La non-participation politique des jeunes: Une étude des barrieres temporaires et permanentes de l'engagement. *Canadian Journal of Political Science, 45*(2), 405–425. https://doi.org/10.1017/S0008423912000388

Marcotte, P., & Bastien, F. (2012). L'influence du mode de financement des medias audiovisuels sur le cadrage des campagnes: Le cas des elections canadiennes de 2005–2006 et 2008. *Canadian Journal of Political Science, 45*(2), 313–336. https://doi.org/10.1017/S0008423904040077

Marschall, M., Shah, Paru, & Anirudh, R. (2011). The study of local elections: Editors' introduction: A looking glass into the future. *PS: Political Science and Politics*, *44*, 97–100. https://doi.org/10.2307/40984492

Martinez, M., & Gill, J. (2006). Does turnout decline matter? Electoral turnout and partisan choice in the 1997 Canadian federal election. *Canadian Journal of Political Science*, *39*(2), 343–362. https://doi.org/10.1017/S0008423906060100

Matthews, J. S., & Pickup, M. (2019). Rational learners or impervious partisans? Economic news and partisan bias in economic perceptions. *Canadian Journal of Political Science*, *52*(2), 303–321. https://doi.org/10.1017/S0008423918000501

Matthews, J. S., Pickup, M., & Cutler, F. (2012). The mediated horserace: Campaign polls and poll reporting. *Canadian Journal of Political Science*, *45*(2), 261–287. https://doi.org/10.1017/S0008423912000327

McGregor, R. M., & Anderson, C. D. (2014). The effects of Elections Canada's campaign period advertising. *Canadian Journal of Political Science*, *47*(4), 813–826. https://doi.org/10.1017/S0008423914001061

McGregor, R. M., & Lucas, J. (2019). Who has school spirit? Explaining voter participation in school board elections. *Canadian Journal of Political Science*, *52*(4), 923–936. https://doi.org/10.1017/S0008423919000088

McGregor, R. M., Moore, A., Jackson, S., Bird, K., & Stephenson, L. (2017). Why so few women and minorities in local politics? Incumbency and affinity voting in low information elections. *Representation*, *53*(2), 135–52. https://doi.org/10.1080/00344893.2017.1354909

McGregor, R. M., Moore, A., & Stephenson, L. (2016). Political attitudes and behaviour in a non-partisan environment: Toronto 2014. *Canadian Journal of Political Science*, *49*(2), 311–333. https://doi.org/10.1017/S0008423916000573

McGregor, R. M., Moore, A., & Stephenson, L. (2021). *Electing a Mega-Mayor: Toronto 2014*. University of Toronto Press.

McGregor, R. M., & Spicer, Z. (2016). The Canadian homevoter: Property values and municipal politics in Canada. *Journal of Urban Affairs*, *38*(1), 123–139. https://doi.org/10.1111/juaf.12178

Meisel, J. (1964). An analysis of the national results. In J. Meisel (Ed.), *Papers on the 1962 election* (pp. 272–288). University of Toronto Press.

Mendelsohn, M. (2003). Rational choice and socio-psychological explanation for opinion on Quebec sovereignty. *Canadian Journal of Political Science*, *36*(3), 511–537. https://doi.org/10.1017/S0008423903778743

Merolla, J. L., Stephenson, L. B., & Zechmeister, E. J. (2008). Can Canadians take a hint? The (in)effectiveness of party labels as information shortcuts in Canada. *Canadian Journal of Political Science, 41*(3), 673–696. https://doi.org/10.1017/S0008423908080797

Mongrain, P. (2019). La prédiction des résultats électoraux au Canada: Un modèle politico-économique sans sondage. *Canadian Journal of Political Science, 52*(1), 97–120. https://doi.org/10.1017/S0008423918000860

Moore, A. A., McGregor, R. M., & Stephenson, L. B. (2017). Paying attention and the incumbency effect: Voting behavior in the 2014 Toronto municipal election. *International Political Sience Review, 38*(1), 85–98. https://doi.org/10.1177/0192512115616268

Nakhaie, M. R. (2006). Electoral participation in municipal, provincial, and federal elections in Canada. *Canadian Journal of Political Science, 39*(2), 363–390. https://doi.org/10.1017/S000842390606015X

Nakhaie, M. R. (2008). Social capital and political participation of Canadians. *Canadian Journal of Political Science, 41*(4), 835–860. https://doi.org/10.1017/S0008423908081055

Ogilvie, M. 2018. What's motivating Torontonians to vote – or not – on Oct. 22 (and it's not the ward fiasco). 19 October. *Toronto Star*. https://www.thestar.com/news/gta/2018/10/19/whats-motivating-torontonians-to-vote-or-not-on-oct-22-and-its-not-the-ward-fiasco.html

Perrella, A. (2005). Long-term economic hardship and non-mainstream voting in Canada. *Canadian Journal of Political Science, 38*(2), 335. https://doi.org/10.1017/S0008423905040242

Perrella, A., Brown, S., & Kay, B. (2012). Voting behaviour among the gay, lesbian, bisexual, and transgendered electorate. *Canadian Journal of Political Science, 45*(1), 89–117. https://doi.org/10.1017/S000842391100093X

Pétry, F., & Bastien, F. (2013). Follow the pollsters: Inaccuracies in media coverage of the horse-race during the 2008 Canadian election. *Canadian Journal of Political Science, 46*(1), 1–26. https://doi.org/10.1017S0008423913000188

Pinard, M. (1971). *The rise of a third party: A study in crisis politics*. Prentice-Hall.

Pinard, M. (1973). Third parties in Canada revisited: A rejoinder and elaboration of one-party dominance. *Canadian Journal of Political Science, 6*(3), 439–460.

Quesnel, L. with Hamel, S. (2007). *Your guide to municipal institutions in Canada*. Federation of Canadian Municipalities, International Centre for Municipal Development.

Raney, T., & Berdahl, L. (2009). Birds of a feather? Citizenship norms, group identity, and political participation in Western Canada. *Canadian Journal of Political Science, 42*(1), 187–209. https://doi.org/10.1017S0008423909090076

Rekkas, M. (2008). Gender and elections: An examination of the 2006 Canadian federal election. *Canadian Journal of Political Science, 41*(4), 987–1001. https://doi.org/10.1017/S0008423908081134

Roy, J. (2009). Voter heterogeneity: Informational differences and voting. *Canadian Journal of Political Science, 42*(1), 117–137. https://doi.org/10.1017/S0008423909090052

Roy, J., & Esselment, A. (2016). Partisans without parties: Party systems as partisan inhibitors? *Canadian Journal of Political Science, 49*(1), 21–39. https://doi.org/10.1017/S0008423916000056

Ruderman, N., & Nevitte, N. (2015). Assessing the impact of political scandals on attitudes toward democracy: Evidence from Canada's sponsorship scandal. *Canadian Journal of Political Science, 48*(4), 885–904. https://doi.org/10.1017/S0008423915001055

Sancton, A. (2015). *Canadian local government: An urban perspective.* 2nd ed. Oxford University Press.

Santin, A. (2018). Poll predicts low turnout – and that could be good news for Motkaluk. 19 October. *Winnipeg Free Press.* https://www.winnipegfreepress.com/civicelection2018/mayor/498070171.html

Schatten, W., Ruderman, N., Zhao, Z, & Nevitte N. (2015). The 2014 Toronto municipal election. Paper presented at the 2015 meeting of the Canadian Political Science Association. Ottawa.

Schimpf, C. (2019). Anticipated election result and protest voting: Why and when Canadian voters signal discontent. *Canadian Journal of Political Science, 52*(4), 847–863. https://doi.org/10.1017/S0008423919000325

Sevi, S., Arel-Bundock, V., & Blais, A. (2019). Do women get fewer votes? No. *Canadian Journal of Political Science, 52*(1), 201–210. https://doi.org/10.1017/S0008423918000495

Sevi, S., Yoshinaka, A., & Blais, A. (2018). Legislative party switching and the changing nature of the Canadian party system, 1867–2015. *Canadian Journal of Political Science, 51*(3), 665–695. https://doi.org/10.1017/S0008423918000203

Siemiatycki, M., & Marshall, S. (2014). *Who votes in Toronto municipal elections?* Report. Maytree.

Silver, D., & Miller, D. (2014). Cultural scenes and voting patterns in Canada. *Canadian Journal of Political Science, 47*(3),425–450. https://doi.org/10.1017/S0008423914000778

Silver, D., Taylor, Z., & Calderon-Figueroa, F. (2020). Populism in the city: The case of Ford Nation. *International Journal of Politics, Culture, and Society, 33*(1): 1–21.

Small, T. A. (2007). Canadian cyberparties: Reflections on internet-based campaigning and party systems. *Canadian Journal of Political Science, 40*(3), 639. https://doi.org/10.1017/S0008423907070734

Snagovsky, F., & Kerby, M. (2018). The electoral consequences of party switching in Canada: 1945–2011. *Canadian Journal of Political Science, 51*(2), 425–445. https://doi.org/10.1017/S0008423917001445

Spicer, Z., McGregor, R. M., & Alcantara, C. (2017). Political opportunity structures and the representation of women and visible minorities in municipal elections. *Electoral Studies, 48*(1), 10–18. https://doi.org/10.1016/j.electstud.2017.01.002

Stanwick, H. (2000). A megamayor for all people? Voting behaviour and electoral success in the 1997 Toronto municipal election. *Canadian Journal of Political Science, 33*(3), 549–568. https://doi.org/10.1017/S0008423900000196

Stephenson, L., McGregor, R. M., & Moore, A. (2018). Sins of the brother: Partisanship and accountability in Toronto 2014. In S. Breux & J. Couture (Eds.), *Accountability and responsiveness at the local level: Views from Canada.* Montreal and Kingston: McGill–Queens University Press.

Studlar, D. (2001). Canadian exceptionalism: Explaining differences over time in provincial and federal voter turnout. *Canadian Journal of Political Science, 34*(2), 299–319. https://doi.org/10.1017/S0008423901777918

Taylor, Z., & Eidelman, G. (2010). Canadian political science and the city: A limited engagement. *Canadian Journal of Political Science, 43*(4), 961–981. https://doi.org/10.1017/S0008423910000715

Taylor, Z., & McEleney, S. (2017). Do institutions and rules influence electoral accessibility and competitiveness? Considering the 2014 Toronto ward elections. *Urban Affairs Review, 55*(1), 210–230. https://doi.org/10.1177/1078087417703753

Tellier, G. (2006). Effect of economic conditions on government popularity: The Canadian provincial case. *Canadian Journal of Political Science, 39*(1), 27–51. https://doi.org/10.1017/S000842390605052

Tessier, C., & Blanchet, A. (2018). Ballot order in cueless elections: A comparison of municipal and provincial elections in Quebec. *Canadian Journal of Political Science, 51*(1), 83–102. https://doi.org/10.1017/S0008423917000701

Tessier, C., & McGregor, M. (Forthcoming). Setting the record straight: Identifying the correlates of split-ticket voting in Montreal and Quebec. In E. Bélanger, C. Anderson, & R. M. McGregor (Eds.), *Voting in Quebec municipal elections: A tale of two cities.* University of Toronto Press.

Tolley, E. (2011). Do women "do better" in municipal politics? Electoral representation across three levels of government. *Canadian Journal of Political Science, 44*(3), 573–594. https://doi.org/10.1017/S0008423911000503

Trimble, L., & Sampert, S. (2004). Who's in the game? The framing of the Canadian Election 2000 by the *Globe and Mail* and the *National Post*. *Canadian Journal of Political Science, 37*(1), 51–71. https://doi.org/10.1017/S0008423904040028.

Walks, R. A. (2005). The city-suburban cleavage in Canadian federal politics. *Canadian Journal of Political Science, 38*(2), 383. https://doi.org/10.1017/S0008423905030842

Wilkins-Laflamme, S. (2016). The changing religious cleavage in Canadians' voting behaviour. *Canadian Journal of Political Science, 49*(3), 499–518. https://doi.org/10.1017/S0008423916000834

2 Calgary

JACK LUCAS AND JOHN SANTOS

On paper, Calgary's 2017 municipal election looks like a sleepy affair. There were no scandals, no surprising candidate entries or sudden withdrawals, no shocking secrets revealed. Candidates spoke of taxes and transit and infrastructure. All of the incumbent councillors, along with Naheed Nenshi, the city's two-term mayor, were re-elected with comfortable margins. What could possibly be more typical?

Yet while Calgarians were actually living it, nothing about the 2017 election *felt* very typical. There was a decidedly un-municipal level of third-party advertising and heavyweight political pressure from the local NHL team. There were accusations of racism and dirty money. There were polls whose controversy was matched only by the confidence with which their pollsters defended them. There was, in the end, the highest turnout ever recorded in a postwar election in Calgary and the most competitive incumbent mayoral race in a generation. It was the most atypical of typical elections. In retrospect, the outcome looks entirely normal. The pathway by which Calgarians got there was anything but.

In this chapter, we'll provide an overview of the Calgary election and reflect on its implications for our understanding of Canadian municipal politics and voting behaviour. We begin with an overview of the campaign: the issues, and the results and then turn to the correlates of mayoral vote choice in Calgary. We will conclude with a brief analysis of the role of political parties and partisanship in Calgary's ostensibly nonpartisan election.

Election Overview

The Mayoral Campaign

In 2013, Mayor Naheed Nenshi's tireless efforts during Calgary's devastating flood earlier in the same year had combined with a surging energy sector to produce a crushing re-election victory, in which he won 74% of the vote. By 2017, however, the atmosphere in Calgary had changed. The immense civic pride in the city's response to 2013 flood was now a distant memory, as were the glory days of the oil boom. After oil prices began to collapse in 2014, tens of thousands of local workers lost their jobs, and even as the local economy regained some momentum, unemployment remained stubbornly high. Friendly Conservative faces in Edmonton and Ottawa had been replaced by a provincial NDP government and a prime minister named Trudeau. These were strange and uncertain times.

For Nenshi, this meant that the path to re-election would be more treacherous in 2017 than it had been in 2013. Still, few doubted that Nenshi would win. Rumours of a star conservative challenger – Calgary MP Michelle Rempel was the most frequently floated name – ultimately amounted to nothing. Neither of the two candidates who emerged to challenge Nenshi – Andre Chabot, a veteran city councillor, and Bill Smith, a provincial PC Party insider with no previous campaign experience – seemed likely to upset a pattern of incumbent mayoral victories in Calgary that stretched back nearly thirty years.

So why did the mayoral election ultimately prove to be so competitive? Each player in the drama is sure to provide a slightly different list of causes: an uninspired campaign by Nenshi, a mammoth fundraising haul by Bill Smith, a set of polls whose conflicting messages seemed to prompt Calgarians to think of the race as highly competitive – and so on. Without denying the significance of any of these explanations, we want to step back from the election drama to highlight two more fundamental factors that combined to generate the most competitive mayoral race in a generation.

The first factor was that a large number of Calgarians were simply fed up with Naheed Nenshi. According to CMES data, almost two in five Calgarians were unhappy with Nenshi's performance, and nearly one third of respondents said they would absolutely *not* vote for him. When we asked respondents to tell us how they felt about Nenshi on a scale of 1 to 100, about 8% of respondents chose the lowest available score: 1.[1] Responses to our open-ended question about what respondents disliked about Nenshi – "arrogant," "smug attitude," "condescending" – suggest that perceptions of Nenshi's weaknesses were more than talking points from pundits and council insiders. After two terms in office, a substantial minority of Calgarians were firmly in the anyone-but-Nenshi camp.[2]

Still, for the anyone-but-Nenshi sentiment to turn into a genuinely competitive race, the election needed more than general disgruntlement among the electorate: it also needed a strong anti-Nenshi candidate. Here the circumstances initially favoured Nenshi, as two broadly conservative challengers, Andre Chabot and Bill Smith, seemed poised to divide the opposition vote. But the three-man race soon evolved into something that was, for the incumbent mayor, a much more dangerous situation: a head-to-head battle with just one major opponent.

While CMES data cannot tell us much about the timing of this coordination effect, we *can* gather some clues from major media sources in Calgary. Figure 2.1 provides an overview of media coverage of the three main contenders – Chabot, Nenshi, and Smith – in the eight weeks leading up to the municipal election. In the first three figures ("Metro," "Postmedia," and "Total"), we report a simple count of the number of times each candidate was mentioned in Metro Calgary and Postmedia newspapers (*Calgary Herald* and *Calgary Sun*) and a sum of the two figures. The final figure in the bottom right ("Postmedia Weighted") displays a weighted count in which a candidate receives three points when mentioned first, two points when mentioned second, and one point when mentioned third. The weighted figure is meant to capture the possibility that the raw count data may misstate the actual levels of media attention paid to each candidate, since a token mention at the end of an article is hardly the same as top billing in the article's headline or opening paragraphs.

Figure 2.1 captures a few important dynamics in the Calgary election. As we would expect of a high-profile incumbent mayor, Nenshi received more coverage than his competitors. For the first six weeks of the campaign, Bill Smith enjoyed a slight coverage advantage over Andre Chabot in the Postmedia newspapers, an advantage that was largely due to *Calgary Sun* columnists who preferred Bill Smith to Andre Chabot from the outset. In Metro Calgary, coverage of Nenshi's two major challengers during this period was roughly equal. Overall, the media data suggest that Bill Smith enjoyed a modest media advantage over Andre Chabot in the first six weeks of the race.

The most important finding in the figure, however, is the clear separation between Bill Smith and Andre Chabot that developed in the sixth week of the campaign. After that point, Andre Chabot receded into the background of the campaign, a trend most evident in the weighted figure on the bottom right; increasingly, Chabot was mentioned, if at all, only after Naheed Nenshi and Bill Smith had been discussed in detail. The principal cause of this separation seems to have been a widely discussed poll – whose release date is marked in the figure with a vertical dotted line – showing Smith leading Nenshi by nine points, with Chabot in a distant third place. The main consequence of the poll may have been that anti-Nenshi voters consolidated in the Bill Smith camp (i.e., a coordination effect). Whatever the exact cause, the media data suggest that the mayoral election entered its seventh week as a clear two-man race.

Figure 2.1. Media coverage of Calgary mayoral candidates

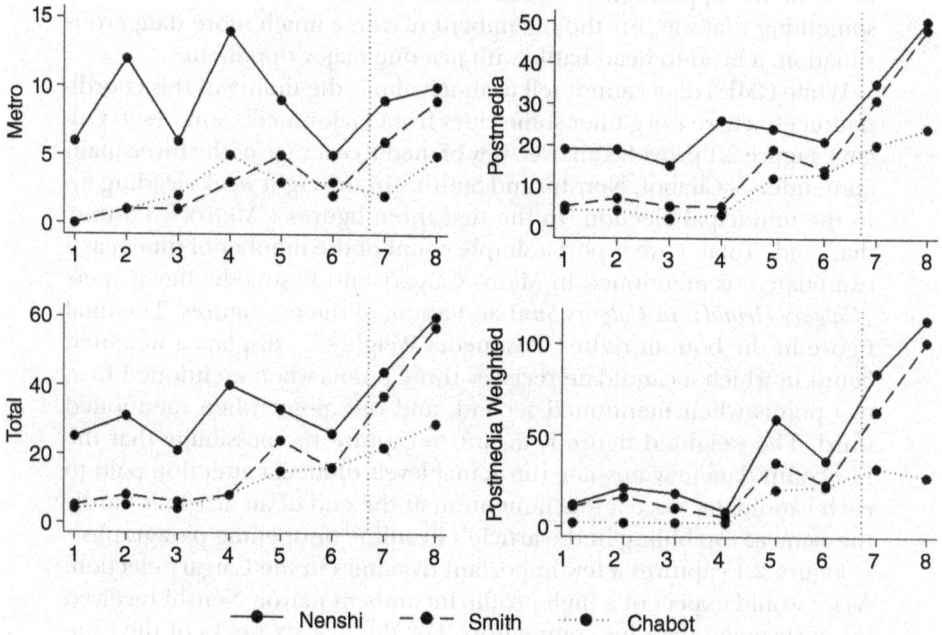

● — Nenshi   − ● − Smith   ···● Chabot

Council Races

As is typical in Canadian municipal elections, Calgary's mayoral race consumed much of the city's media attention and public conversation. In recent years, however, a number of local leaders in Calgary have realized that the city's weak-mayor system makes ward-level races almost as important as the mayoral race. "As long as you have eight votes," said Cal Wenzel, a Calgary developer, in an infamous secretly recorded video in 2013, "you can control whatever happens."[3] This increased recognition of the importance of ward races has led to significant increases in campaign contributions and political efforts in ward contests. The result has been a number of contentious and potentially competitive elections.

While much could be said about the local controversies and idiosyncrasies in particular ward races, we will confine ourselves to a few broad observations. Perhaps the most important relates to a pattern that had begun to develop in earnest in 2013: a set of loosely coordinated conservative candidates who were critical of Nenshi on the one hand, and the incumbent councillors who were seen as supporting his agenda on the other. A new third-party organization calling itself "Save Calgary" campaigned actively against a handful of city councillors who it viewed as fiscally irresponsible, and some ward candidates used similar public advertising (such as lawn signs) and backroom connections (such as connections between Bill Smith's campaign strategists and ward-level campaigns) to maximize their likelihood of success.

These campaign tactics gave many ward races a distinctly ideological hue. In some wards (such as Wards 7 and 11), candidate lawn signs resembled those of the federal Conservative Party, with the words "Your Conservative Choice" printed on each sign to ensure that no one missed the message. In another race, Ward 4, a high-profile progressive candidate ran a serious campaign against the city's most openly conservative incumbent councillor. While some ward candidates stuck close to traditional municipal rhetoric – the need for pragmatism, the inappropriateness of ideology in municipal politics, and so on – many ward races were notable for the explicitly ideological terms in which conservative or progressive candidates faced off against incumbent candidates.

A final observation to make about Calgary's ward races is that none of the ideological contestation or third-party advertising ultimately mattered: every incumbent councillor, whether an "ally" of Mayor Nenshi or not, was safely re-elected to office. This did not come as a surprise to Calgarians; when we asked CMES respondents to estimate their incumbent's probability of re-election, their average estimate was above 50% in every ward in the city.

Issues and Events

Calgary's municipal election was not dominated by a single issue. As we will discuss later on, the most important "issue" in the election, to the extent there was one, was probably the voters' feelings about the performance of Nenshi himself. Nevertheless, the election did feature a number of issue controversies, many of which are important urban policy issues more generally and thus worth discussing briefly.

The issue content of the Calgary election as it unfolded can be divided into three clear phases: pre-arena, arena, and post-arena. In the pre-arena phase, from mid-summer up to 12 September, a number of issues percolated to the surface, each with the potential to generate serious controversy during the election, though in the end they did not. These included a looming municipal budget shortfall, arts and culture policy in Calgary, and a potential Olympic bid. While some of these issues provoked controversy – a new and unpopular public art installation was particularly salient – none was so important as to dominate the election-related conversation in Calgary.

All of this changed on Tuesday, 12 September, when the Calgary Flames organization announced that it was permanently withdrawing from talks with the city about a new arena. The story had begun a day earlier, when Nenshi introduced a campaign proposal for a "cultural and economic hub" in Calgary that would include an NHL arena. The city and the Flames organization had been far apart in their negotiations until that point, so Ken King, the president and CEO of Calgary Sports and Entertainment (CSEC), called Nenshi's office to ask whether the new announcement meant that Nenshi was ready to support something closer to CSEC's financial proposal for the arena.[4] The answer: not a chance.

CSEC's ownership was reportedly furious, and King quickly organized a press conference, accompanied by NHL Commissioner Gary Bettman, to announce that the conversation was over; there would be no new arena in Calgary. King insisted that his motive was not political and that he was not threatening to move the team. Gary Bettman was less measured. Without a new building, he said, "there will be consequences that everybody is going to have to deal with."

King's announcement came as a surprise to Nenshi, who rushed past reporters without comment on the evening of the 12th. But by the next day, he was ready to respond: the city's offer had been "eminently reasonable," he argued, and CSEC's offer was "eminently unreasonable." Mayoral challenger Bill Smith claimed that the whole episode spoke to Nenshi's inability to translate ideas into reality; city councillor Diane Colley-Urquhart spoke of a "vacuum of leadership" at City Hall. King claimed repeatedly that no political strategy was involved in the announcement; most local observers were unconvinced.

For the next few weeks – a substantial portion of the election period – the arena controversy dominated, so much so that one local columnist complained that election reporters would "be covering tiddlywinks" were it not for the arena debate. Nenshi sought to connect the issue to Smith's past role as president of the PC Party of Alberta during the period in which the party was receiving major donations from Edmonton Oilers owner Daryl Katz. Smith worked to link the arena issue to Nenshi's perceived arrogance and unwillingness to compromise. Voters, meanwhile, were bored by the whole spectacle: among the six issues included in the CMES survey, more than 80% of respondents listed the NHL arena *last* in importance (see Figure 2.2). The most important effect of the weeks-long arena controversy may thus have been its opportunity cost: more time spent on the NHL arena meant less time for other issues, such as

Figure 2.2. Issue importance in the 2017 Calgary election

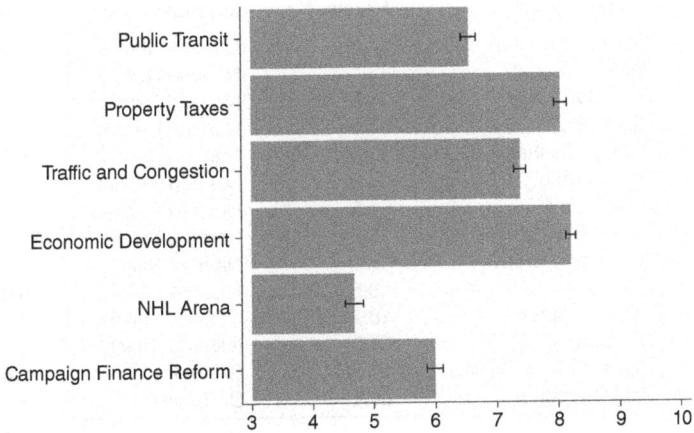

economic development and property taxes (the issues that Calgarians rated as most important).

In the closing weeks of the campaign, attention finally shifted away from the NHL arena, ultimately converging in the closing days on the issue of character: Nenshi's "arrogance" against Smith's "inexperience." Video clips of Nenshi seeming to call some of his opponents' supporters racists squared off against talk of financial difficulties and administrative incompetence at Smith's law firm. The closing minutes of the campaign's final public mayoral debate, less than a week before Election Day, captured the fervid tone of the election's final days: Nenshi, storming to the microphone to respond to a fringe candidate's claim that Nenshi had called him a racist; another fringe candidate rising to his feet to shout social conservative platitudes at the crowd; Smith, oddly separated from the other candidates on the other side of the lectern, gazing bemusedly at the whole scene; and Chabot, once considered a major challenger, now sitting silently, staring at the floor. It had not been the election that anyone on the stage had expected.

The Election Result

Table 2.1 surveys the election results in Calgary; incumbent races are marked with asterisks. In the mayoral race, the outcome was a clear victory for Nenshi, whose 7.6% margin of victory would be considered comfortable in most settings but was very close by the standards of Calgary's incumbent mayoral elections. In the ward races, all nine incumbent

Table 2.1. Election results, by ward

Ward	Council winner	Margin (%)	Mayoral winner	Margin (%)
1	Ward Sutherland*	11.8	Naheed Nenshi	8.5
2	Joe Magliocca*	13.1	Naheed Nenshi	7.6
3	Jyoti Gondek	15.6	Naheed Nenshi	4.4
4	Sean Chu*	7.0	Naheed Nenshi	8.3
5	George Chahal	17.5	Naheed Nenshi	24.9
6	Jeff Davison	23.2	Naheed Nenshi	4.1
7	Druh Farrell*	3.5	Naheed Nenshi	31.4
8	Evan Woolley*	25.7	Naheed Nenshi	29.2
9	Gian-Carlo Carra*	8.1	Naheed Nenshi	9.7
10	Ray Jones*	8.5	Naheed Nenshi	9.0
11	Jeromy Farkas	16.2	Naheed Nenshi	4.2
12	Shane Keating*	61.2	Naheed Nenshi	3.1
13	Diane Colley-Urquhart*	17.3	Bill Smith	2.6
14	Peter Demong*	80.5	Bill Smith	7.1
Overall			Naheed Nenshi*	7.6

candidates were re-elected, with margins of victory ranging from a competitive 3.5% to a crushing 80.5%. The city's open races, which tend to be competitive, were in fact rather uncompetitive in 2017, with margins of well over 10% in every race.

The overall competitiveness of the mayoral race was not reflected in all of the city's geographic subregions. Figure 2.3 provides an overview of the geographic variation, plotting the distribution of Nenshi's vote share in each ward. In three wards, Nenshi trounced his competitors: Ward 5, his geographic "home base" in the northeastern corner of the city, along with Words 7 and 8, which comprise the city's inner core. In Wards 13 and 14, in the city's south end, the opposite was true, with vote share results for Nenshi that were consistently below his overall result. Taken as a whole, Figure 2.3 clarifies the geographic landscape of Nenshi's support in 2017: strong in the northeast and urban core; weak in the deep south end of the city; and competitive races everywhere else.

A final noteworthy feature of the election result is the turnout: at 58%, the 2017 election saw the highest municipal turnout of any postwar election. This exceptionally high rate by municipal standards was likely the result of the very competitiveness we identified earlier, competitiveness that voters themselves appear to have keenly perceived. When we asked CMES respondents about the mayoral candidates' chances of winning the election, the average odds were very close between Nenshi and Smith. Perhaps most revealing are respondents' estimates of the chances for the candidate they *opposed*: Nenshi supporters put Smith's chances at

Figure 2.3. Vote share for Nenshi, by ward

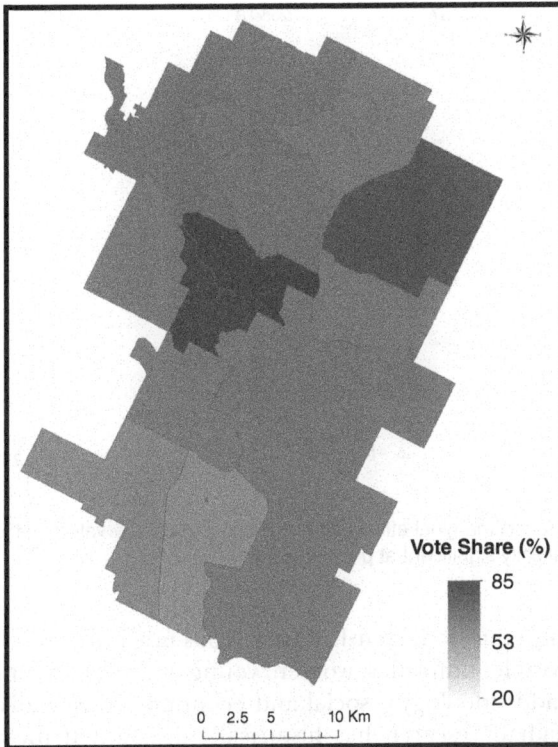

about 47%, and Smith's supporters put Nenshi's chances at a very similar 46%. This perception appears to have motivated Calgarians to turn out in record numbers.

Vote Choice

We now turn to a more detailed examination of mayoral vote choice in the Calgary election. provides a visual summary of a series of logistic regression models, each of which adds a new block of variables. Model A presents demographic characteristics, the importance of which has long been recognized in studies of voting behaviour. The Calgary municipal election is no exception. Smith's voter coalition looks very much like the norm for conservative candidates: white, male, older,

Figure 2.4. Vote choice for Nenshi – marginal effects

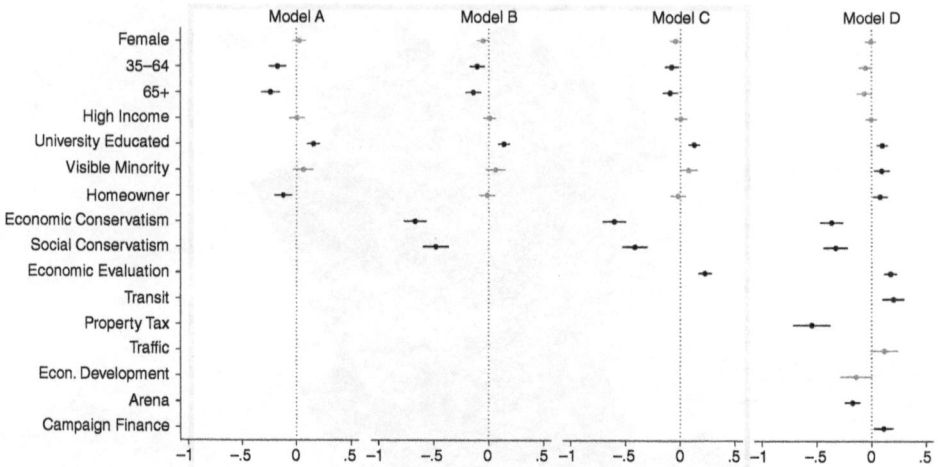

Notes: Entries report marginal effects and 95% confidence intervals. Coefficients in black are statistically significant at p < 0.1.

non-university-educated. Nenshi's base looks much like those of parties on the left: visible minorities, women, younger, university-educated.

Model B adds ideology – social and economic conservatism – to the model. Canadian research has historically discounted the salience of such a left–right dimension among voters (Lambert et al., 1986); more recent research, however, suggests that voters not only understand left and right but can locate parties and themselves in that abstract space (Cochrane, 2015). The extraordinarily large coefficients for both variables in Model B suggest that this more recent argument certainly applied in Calgary in 2017: increased social or economic conservatism was strongly associated with decreased probability of support for Nenshi. Moreover, the effects of some of the demographic characteristics are no longer significant in Model B (gender, income, homeownership). This is because those demographic characteristics' effects on vote choice are explained by members of those groups tending to have similar ideological orientations – women and atheists are more likely to be on the left, and the wealthy (with homeownership as a proxy for wealth) are more likely to be on the right.

Model C adds retrospective economic evaluations to the model – a particularly important variable to include in Calgary, where the collapse of the city's predominantly oil-and-gas economy had produced considerable economic difficulty for Calgarians in the years leading up to the 2017 election. A municipal government has only a limited ability to influence the national or provincial economy; even so, voters may punish their municipal government for a poor economy – a phenomenon some political scientists have called "blind retrospection" (Achen and Bartels, 2015). In our analysis, this economic voting effect proved to be small but statistically significant; those who thought that economic conditions in Calgary had improved were seven points more likely to vote for Nenshi than those who thought the economy had gotten worse. Notice also that other variables do not change when economic evaluations are added to the model; the marginal effects for the significant predictors in Model C continue to be significant in Model D. This suggests that economic evaluations do not mediate the effect of prior variables.

Finally, Model D adds policy issues to the analysis. Such variables represent how important particular issues are for individual voters. The clear ideological distinctions between the two mayoral candidates – as well as their opposite positions on the arena deal – can be seen in the issues that were considered most important by each candidate's supporters. Those who believed that property taxes were an extremely important issue were 58 points more likely to vote for Smith than those who were not concerned about property taxes. Conversely, those who said transit was extremely important were 18 points more likely than those who were not at all concerned about transit to vote for Nenshi. In both cases, these findings accord with a general tendency for right-leaning candidates to "own" fiscal and tax issues while left-leaning candidates "own" issues such as public transit. Finally, as expected given Smith's more favourable stance toward an arena deal with the Calgary Flames, voters who felt the arena issue was very important were 15 points more likely to vote for Smith than voters who did not.

Model D is also interesting because of how the other predictors respond to the introduction of issue importance. In the final model, only three of the original seven significant demographic predictors of vote choice continue to be significant: university education, visible minority status, and homeownership.[5] Similarly, the effect of other predictors has weakened. The size of the ideological self-placement coefficient, while still clearly very important and statistically significant, has come down slightly from Models C and D. The effect of Conservative Party identification (versus no partisanship or Liberal or Alberta Party identification) is now 14 points in favour of Smith, down from about 22 points in the previous models. The effect of NDP identification is now 12 points, down from 14 points in the previous two models. Again, this shows how different issues are associated with different sides of the political spectrum, whether that is in terms of symbolic, abstract left–right ideology or in terms of parties.

On the whole, these findings echo what McGregor, Moore, and Stephenson (2015) and Cutler and Matthews (2005) have found in past research: municipal voting behaviour is broadly similar to provincial and federal voting behaviour. The same factors matter, and they play out in largely the same way, with more distant factors being mediated by more proximate ones. This holds true even in the absence of a formal party system in Calgary.

Within the vote choice models, two factors are particularly noteworthy, and we examine these more closely in the next session. Ideology exerts a very strong effect, which continues to be strong even after a high degree of mediation from other, more proximate variables. Partisanship also exerts strong effects, and this is despite the absence of municipal parties in Calgary. These are the topics of the third section of this chapter.

Parties and Partisanship in a Non-Partisan Election

Without political parties, E.E. Schattschneider once famously declared, modern democracy is unthinkable (Schattschneider, 1942). In most elections today, political parties are indeed crucial: they frame the issues around which partisan activists mobilize (Bawn et al., 2012), they provide political identities for voters (Green et al., 2002), and they provide voters with a simple heuristic for vote choice (Sniderman et al., 1991). Most democratic elections today really *are* unthinkable save in terms of parties.

In Calgary's 2017 election, however, parties were nowhere to be found. This was not always the case – back in the mid-twentieth century, municipal candidates in Calgary organized themselves into two main parties, Labour and the more business-oriented Civic Government Association. But since the mid-1960s, civic political parties have been non-existent in Calgary (Lucas, 2019; Masson and LeSage, 1994). The city's municipal electoral machinery is entirely non-partisan: fundraising is entirely on an individual basis, lists of municipal candidates are organized on the city's website in a simple ward-by-ward manner, and the municipal ballot contains no information about candidates except for their names. Calgary's municipal elections give every appearance of being genuinely non-partisan affairs.

But are non-partisan municipal elections *really* non-partisan? The municipal ballot may not include party labels, and municipal candidates may work to hide rather than highlight their partisan affiliations, but the men and women who vote in Canadian municipal elections are the same people who vote in provincial and federal elections. Do these voters "switch off" their partisan loyalties when they turn their attention to municipal politics? If the formal institutions of Calgary's municipal election are non-partisan, does this mean that municipal voting behaviour is non-partisan as well (Stephenson et al., 2018)?

The progressive reformers, who worked hard a century ago to rid municipal elections of political parties (Copus et al., 2012), might have hoped that the answer to these questions would be yes – that voters would indeed switch off the partisan portion of their brains when they turned their attention to municipal politics. But the reality, at least in Calgary, does not fit with this vision. As we will show in this section, partisanship plays an important role in municipal elections even when municipal parties don't exist. It seems that parties and party labels are so useful to voters – especially voters who are partisans themselves – that the progressive vision of municipal politics as a non-partisan island, standing proudly alone in a vast partisan sea, is, we will argue, little more than a mirage.

Partisan Calgarians, Partisan Candidates

While Calgary's mayoral election was officially non-partisan, the candidates who sought the office were connected to varying degrees with provincial and federal provincial parties. Bill Smith, who had been president of the Progressive Conservative Party of Alberta, had the clearest partisan connections, a fact he neither hid nor advertised during the municipal election. Andre Chabot also had connections with provincial and federal Conservative parties, though his involvement was more modest and was not widely discussed during the campaign. Naheed Nenshi, while a long-time political animal, has kept his partisan affiliations closer to the vest. Many Calgary politicos associate Nenshi with the Liberals, while others emphasize his long-standing connections with the Alberta Party. Few doubt, however, that he was engaged and interested in partisan politics, both as an observer and as a potential participant, prior to his election to the mayor's office in 2010.

Calgarians were aware of these general patterns during the 2017 election. In Table 2.2, we summarize the CMES respondents' replies to the question of which provincial party, if any, they associated with each candidate. On Nenshi, respondents were divided into four roughly equal camps: those who associated him with the NDP, those who associated him with the Liberals, those who didn't know, and those who associated him with a different party. Nenshi's "purple party" rhetoric (neither red nor blue, but a mix of the two) was also reflected in the modestly higher proportion of respondents who placed him in the "none" category. Smith, unsurprisingly, gave CMES respondents less difficulty;

Table 2.2. Partisan attributions, by candidate (%)

	Nenshi	Smith	Chabot
NDP	24.3	1.1	4.3
PC	7.5	34.1	12.7
Wildrose	1.4	5.9	3.9
UCP	2.0	25.5	8.5
Liberal	24.3	2.9	6.8
Alberta Party	4.0	0.7	1.8
Other party	0.5	0.1	0.7
None	12.2	4.5	7.8
Don't know	23.8	25.1	53.7

more than half associated him with either the PC Party or the United Conservative Party (the outcome of a merger of the PC and Wildrose Parties). On Chabot, fewer than one sixth of respondents associated him with the PC Party and more than half were unsure, reflecting the lower levels of overall coverage of Chabot as well as his more distant party connections.

Calgarians, then, were generally willing and able to answer questions about the partisanship of the mayoral candidates despite the ostensibly non-partisan character of the race. This finding is even more emphatic when we consider the partisanship of the respondents themselves. In Figure 2.5, we display the answer to a simple question: did *partisan* respondents have an easier time than non-partisan respondents associating Nenshi or Smith with a political party? In both of the subfigures, the vertical axis indicates the proportion of respondents who associated Nenshi or Smith with a political party – any political party – rather than choosing "none" or "don't know." In each case we compared the respondents who were partisans (i.e., who identified fairly or very strongly with any political party) to those who were not. In both cases, the result was clear: while a majority of all respondents associated Nenshi and Smith with a political party, an *overwhelming* majority of partisans did so: more than 70% of respondents in both cases. Partisans see the political world in partisan colours, even when the election itself is non-partisan.

Partisan Votes

We have established so far that Calgarians tended to see some partisanship in the city's non-partisan mayoral race, especially when they were partisans themselves. But did this actually affect their vote choice? After all, voters may *perceive* a partisan landscape in municipal politics while still adhering to the progressive credo when the time comes to cast a

Figure 2.5. Partisan attribution, by candidate and respondent partisanship

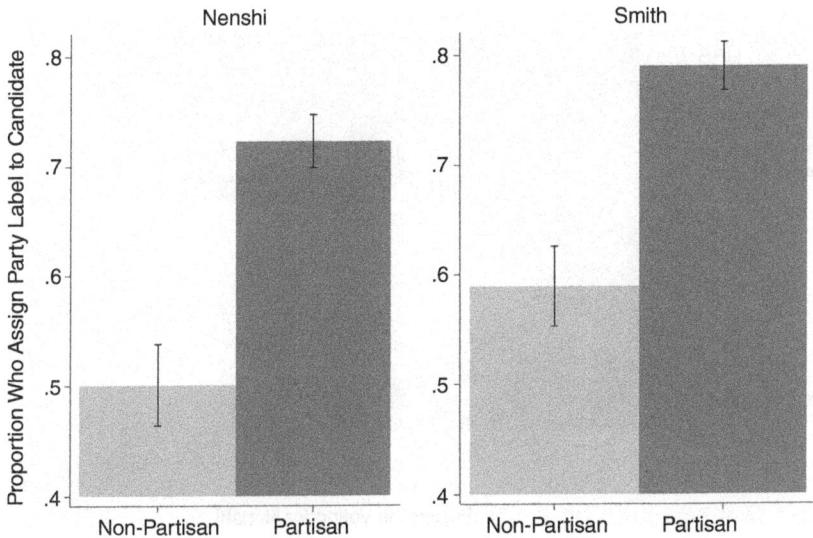

vote. If this is the case, then we should find that partisanship was generally unimportant for mayoral vote choice in Calgary in 2017a.

Figure 2.6 provides telling preliminary evidence that partisanship does indeed shape vote choice at the municipal level. The figure displays the proportion of party identifiers (along with non-partisans) who cast a vote for Nenshi in the 2017 mayoral election. The partisan patterning in the figure is obvious: some partisans (NDP, Liberal, Alberta Party) overwhelmingly supported Nenshi, while others (PC, Wildrose, UCP) overwhelmingly did not. Non-partisans were between the two extremes but were more likely to support Nenshi. Once again, it appears that voters were decidedly *not* setting partisan considerations aside in making their municipal voting decisions.

Of course, the apparent patterns in Figure 2.6 may be misleading; perhaps they are merely a reflection of respondent *ideology*. Since Smith ran a campaign to the right of Nenshi, those on the ideological right probably tended to support Smith – the very same people who were also likely to identify with the PCs, Wildrose, or the UCP. Patterns of partisan support and opposition may simply reflect ideological proximity rather than partisan alignment.

To test this possibility, we carried out an additional analysis. We began by generating two new variables. The first was a measure of ideological distance: the absolute value of the distance between a respondent's

Figure 2.6. Nenshi vote, by respondent partisanship

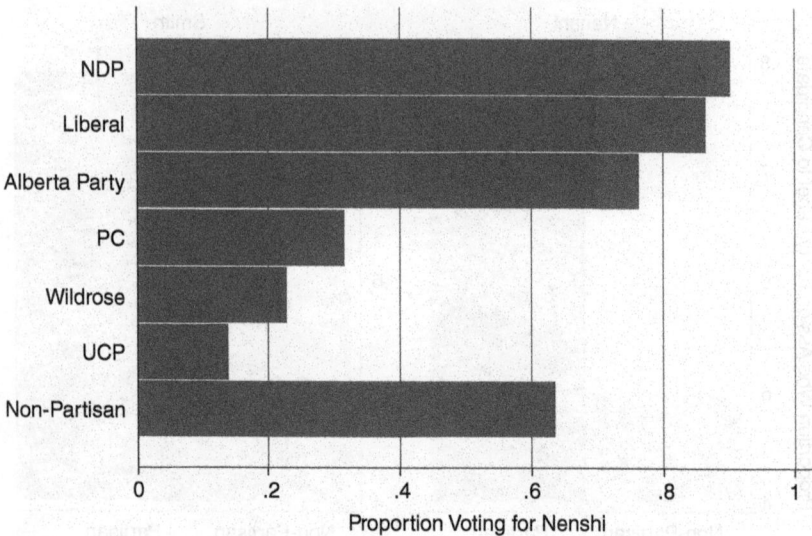

own self-reported ideology (on a 0 to 10 scale) and their perception of each *candidate's* ideology on the same scale. This ranged from 0 (for those who placed themselves and the candidate at the same point on the scale) to 10 (for those who placed themselves at one extreme and the candidate at the other extreme). The second variable was a measure of co-partisanship. This variable was coded 1 if a respondent identified with a party *and* associated a mayoral candidate with the same party; it was coded 0 if a respondent did not perceive a particular mayoral candidate as a "co-partisan."

Having created the ideological distance and co-partisanship variables, we could now tease out the difference between ideological proximity and partisanship in mayoral vote choice. To do so, we have regressed the Nenshi and Smith vote choices on the ideological distance and co-partisanship variables and reported the associated marginal effects in Figure 2.7. For each ideological distance score, the figure reports the predicted probability of a Nenshi or Smith vote, depending on whether the respondent is a co-partisan (solid line) or not a co-partisan (dashed line).

Figure 2.7 demonstrates clearly that ideological distance is a crucial component of mayoral vote choice: as a respondent's perceived ideological distance from Nenshi increased from 0 to 3, for instance, their predicted probability of voting for Nenshi declined by about 33%. The

Figure 2.7. Predicted probability of vote, by ideological distance and co-partisanship

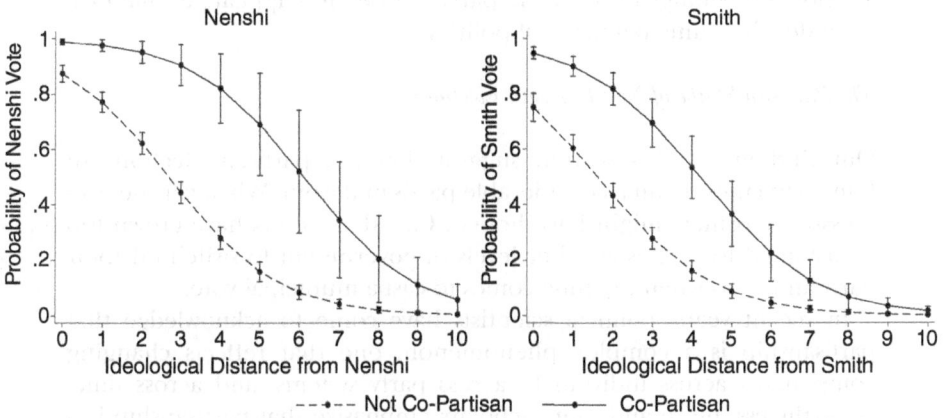

downward slope of the lines in both figures indicates, unsurprisingly, that a respondent's probability of choosing a candidate declined as the perceived ideological distance between the respondent and the candidate grew.

For our purposes, however, the big story of Figure 2.7 is the consistent distance between the solid and dashed lines: for practically all possible ideological distance scores, co-partisans were consistently more likely to vote for a particular candidate than those who did not see the candidate as a co-partisan. The distance between the two lines is remarkable, particularly in the Nenshi figure; even co-partisans with very large ideological distance scores remained quite likely to vote for their co-partisan candidate. For Nenshi voters, the increase in the predicted probability of a Nenshi voter being a co-partisan (35%) is equivalent to moving more than 3 points closer to Nenshi in ideological distance; for Bill Smith, the co-partisan boost (24%) is equivalent to a decreased ideological distance score of about 3 points.

These are remarkable numbers, particularly because the partisan affiliations we are discussing in these analyses are drawn from another level of government altogether (Cutler and Matthews, 2005). This means that the chance that the co-partisan variable is capturing something other than shared partisan identity – such as shared issue positions – is attenuated by the fact that it is difficult to impute municipal issue positions from provincial partisanship. In fact, when we ran the same analysis using federal partisanship, where the link between federal partisanship and municipal issue positions was even *more* attenuated, our substantive findings were identical. Simply put, co-partisanship – a perception that a candidate belongs to the same party as oneself – appears to matter a great deal in municipal mayoral politics.

The Partisan Shape of Non-Partisan Elections

Our findings in this section suggest that non-partisan elections in Canadian cities retain a considerable partisan flavour. Whatever the progressive reformers might have hoped, Canadian voters have grown too accustomed to parties at other levels of government to switch off their partisan brains when the time comes to cast a municipal vote.

In recent years, political scientists have come to acknowledge that partisanship is a complex phenomenon, one that reflects changing components across individuals, across party systems, and across time. Nevertheless, more and more scholars emphasize that partisanship is a *social identity*, one that reflects a voter's conception of the social groups to which he or she belongs (Green et al., 2002; Mason, 2018). Our findings in this brief analysis lend some support to this view. When an individual is more likely to vote for a mayoral candidate because she believes that she and the candidate belong to the same federal or provincial party, what is partisanship actually *doing* to produce this effect? The simplest answer, we would argue, is social identity: co-partisanship reflects a perception that the voter and a mayoral candidate are on the same political team. Like a thermos with a lingering coffee flavour, partisanship is not easily expunged from voters for whom political party labels are a valuable tool for interpreting and understanding their place in the political landscape.

Conclusion

In retrospect, Calgary's 2017 municipal election result looks typical of Canadian city elections, particularly with regard to the dominance of the incumbent candidates who sought re-election. Beneath the surface, however, the election was far from typical: hotly contested, generously funded, deeply competitive, and – if turnout is any indication – more engaging to Calgarians than any other municipal election in recent memory.

In this chapter, we have sought to provide an overview of what happened in Calgary in the weeks leading up to the election, as well as an analysis of the factors that were most important for understanding who supported each of the major mayoral candidates, Naheed Nenshi and Bill Smith. We then highlighted the importance of ideology and partisanship for mayoral vote choice. While municipal candidates and pundits may continue to insist that municipal politics is wholly non-partisan and that ideology has no place at the municipal level ("there's no left-wing or right-wing position on how to fill a pothole"), our findings in this chapter suggest that municipal voters did not hesitate to draw on their ideological or partisan identities when they cast a ballot in Calgary.

NOTES

1 Reassuringly for Nenshi, about the same number chose the *highest* possible score.
2 For a discussion of changing views of Nenshi in Calgary, see Markusoff (2020). See also Lucas and McGregor (2020) for more detail on coalitions of support for and opposition to Nenshi.
3 According to Wenzel's remarks in this video, the quote is a paraphrase of advice given to Wenzel by former Calgary mayor Dave Bronconnier.
4 See Rieger (2019) for an overview of the original proposals, as well as the more recent agreement on the NHL arena.
5 Homeownership is significant and positively associated with Nenshi support in the final model. This is because of the property tax issue importance variable: among those who do not consider property taxes important, homeowners are slightly more likely to support Nenshi than renters. Given the very small number of respondents who selected values in the 0–6 range for property tax issue importance, however, we believe that this particular finding should be interpreted with caution.

REFERENCES

Achen, C. H., & Bartels, L. M. (2016). *Democracy for realists: Why elections do not produce responsive government.* Princeton University Press.
Bawn, K., Cohen, M., Karol, D., Masket, S., Noel, H., & Zaller, J. (2012). A theory of political parties: Groups, policy demands and nominations in American politics. *Perspectives on Politics, 10*(3), 571–597. https://doi.org /10.1017/S1537592712001624
Cochrane, C. (2015). *Left and right: The small world of political ideas.* McGill–Queen's University Press.
Copus, C., Wingfield, M., Steyvers, K., & Reynaert, H. (2012). A place to party? Parties and nonpartisanship in local government. In *Oxford Handbook of Urban Politics* (pp. 210–230). Oxford University Press.
Cutler, F., & Matthews, J. S. (2005). The challenge of municipal voting: Vancouver 2002. *Canadian Journal of Political Science, 38*(2), 359–382. https://doi.org/10.1017/S0008423905040151

Green, D., Palmquist, B., & Schickler, E. (2002). *Partisan hearts and minds.* Yale University Press.

Lambert, R. D., Curtis, J. E., Brown, S. D., & Kay, B. J. (1986). In search of left/right beliefs in the Canadian electorate. *Canadian Journal of Political Science, 19*(3), 541–564.

Lucas, J. (2019). The size and sources of municipal incumbency advantage in Canada. *Urban Affairs Review.* https://doi.org/10.5683/SP2/8BLD2I

Lucas, J., & McGregor, R. M. (2020). Are city elections unique? Perceptions of electoral cleavages and social sorting across levels of government. *Electoral Studies.* https://doi.org/10.1016/j.electstud.2020.102165

Markusoff, J. (2020). Naheed Nenshi falls back to earth. *Maclean's.* 26 February.

Mason, L. (2018). *Uncivil agreement: How politics became our identity.* University of Chicago Press.

Masson, J., & LeSage, E. C. (1994). *Alberta's local governments: Politics and democracy.* University of Alberta Press.

Rieger, S. (2019). What's new in Calgary's tentative arena deal. *CBC News Calgary.* https://www.cbc.ca/news/canada/calgary/calgary-proposed-arena-deal-1.5221185

Schattschneider, E. E. (1942). *Party government.* Transaction.

Sniderman, P. M., Brody, R. A., & Tetlock, P. E. (1991). *Reasoning and choice: explorations in political psychology.* Cambridge University Press.

Stephenson, L. B., McGregor, R. M., & Moore, A. A. (2018). Sins of the brother: Partisanship and accountability in Toronto, 2014. In S. Breux & J. Couture (Eds.), *Accountability and responsiveness at the municipal level: Views from Canada* (pp. 23–48). McGill–Queen's University Press.

3 Montreal

ÉRIC BÉLANGER AND JEAN-FRANÇOIS DAOUST

Just four months before the 2017 Montreal municipal election, incumbent mayor Denis Coderre seemed well-positioned to win a second consecutive mandate. A Léger poll published in late June 2017 suggested that 43% of voters intended to support his party versus 29% for Projet Montréal, with only 14% of respondents intending to support a third party. Yet on Election Day, Coderre was narrowly defeated by Projet Montréal candidate Valérie Plante, who became Montreal's first-ever female mayor.

How can we account for this surprising turn of events? How could it be that a relatively popular incumbent mayor like Denis Coderre, who by most accounts had a good record that was untainted by corruption scandals like those that plagued previous administrations, was not rewarded by voters for his performance? We might first note that Coderre's satisfaction score, as recorded in the Canadian Municipal Election Study (CMES) pre-election survey, stood at 54%, which was high but not overwhelmingly so. In addition, the same June Léger poll revealed that while 44% of Montrealers said they had a positive opinion of his party, Équipe Denis Coderre, 37% said they had a negative opinion of it. These numbers suggest that the public's opinion of Coderre was perhaps more polarized than we might have expected. In comparison, positive opinions of Projet Montréal stood at 37% in the June poll and negative ones at only 12%, with as many as 40% not yet having an opinion about Plante's party. These numbers suggest that she had significant room for growth during the Montreal 2017 campaign, provided that she could effectively attack Coderre's image and invite voters to think more positively and more prospectively when deciding whom they wanted in office for the next four years.

This chapter provides an overview of Montreal's 2017 municipal campaign. It also summarizes the election's outcome and analyses the factors that explain the support eventually received by the two main mayoral candidates, Plante and Coderre. We then examine more closely the possibility that support for these candidates relied on prospective considerations, such as anticipation of the race's outcome, in addition to retrospective ones, such as the incumbent mayor's performance in office.[1]

Election Overview

The Mayoral Campaign

In 2012, revelations made during the hearings of the Commission of Inquiry on the Awarding and Management of Public Contracts in the Construction Industry (also known as the Charbonneau Commission) put an end to the political career of then mayor Gérald Tremblay, leader of Union Montréal. Having served as mayor since 2002, Tremblay was suspected of public fraud linked to organized crime in the awarding of city construction contracts. In November 2012, he resigned and left politics. Michael Applebaum was then selected by the Municipal Council to serve as interim mayor. However, Applebaum failed to remove the taint of corruption surrounding his party. In fact, a few months later, in June 2013, Applebaum himself was arrested and indicted for breach of trust, corruption in municipal affairs, and 14 counts of fraud. He resigned the day after his arrest, just a few months before the upcoming municipal election. In short, back in 2013, turmoil characterized Montreal politics.

The resignations of Tremblay and Applebaum created an opportunity for an outsider candidate to take the lead in Montreal and change both the city's direction and its reputation for corruption. Denis Coderre, a former federal minister and a prominent member of the federal Liberal caucus, seized it. With a 5.7% lead over his closest rival (Mélanie Joly, from the party Vrai Changement pour Montréal), Coderre quite easily won the mayoral election of 2013. He would govern without any major scandal. His record was also relatively positive, notably in terms of economic prosperity. Unsurprisingly, his 2017 re-election campaign emphasized these positive aspects of his tenure and the need to elect him to a second term so as to maintain this direction.

Coderre's main opponent in the 2017 election was Valérie Plante. Coming from the not-for-profit sector, Plante was first elected in 2013 as City Councillor for the Sainte-Marie district of the Ville-Marie borough, running under the banner of Projet Montréal. In December 2016 she was unexpectedly chosen as the party's new leader and mayoral candidate for the upcoming election (she received 52% of the party membership vote). Although Plante was well-known and -appreciated by the party's membership, she suffered a name recognition deficit vis-à-vis Coderre. Plante therefore used her time during the lead-up to the election campaign to make herself better-known to Montrealers. Perhaps her most daring attempt at this involved a publicity stunt in mid-August 2017 – just a few weeks before the official start of the election campaign – that used a large picture of her with a caption presenting her as "the right man for the job" ("L'homme de la situation"). The ad was eye-catching, cleverly upending gendered expectations about what made a candidate fit for the job of city mayor. At the very least, the ad had people talking about Plante and her party.

The electoral campaign officially started on 22 September. A poll published on the first day of the race gave Coderre a five-point lead over Plante but also indicated that as many as 41% of respondents had yet to decide whom they would support. The poll numbers also suggested that the mayoral campaign was, in effect, a two-way race between the two.[2] In fact, as many as six other candidates were also in the race. Five of them ran as independents[3] and, in the end, would collectively receive less than 2% of the final vote. The sixth candidate was Jean Fortier of the party Coalition Montréal. After campaigning for nearly a month, Fortier abandoned the race on 18 October. Estimating that Plante was the candidate who was better positioned to defeat the incumbent, Fortier called on his supporters to rally behind her and Projet Montréal.[4]

In the end, Montrealers were left to choose between two main candidates who appeared to represent significantly different political projects and ideologies. This impression is confirmed by the CMES data. Respondents were asked to locate each candidate on a general left–right ideological scale where 0 means left, 10 means right and 5 represents the centre. According to these data, Plante (4.2) was clearly viewed by respondents as being ideologically to the left of Denis Coderre (6.0).[5]

According to many observers, Plante was clearly running a better campaign than Coderre (e.g., Castonguay, 2017; Normandin, 2017), and many praised the effectiveness of her ad campaign (e.g., Martellini, 2017). As Election Day neared, it became obvious that Plante had become a genuine threat to Coderre. Indeed, two weeks before Election Day, two polls published by two different firms showed a statistical tie between the two candidates. Table 3.1 summarizes these polls' results, showing the progress made by Plante and suggesting that the race had become too close to call.

Table 3.1. Campaign vote intention polls (%)

	Plante	Coderre	Undecided	Polling firm
22 September	25	30	41	Mainstreet
22 October	38	38	21	Léger
24 October	39	37	17	Crop

Plainly, the election campaign clearly mattered for Plante. She ran a very good and mostly positive campaign around ambitious projects such as the creation of a brand-new subway line (see below). She was able to make herself and her party better known to Montrealers, which allowed Projet Montréal to build upon the ideological base of support it had established in previous elections.

Council Races

Elections in Montreal are structured differently than in the other municipalities in this volume. Most Montrealers cast three votes when going to the polls: for city mayor, city councillor, and borough mayor. In all, there are 65 elected officials on the Montreal City Council: 46 city councillors, 18 borough mayors, and the mayor of Montreal (who also serves as mayor of the Ville-Marie borough).[6]

As in most Canadian municipal elections, the media focused on the mayoral race. However, council races are also important for providing a majority of council seats in support of the mayor; without such support, it is much more difficult for the mayor to implement his or her program. In addition, because Montreal is an amalgamated city, borough mayors – who also sit on the City Council – are key for consolidating a popular support base for the mayor and his or her party.

The borough mayoral race that received the most attention was in Plateau Mont-Royal, where the incumbent Luc Ferrandez (Projet Montréal) was well-known for his straight talk and his radical ecological agenda, which was appreciated by many of his constituents (Ferrandez was elected with 45%, 51%, and 66% of the votes in 2009, 2013, and 2017, respectively). This was a non-trivial borough race, for Ferrandez's record was often viewed as an indicator of what Projet Montréal might do at the city level if elected. His work was cast in a very negative light by Projet Montréal's opponents and was framed as the product of extreme policy views. For example, during the campaign, Denis Coderre frequently argued that a victory by Valérie Plante would bring about a "Plateau-ization" of Montreal, by which he meant that Projet Montréal would greatly extend the kind of pro-environment, anti-car policies that

Ferrandez had implemented in his borough since becoming its mayor in 2009. In fact, Ferrandez ended up quitting his position in 2019 in part because he viewed Projet Montréal under Plante as not radical enough in its implementation of environmental policy.

The City of Montreal covers a vast and heterogeneous territory, and it is no wonder that competition in some areas of the city tends to depart from general patterns. So it should be noted that competition in two of the city's boroughs involved political parties that only presented candidates in those areas. These borough-based parties are Équipe Anjou (in the borough of Anjou) and Équipe Barbe (in the borough of LaSalle). Candidates from each of these two parties managed to get re-elected as borough mayors (Luis Miranda in Anjou and Manon Barbe in LaSalle). In addition, each party has controlled its borough's council since 2013. All City Councillors and Borough Councillors from LaSalle are affiliated with Équipe Barbe. In the case of Anjou, the sole City Councillor is with Équipe Anjou, as are two of the three Borough Councillors (the third Borough Councillor, Lynne Shand, was elected as an independent candidate). These boroughs thus form two politically distinct "islands within the island," so to speak, and are governed by parties that were created to defend their respective boroughs' autonomy vis-à-vis the city centre.

Issues and Events

As in any electoral campaign, the candidates debated a variety of issues, although some certainly stood out more than others. Among the salient issues in the 2017 Montreal mayoral campaign, one in particular seems to dented Denis Coderre's image. Early in the campaign, Valérie Plante put him on the spot for having authorized the organization of a Formula E (electric car) race held in downtown Montreal in July 2017, just a few weeks before the start of the election campaign. Rumours were circulating that the race had failed to attract crowds and that a massive number of tickets had remained unsold. Suspected by the opposition of having wasted public funds on this event, which had also inconvenienced residents of the neighbourhood where the race was held, Coderre refused to disclose the number of tickets sold. On 1 November, just four days before Election Day, the organizers of the Formula E event revealed that as many as 20,000 tickets had been distributed free of charge and that the remaining 25,000 tickets had been either sold to the public or made available to the event's partners and sponsors. With the rumours confirmed, Coderre simply replied that he regretted not having disclosed these numbers himself sooner. Though some might see this as a minor scandal at most, it painted the incumbent mayor as somebody who had things to hide and who was stubborn and/or untrustworthy.

Fuelling Plante's criticisms of Coderre as being an old-school politician who was not transparent enough, the Société Radio-Canada (SRC) made public near the end of the campaign (on 23 October) several testimonials from journalists and public officials claiming that Coderre had tried to control information on a regular basis since his election as mayor in 2013. According to the SRC report, journalists covering municipal affairs had been pressured, some even intimidated, by the mayor himself or by people from his entourage. Also, City Hall employees had been reprimanded when it was found that they had spoken to the media without the mayor's authorization. These revelations added to a scandal from a year prior when it was revealed that the Montreal police (SPVM) had spied on well-known *La Presse* journalist Patrick Lagacé after the latter published embarrassing stories about Coderre – many suspected at the time that these spying activities had been requested by the mayor himself. Coderre denied the SRC report's allegations. Yet together with the Formula E controversy, these allegations may have fostered more strongly negative opinions of Coderre relative to Plante. For example, when the CMES survey asked whether there was anything in particular that the respondents disliked about each of the mayoral candidates, 29% indicated that there was nothing they disliked about Valérie Plante; this percentage dropped to 15% in the case of Denis Coderre – in other words, Montrealers were twice as likely to be able to name something they disliked about the incumbent as they were about the challenger. There is little doubt that Coderre's record contributed to this.

Plante distinguished herself from Coderre by presenting the image of a grassroots candidate who was deeply concerned about transit issues. She claimed that if elected she would be the "mobility mayor" ("la mairesse de la mobilité"). To drive her point home, she pledged that she would create a new subway line (the Pink Line) that would provide relief to the overcrowded Orange Line. Plante also emphasized environmental issues, declaring that she wished to create and protect more "green" areas across the city. Her emphasis on transit, environmental protection, services to families, and decentralization to the boroughs as the best way to implement these projects aimed at making clear her vision for improving Montrealers' quality of life. Plante's emphasis on quality of life for families also addressed growing concerns about housing affordability in Montreal, where the prices for existing and new stocks of housing have increased in recent years.

Figure 3.1. Issue importance in the 2017 Montreal election

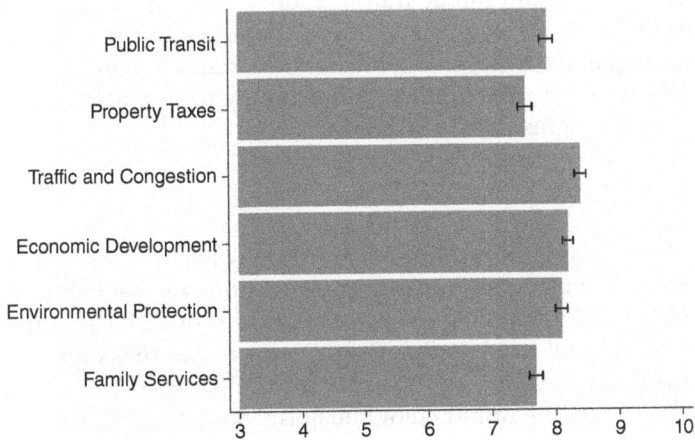

Note: 95% confidence intervals are displayed.

All of these issues came to the fore during the leaders' debates. Two official debates were held, one in French (19 October), the other in English (23 October). In addition, the two mayoral candidates debated each other less formally on the set of the televised talk show *Tout le monde en parle* on 15 October. During these debates, Coderre's lack of transparency, his centralizing tendencies, and his failure to address transit problems efficiently were raised by Plante as important weaknesses of her opponent. In response, Coderre criticized Plante's and Projet Montréal's promises as unrealistic and as having the potential to lead to a "Plateau-ization" of Montreal (that is, they would make the entire city unfriendly to car traffic).

Figure 3.1 presents a summary of issue importance in the 2017 Montreal election, as reflected in the views of CMES respondents. To the standard battery of four issues examined in all cities in this volume, we add two Montreal-specific ones: environmental protection and family services. These two issues were selected for this city because they proved to be important in the early days of the campaign, with Projet Montréal making several environment-friendly proposals (such as a car-free Mount Royal Park) and pushing for a better quality of life for Montreal families (related to, for instance, the presence of schools and recreational facilities in some redeveloping areas of the city). According to the data from Figure 3.1, the issue of traffic and congestion was the most salient to

Montrealers in this election, followed closely by economic development, the environment, and public transit. Property taxes and family services were the least salient issues out of the six. These data suggest that the voters' issue agenda was perhaps a bit closer to Plante's than to Coderre's, although economic development was certainly an issue that tapped into the latter's strengths.

The Election Result

About 42.5% of registered Montrealers turned out to vote on 5 November 2017. Despite the race's competitiveness, turnout was not higher than in 2013 (43.3%). Valérie Plante won the election with 51.4% of the vote; Denis Coderre received 45.7%. Plante became the first woman to win a Montreal mayoral election. Moreover, with 33 seats out of 64 going to Projet Montréal, she would enjoy a majority on the City Council (a gain of 14 seats from 2013 for her party).

Figure 3.2 illustrates the geography of the vote share. As the map shows, Plante's support was highest in five areas of the island: in Rosemont and Plateau Mont-Royal, in Hochelaga-Maisonneuve, in the Sud-Ouest, in Lachine, and in Île Bizard. Most of these areas, on the eastern side of the island, had long leaned toward Projet Montréal. The areas where Plante received the least support (and where, by extension, Coderre received his strongest support) were in Saint-Léonard and Montréal-Nord (which Coderre represented as a Member of Parliament in Ottawa from 1997 to 2013), as well as in Saint-Laurent. He and his party also performed well in the western and northern parts of the city in 2013.

Table 3.2 displays the election results for the City Councillor races; re-elected incumbents are marked with an asterisk. Overall, Projet Montréal managed to elect 23 City Councillors. Équipe Denis Coderre saw 19 of its candidates elected. Three well-known incumbent councillors from other parties who had decided to run for Équipe Denis Coderre in 2017 were defeated: Richard Bergeron (former leader of Projet Montréal, from 2004 to 2014), Elsie Lefebvre (formerly with Coalition Montréal), and Lorraine Pagé (formerly with Vrai Changement pour Montréal). One candidate from Coalition Montréal, Marvin Rotrand, managed to keep his seat (district of Snowdon). The remaining three City Councillor seats went to candidates from the borough-based parties Équipe Anjou and Équipe Barbe.

Table 3.3 shows the results for borough mayoral races in the 2017 election. Many borough incumbent losses were by candidates who had run for Équipe Denis Coderre. Two high-profile borough mayors

Figure 3.2. Vote share for Plante, by district

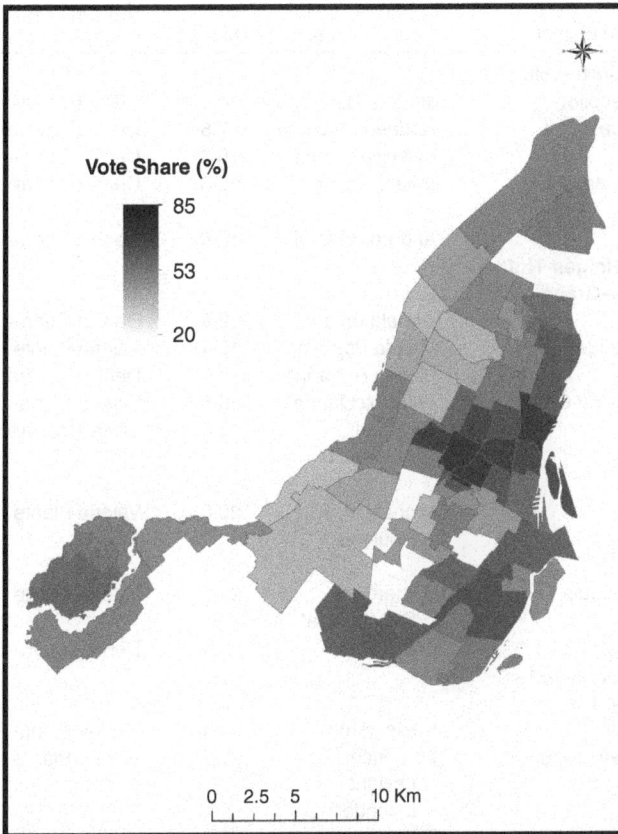

Note: The blank areas are independent cities and not part of the Montreal election.

who had also decided to run under the banner of Coderre's party in 2017 lost their re-election bids: Réal Ménard and Russell Copeman (both formerly with Coalition Montréal). Anie Samson, who switched to Coderre's party in 2013, was also defeated. All of them lost to Projet Montréal candidates. Overall, 10 boroughs elected a representative from Projet Montréal, bringing that party's total of City Council seats to 33. As for Équipe Denis Coderre, six of its candidates won their borough mayoral races, providing Coderre with a total of 25 City Council seats. Finally, as mentioned earlier, Anjou and LaSalle were the only boroughs having elected a mayor not affiliated with one of the two main parties.

Table 3.2. Election results, by district (asterisks denote incumbent candidates)

Borough and district	Council winner	Margin	City mayoral winner	Margin
Ahuntsic–Carterville				
Sault-au-Récollet	Jérôme Normand	4.5	Denis Coderre	0.7
Saint-Sulpice	Hadrien Parizeau	7.5	Denis Coderre	4.3
Ahuntsic	Nathalie Goulet	16.1	Denis Coderre	1.5
Bordeaux–Cartierville	Effie Giannou	25.3	Denis Coderre	28.2
Anjou				
Anjou	Andrée Hénault*	18.5	Denis Coderre	5.3
Côte-des-Neiges–Notre-Dame-de-Grâce				
Darlington	Lionel Perez*	9.8	Denis Coderre	17.3
Côte-des-Neiges	Magda Popeanu*	18.4	Valérie Plante	1.1
Snowdon	Marvin Rotrand*	8.6	Denis Coderre	2.4
Notre-Dame-de-Grâce	Peter McQueen*	35.5	Valérie Plante	12.4
Loyola	Christian Arsenault	11.4	Denis Coderre	0.6
Lachine				
Lachine	Micheline Rouleau	20.8	Valérie Plante	20.0
LaSalle				
Sault-Saint-Louis	Richard Deschamps*	24.3	Valérie Plante	4.2
Cecil-P.-Newman	Lise Zarac	5.1	Denis Coderre	2.4
Mercier–Hochelaga–Maisonneuve				
Tétreaultville	Suzie Miron	16.4	Valérie Plante	8.3
Maisonneuve–Longue-Pointe	Laurence Lavigne-Lalonde*	27.7	Valérie Plante	19.6
Hochelaga	Éric Alan Caldwell*	43.0	Valérie Plante	36.7
Louis-Riel	Karine Boivin-Roy*	8.1	Denis Coderre	2.2
Montréal-Nord				
Marie-Clarac	Abdelhaq Sari	9.0	Denis Coderre	21.3
Ovide–Clermont	Denis Coderre/ Chantal Rossi	30.9	Denis Coderre	28.3
Pierrefonds–Roxboro				
Bois-de-Liesse	Benoit Langevin	5.4	Denis Coderre	1.6
Cap-Saint-Jacques	Catherine Clément-Talbot*	7.6	Valérie Plante	0.9
Plateau-Mont-Royal				
Mile-End	Richard Ryan*	45.1	Valérie Plante	37.5
De Lorimier	Marianne Giguère	41.7	Valérie Plante	33.9

Table 3.2 (*continued*)

Borough and district	Council winner	Margin	City mayoral winner	Margin
Jeanne-Mance	Alex Norris*	30.4	Valérie Plante	20.7
Rivière-des-Prairies– Pointe-aux-Trembles				
La Pointe-aux-Prairies	Richard Guay*	0.7	Denis Coderre	1.9
Pointe-aux-Trembles	Suzanne Décarie*	10.1	Valérie Plante	3.0
Rivière-des-Prairies	Giovanni Rapanà*	19.9	Denis Coderre	17.4
Rosemont–La Petite-Patrie				
Saint-Édouard	François Limoges*	54.8	Valérie Plante	40.4
Étienne-Desmarteau	Stéphanie Watt	34.8	Valérie Plante	30.7
Vieux-Rosemont	Christine Gosselin*	35.1	Valérie Plante	21.9
Marie-Victorin	Jocelyn Pauzé	5.3	Valérie Plante	1.2
Saint-Laurent				
Côte-de-Liesse	Francesco Miele*	36.8	Denis Coderre	23.5
Norman-McLaren	Aref Salem*	13.5	Denis Coderre	15.9
Saint-Léonard				
Saint-Léonard-Est	Patricia Lattanzio*	34.9	Denis Coderre	24.6
Saint-Léonard-Ouest	Dominic Perri*	33.8	Denis Coderre	22.8
Sud-Ouest				
Saint-Henri-Est–Petite- Bourgogne–Pointe- Saint-Charles– Griffintown	Craig Sauvé*	34.1	Valérie Plante	19.0
Saint-Paul–Émard–Saint- Henri-Ouest	Anne-Marie Sigouin*	32.1	Valérie Plante	22.6
Verdun				
Champlain–L'Île-des- Soeurs	Marie-Josée Parent	5.8	Denis Coderre	5.7
Desmarchais–Crawford	Sterling Downey*	16.0	Valérie Plante	22.5
Ville-Marie				
Peter-McGill	Cathy Wong	12.7	Denis Coderre	14.8
Saint-Jacques	Robert Beaudry	6.7	Valérie Plante	9.5
Sainte-Marie	Valérie Plante/ Sophie Mauzerolle	35.7	Valérie Plante	29.3
Villeray–Saint-Michel– Parc-Extension				
Saint-Michel	Frantz Benjamin*	23.9	Denis Coderre	23.5
François-Perrault	Sylvain Ouellet*	18.4	Valérie Plante	10.9
Villeray	Rosannie Filato	2.4	Valérie Plante	34.2
Parc-Extension	Mary Deros*	5.8	Valérie Plante	4.5

Table 3.3. Borough mayoral election results (asterisks denote incumbent candidates)

Borough	Borough mayoral winner	Margin	City mayoral winner	Margin
Ahuntsic–Cartierville	Émilie Thuillier	5.0	Denis Coderre	7.7
Anjou	Luis Miranda*	28.9	Denis Coderre	5.3
Côte-des-Neiges–Notre-Dame-de-Grâce	Sue Montgomery	3.8	Denis Coderre	0.0
Lachine	Maja Vodanovic	15.2	Valérie Plante	20.0
LaSalle	Manon Barbe*	31.2	Valérie Plante	1.1
L'Île-Bizard–Sainte-Geneviève	Normand Marinacci*	6.7	Valérie Plante	5.3
Mercier–Hochelaga–Maisonneuve	Pierre Lessard-Blais	10.1	Valérie Plante	15.5
Montréal-Nord	Christine Black*	32.6	Denis Coderre	23.8
Outremont	Philipe Tomlinson	15.8	Valérie Plante	10.3
Pierrefonds–Roxboro	Dimitrios Jim Beis*	12.7	Denis Coderre	0.4
Plateau-Mont-Royal	Luc Ferrandez*	31.4	Valérie Plante	31.3
Rivière-des-Prairies–Pointe-aux-Trembles	Chantal Rouleau*	14.7	Denis Coderre	5.5
Rosemont–La Petite-Patrie	François William Croteau*	36.6	Valérie Plante	24.2
Saint-Laurent	Alan De Sousa*	33.9	Denis Coderre	20.1
Saint-Léonard	Michel Bissonnet*	34.1	Denis Coderre	23.6
Sud-Ouest	Benoît Dorais*	42.8	Valérie Plante	20.7
Verdun	Jean-François Parenteau*	8.4	Valérie Plante	7.2
Ville-Marie	Valérie Plante	–	Valérie Plante	11.2
Villeray–Saint-Michel–Parc-Extension	Giuliana Fumagalli	8.1	Valérie Plante	11.6

Vote Choice

We now examine Montrealers' vote choice calculus in the 2017 municipal election. As in other chapters, Figure 3.3 provides a visual summary of the marginal effects based on logistic regression models, with each model successively adding a new bloc of variables to the equation. As elsewhere in this volume, these models predict the vote for the winning candidate as their dependent variable, meaning in our case that these models estimate the vote in favour of Valérie Plante as opposed to Denis Coderre. Hence, positive effects indicate a vote in favour of Plante while negative effects indicate a vote against Plante (so in favour of Coderre, as the two candidates accounted for over 97% of the vote). All the variables are coded on a 0–1 scale.

Figure 3.3. Vote choice for Plante – marginal effects

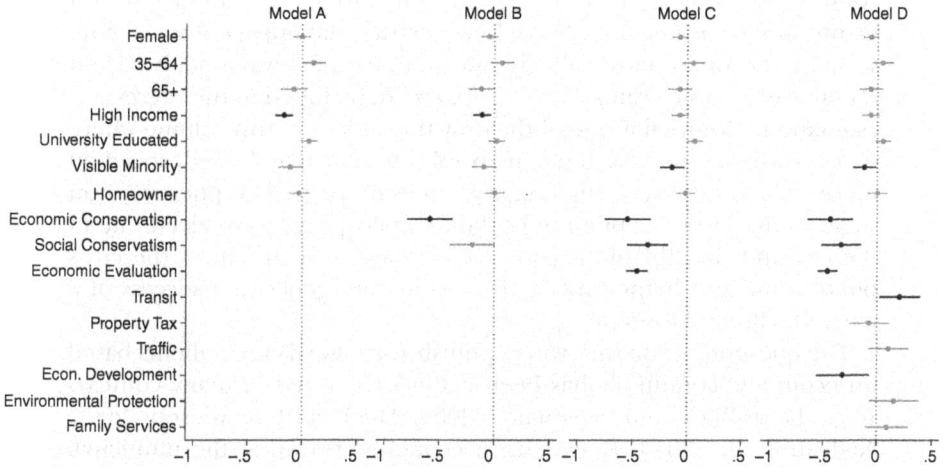

Notes: Entries report marginal effects and 95% confidence intervals. Coefficients in black are statistically significant at p < 0.1.

Model A considers the impact of socio-demographic variables on the vote decision. Among this set of characteristics, only household income has a statistically significant impact. The result indicates that more afflu-ent voters were less likely to vote for Plante than less affluent ones (an average marginal effect of –16 percentage points if we compare the least affluent with the most affluent). We note the absence of a gender gap in voting, which may be somewhat surprising given that the 2017 mayoral race pitted a woman against a man. Finally, it is worth pointing out that, when economic evaluations and issues are introduced (see Models C and D), the income effect vanishes, while a significant impact of visible minority status emerges, favouring Denis Coderre (the p-value for this variable in Model A is 0.11).

Model B adds two ideological self-identification variables. The first one, economic conservatism, is strongly associated with a vote against Plante (maximum average marginal effect of –59 percentage points). That said, this variable's distribution (mean of 0.24 on a 0–1 scale) indi-cates that ideological positioning on the economic dimension proved to be a huge reservoir of support for Plante, given that few Montreal-ers position themselves as economic conservatives. The second ideologi-cal variable, social conservatism, is just shy of statistical significance in Model B. Much as with economic conservatism, CMES respondents in

Montreal tend to locate themselves closer to the lower end of the social conservatism scale (mean of 0.3), and this variable's relationship with Plante support is negative. Note, however, that the impact of social conservatism becomes statistically significant in the next two models (C and D) once economic evaluations and issues are included in the regression estimation. Montreal is one of the only three cities in this volume where social conservatism is related to mayoral vote choice in the fully specified model (the other two being Calgary and Winnipeg). This phenomenon suggests the presence of an important socially progressive electorate in the city and that this non-economic cleavage also structures the city's political life and helps explain the recent emergence and success of a party like Projet Montréal.

The question of whether voters punish (or reward) incumbents based on economic conditions has been extensively tested in many contexts (e.g., Lewis-Beck and Stegmaier, 2000; Duch and Stevenson, 2008; Nadeau et al., 2013). Research on economic voting at the municipal level has been sparser but has tended to confirm the presence of economic voting at this level too (Martins and Veiga, 2013; Dassonneville et al., 2016; Anderson et al., 2017; Bélanger and Tessier, forthcoming). Model C incorporates a variable that taps voters' retrospective evaluations of the state of Montreal's economy. The variable indicates that economic evaluations had a strong effect on vote choice. Respondents with a positive outlook on Montreal's economy were less likely to support challenger Plante over incumbent Coderre (maximum average marginal effect of –46 percentage points). The extent to which this variable played in favour of Coderre remains in question, however, since "only" 46% of CMES respondents viewed Montreal's economy as having improved over the year prior. As many as 36% indicated that they had perceived no change in the city's economic conditions (the variable's mean is 0.65 on a 0–1 scale). In short, this retrospective variable did help Coderre but perhaps not as much as it ought to have, given that Montrealers' perceptions of the city's economy were not uniformly positive.

Model D is the fully specified model and adds to the analysis the six policy issue variables presented earlier in Figure 3.1. Recall that environmental protection and family services were two Montreal-specific issues. In the multivariate regression model these two issues are positively associated with a vote for Plante, as one might expect; however, their relationship is not statistically significant. The regression estimates indicate that only two of the six issue variables had a significant relationship with Montrealers' vote choice. First, the importance of the public transit issue is positively linked with supporting Plante – a relationship that likely taps into, among other things, the appeal of her proposal to build a new subway line. Second, the importance of economic development is negatively associated with a vote for Plante, indicating that this issue was more of a priority for Coderre supporters. The two issues were viewed as almost equally important by voters (see Figure 3.1), and their impact on vote choice was of similar magnitude, although slightly greater for the latter (average marginal effect of –32 percentage points as opposed to 21 for public transit).

Did Expectations about Competitiveness Matter to the Montreal Election?

As we have just seen, electoral behaviour at the local level involves retrospective assessments of economic performance. Can municipal vote choice also be shaped by considerations that are more prospective in nature? More precisely, could perceptions about the candidates' chances of winning have been a factor in the Montreal mayoral contest of 2017? If so, what was their weight in citizens' vote choice calculus? Prospective voting has been studied in a variety of contexts but has received scant attention in the context of local elections. In the following section, we consider the role of competitive expectations in the Montreal municipal election and discuss the implications of our findings.

Prospective Voting and the State of the Race

The results presented in Figure 3.3 revealed the presence of a substantial economic voting effect in Montreal's mayoral election of 2017. Since citizens' economic perceptions were not overly optimistic, this means that incumbent Coderre was not able to reap as much electoral benefit from his economic management of the city as he might have hoped. His defeat can certainly be attributed in part to this. Yet it may also be that Montreal voters were not as retrospectively oriented in their behaviour as electoral accountability theory would lead one to expect.

Local elections are usually not as information-rich as those held at higher levels of government (Cutler and Matthews, 2005; Matson and Fine, 2006). Whether Montreal's municipal elections are "low information" contests might be debatable, but they surely constitute a *lower*-information context compared to federal and provincial elections. A major implication of this relative lack of information is that it leaves room for heuristics (or "cues," cognitive shortcuts) to play a greater role in explaining how voters decide which local candidate to support.

Voters rely on a range of heuristics when making their decisions. The best-known and most powerful of these is partisanship (Campbell et al.,

1960). However, the application of this concept at the municipal level is not necessarily obvious. Citizens may well identify with a municipal political party, but this psychological attachment is less prevalent and less intense than at the provincial or federal levels, in part because municipal parties are often short-lived and leader-centred (Bélanger and Stephenson, forthcoming). Another heuristic, which may be especially salient at the local level, is ethnic or gender affinity. For example, Bird et al. (2016) showed a strong affinity-voting effect based on race and sex during the 2014 Toronto mayoral election in favour of Olivia Chow, a Chinese and female candidate. By comparison, Dabin et al. (2019) found that affinity voting among Indigenous voters is much weaker[7] in the high-information context of Canadian federal elections. Finally, in low-information contexts, seemingly uninformative heuristics such as ballot position may affect vote choice. Comparing ballot position effects in municipal and provincial elections, Tessier and Blanchet (2018) found that ballot order (that is, listing names in alphabetical order) in the 2009 and 2013 Montreal municipal elections did affect citizens' vote choices, benefiting upper-ordered candidates, while it had no effect in provincial (i.e., high-information) elections.

Other types of heuristics are not related to policy preferences and involve the anticipation of future outcomes. One such prospectively oriented heuristic is what the literature refers to as the "bandwagon effect," that is, the psychological phenomenon inciting people to do something because others are doing it. Simply put: if I perceive my fellow citizens as more inclined to support a particular candidate, I may be inclined to support that same candidate. The literature on the presence or absence of this effect in electoral politics is mixed. Research showing positive results is mostly based on experimental designs (Ceci and Cain, 1982; Cloutier et al., 1989; Nadeau et al., 1993; van der Meer et al., 2016; Dahlgaard et al., 2016), and in most cases, the authors point out that the effect appears only when respondents are exposed to clear trends in public opinion. A meta-analysis conducted by Hardmeier (2008, p. 510) covered 45 studies of bandwagon effects and reached the conclusion that "the fears of many politicians and some researchers about the impact of published opinion polls are exaggerated." However, more recent work by Morton et al. (2015) indicated the presence of a bandwagon effect using aggregate-level data from France. Relying on individual-level survey data from Germany and Austria, Meffert al. (2011) also found evidence of a bandwagon effect but concluded that the effect was "fairly small" and that it seemed to affect mainly low-knowledge voters.

The CMES includes ideal questions to verify the presence of a bandwagon effect. Indeed, the pre-electoral wave of the CMES survey

Figure 3.4. Citizens' perceptions of the 2017 Montreal mayoral race

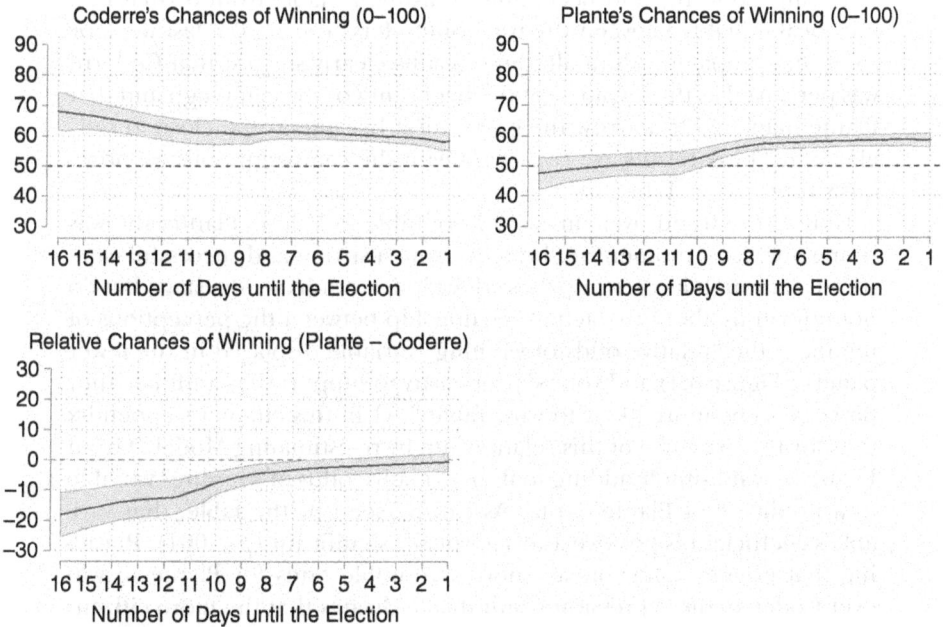

Coderre's Chances of Winning (0–100)

Plante's Chances of Winning (0–100)

Number of Days until the Election

Number of Days until the Election

Relative Chances of Winning (Plante – Coderre)

Number of Days until the Election

Note: Estimations from a loess regression and 95% confidence intervals using Stata's default bandwidth (.8).

provides a measure of citizens' subjective perceptions about the race. This is the question asked: "What are the following candidates' chances of winning the mayoral race? Please use the sliders to indicate your expectations on a scale from 0 to 100, where zero means the candidate has NO CHANCE of winning, and one hundred means the candidate is CERTAIN TO WIN."

Figure 3.4 displays the results from a loess regression illustrating citizens' perceptions of the race between Coderre and Plante over the 16 fieldwork days of the CMES pre-election survey. Interviews were conducted during the last two weeks or so of the campaign, between 20 October and 4 November. The upper panels show three interesting findings: (1) there was some movement over that period in the perceptions of Coderre's and Plante's chances of winning the mayoral election, (2) this movement was of about 10 percentage points in both cases, and (3) this movement was negative for Coderre and positive for Plante. Hence, it is not surprising that when we subtract the individual score given to Plante from the one attributed to Coderre, we get a relative indicator of viability beginning at around –20 percentage points (that is, favouring Coderre) and becoming undistinguishable from 0 (that is, a statistical equality between the two contenders) during the last week or so of the campaign. All in all, these results clearly suggest that Coderre was perceived as the favourite at the beginning of the campaign and that Plante managed to narrow the gap until it became a "too close to call" election. These results are consistent with the campaign polls we previously reported in Table 3.1.

Hence, the trend over time was favourable to Valérie Plante: she was riding a wave of momentum built up from a strong and successful campaign. Although interesting, these descriptive results set the stage but do not inform us about the actual relationship between the perceptions of the race (the "relative odds of winning" variable displayed in the lower panel of Figure 3.4) and voters' propensity to support the candidate they perceive to be more likely to win. Table 3.A1 in this chapter's appendix tests for the presence of this relationship by re-estimating Model D from Figure 3.3 and simply adding to it the "relative odds of winning" variable as a predictor of Plante's vote. As can be seen in the table, that variable's coefficient is positive and statistically significant ($p < .001$). Recalling that greater values mean more favourable odds for Plante to win over Coderre, the regression result thus indicates that the more citizens believed that Plante was going to win the election, the more likely they were to support her and the less likely they were to support Coderre. The empirical relationship and its magnitude are illustrated in Figure 3.5.

As can be seen in the figure, the distribution of the relative-odds-to-win variable ranges from –100 to +100. Simply put, the estimated relationship suggests that, going from one extreme to the other, a voter is almost certain to support Coderre (i.e., probability of .04 to vote for Plante when located at –100) or to support Plante (probability of .99 when located at +100). While partisan bias obviously colours the perceptions of the candidates' chances of winning the election (Blais and Bodet, 2006), the relationship remains strong even when controlling for all the previous blocs of predictors (those from Model D in Figure 3.3; see Table 3.A1 for full regression results). Another feature of our model that helps mitigate partisan bias is that perceptions of winning are measured in the pre-election wave of the CMES whereas the dependent variable (vote choice) comes from its post-election wave.[8]

That said, since only very few people are actually located at these two extremes, a more realistic way to look at the estimated relationship is, following Daoust and Bol (2020), to focus on the values of the distribution located above and under one standard deviation of the mean. This roughly corresponds to –30 to +30, identified by the two vertical lines in

Figure 3.5. Relationship between Plante vote and relative odds of Plante victory

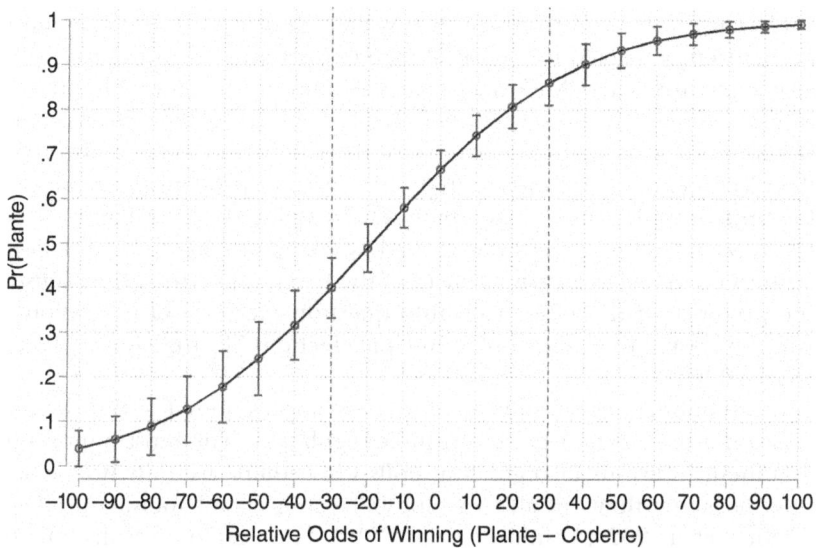

Notes: Predicted probabilities with 95% confidence intervals are based on Model 1 of Table 3.A1. Dashed vertical lines indicate the values comprised within one standard deviation around the mean.

Figure 3.5. The probability of voting for Plante goes from .36 when, all things being equal, a respondent perceives her to be trailing by 30 points behind Coderre, to .86 when she is perceived to be 30 points in advance over her opponent. This 50-percentage-point relationship to vote choice is impressive, although as stated above, we must remain cautious due to the partisan bias associated with these perceptions.

A Wave of Irrational Voting?

Retrospective voting has the virtue of keeping governments – including mayors and City Councillors – accountable for their policy decisions. They govern and are then judged based on their record. When evaluating incumbents, citizens can either reward or punish them with their vote. In the Montreal 2017 election, voters were relatively satisfied with the way things were being managed in the city (with 46% saying the economy had improved in the past year). Most importantly, as predicted by economic voting theory, voters who perceived local economic conditions to have improved were more likely to reward incumbent Denis

Coderre, while those who were less optimistic about the city's economy were more likely to punish him and support challenger Valérie Plante. This is good news from the point of view of democratic accountability.

However, a look into prospective voting, and more specifically into how citizens expected the mayoral race to turn out, provides a very different picture. The CMES data reveal a phenomenon for which there is little evidence in provincial or federal elections. Using citizens' perceptions, we show that expectations of the candidates' odds of winning the election are strongly associated with a greater propensity to support the prospectively winning candidate. The magnitude of this bandwagon effect is important, even when assessed by taking one standard deviation around the mean as a basis (instead of the maximum effect). In a sense, the presence of this effect calls into question the ideal of the rational voter, at least in the context of municipal elections like the Montreal one analysed here.

In addition, these results have serious implications for the debate regarding pre-election polls and their regulation. The most important argument in favour of regulating polls when there are only two viable options is that they can affect voting behaviour via a bandwagon effect (Daoust et al., 2020; Frankovic et al., 2018). However, our results hint at the presence of a bandwagon effect in a context of low information in terms of pre-election polls. As mentioned, there were only three polls published during the 2017 Montreal campaign, and it was clear from the final polls that they could not trigger a bandwagon effect since no candidate was ahead. Hence, the relationship between competitiveness and vote choice we observed could *not* have come from the polls. It was rather based on citizens' own subjective perceptions of the state of the race, which were themselves based on many different sources (pre-election polls, political discussions with family and friends, media coverage, political ads, etc.). Our results do not show that polls cannot trigger a bandwagon effect, but they do indicate that having fewer polls does not necessarily mean that the likelihood of a bandwagon effect is reduced.

Conclusion

The outcome of the 2017 Montreal municipal election turned out to be a surprise. Denis Coderre was widely expected to be re-elected for a second consecutive mandate but ended up losing the election to challenger Valérie Plante, who had been largely unknown just a few months before the election. Our chapter proposed an examination of this local election's outcome using the CMES survey data. Analysis of the motivations behind Montrealers' vote decision showed that the economy played a major role. No less than three economic variables from our model had a significant and substantial impact on the vote. Citizens who thought that economic development was an important issue in that election strongly supported Coderre. The other two economic variables – economic conservatism and retrospective assessments of the city's economic condition – also had an important effect but played more in favour of Plante. Indeed, CMES data revealed, in the former case, that not many Montrealers qualify as economic conservatives. In the case of retrospective economic evaluations, while they did slightly tend toward the positive, they were not overwhelmingly optimistic.

Our chapter further showed that the vote decision in Montreal may also have involved prospective considerations. In particular, we found that voters' subjective perceptions of the state of the race mattered to their decision and that Montrealers were more likely to support the prospectively winning candidate, Valérie Plante. This phenomenon may have helped trigger a bandwagon effect in favour of the challenger. The presence of such an effect raises important issues about voting behaviour in the low-information environment of municipal elections.

APPENDIX TO CHAPTER 3

Table 3.A1. The impact of candidates' relative chances of winning

	Model 1	Model 2	Model 3
Female	−0.388	−0.277	−2.574*
	(0.270)	(0.286)	(1.096)
35–64	0.629	1.111**	0.499
	(0.377)	(0.386)	(1.079)
65+	0.180	0.697	1.259
	(0.428)	(0.466)	(1.174)
High income	−0.531	−0.571	−3.346**
	(0.308)	(0.336)	(1.162)
University educated	0.344	−0.045	−0.631
	(0.296)	(0.341)	(0.837)
Visible minority	−0.736	−0.266	−1.125
	(0.422)	(0.419)	(1.004)
Homeowner	0.034	−0.057	1.166
	(0.334)	(0.385)	(1.391)
Economic conservatism	−2.215**	−1.719	−6.886
	(0.813)	(0.991)	(3.588)
Social conservatism	−2.278**	−1.546*	0.012
	(0.710)	(0.768)	(2.413)
Economic evaluation	−2.318***	−1.747***	−3.530**
	(0.411)	(0.435)	(1.188)
Transit	1.935**	0.636	−0.917
	(0.702)	(0.791)	(3.029)
Property tax	−1.169	−0.962	1.852
	(0.634)	(0.837)	(2.011)
Traffic	1.182	1.380	2.744
	(0.654)	(0.729)	(3.044)
Econ. development	−2.122*	−0.975	0.804
	(0.900)	(0.876)	(1.990)
Environmental protection	0.667	−0.646	−6.444**
	(0.792)	(0.907)	(2.256)
Family services	0.639	1.382	−2.004
	(0.669)	(0.793)	(2.138)
Relative chances of winning	0.050***	0.036***	0.053**
	(0.007)	(0.007)	(0.021)
PID Équipe Coderre	−	−1.474***	−
	−	(0.346)	−
PID Projet Montréal	−	2.162***	−
	−	(0.433)	−
Constant	2.517*	1.625	9.639*
	(1.048)	(1.129)	(4.597)
Observations	553	553	68

Notes: Logistic regressions where Plante vote = 1. Coefficients are displayed with standard errors in parentheses. The reference category for party identification in Model 2 is no party identification.

NOTES

1 We thank Philippe Chassé and Andréa Febres-Gagné for their research assistance.
2 The calculated effective number of candidates in this mayoral election was 2.19.
3 They were Bernard Gurberg, Fabrice Ntompa Ilunga, Tyler Lemco, Philippe Tessier, and Gilbert Thibodeau.
4 Fortier's decision to abandon the race was made too late in the campaign for his name to be removed from the ballot. He ended up receiving 1.26% of the vote on Election Day.
5 A t-test reveals that this difference is statistically significant at $p < 0.001$; $N = 1,414$.
6 In addition, there are 38 elected borough councillors, which means that some Montrealers had to cast a fourth vote to select them. However, because borough councillors do not sit on City Council, they were not included in the CMES study and will not be considered in this chapter.
7 With the sole exception of the NDP (see their Table 3.4).
8 In addition, we conducted two checks for robustness. First, we added two dummy variables measuring party identification (one for Projet Montréal, the other for Équipe Denis Coderre) to reduce the partisan bias inherent in the relationship. Doing so slightly mediated the competitiveness variable's relationship to vote choice (coefficient of .036 compared to .050) but it remains statistically significant ($p < .001$) and substantially important. Second, we re-estimated our model on a sample restricted to respondents who indicated that they had made their vote decision on Election Day. This reduced the sample to 68 respondents, yet it shows that the coefficient for competitiveness was .053. The fact that this coefficient is significant ($p < .01$) and is virtually the same as the one estimated in our initial model is reassuring regarding the robustness of the relationship. The results for these two additional tests are shown in Table 3.A1 (Models 2 and 3).

REFERENCES

Anderson, C. D., McGregor, R. M., Moore, A. A., & Stephenson, L. B. (2017). Economic voting and multilevel governance: The case of Toronto. *Urban Affairs Review, 53*, 71–101. https://doi.org/10.1177/1078087415617302

Bélanger, É., & Stephenson, L. B. (Forthcoming). Understanding municipal partisanship. In É. Bélanger, C. Anderson, & R. M. McGregor (Eds.), *Voting in Quebec municipal elections: A tale of two cities*. University of Toronto Press.

Bélanger, É., & Tessier, C. (Forthcoming). Economic voting in the 2017 Montreal and Quebec City municipal elections. In É. Bélanger, C. Anderson, & R. M. McGregor (Eds.), *Voting in Quebec municipal elections: A tale of two cities*. University of Toronto Press.

Bird, K., Jackson, S., McGregor, M., Moore, A., & Stephenson, L. B. (2016). Sex (and ethnicity) in the city: Affinity voting in the 2014 Toronto mayoral election. *Canadian Journal of Political Science, 49*, 359–383. https://doi .org/10.1017/S0008423916000536

Blais, A., & Bodet, M.-A. (2006). How do voters form expectations about the parties' chances of winning the election? *Social Science Quarterly, 87*, 477–493. https://doi.org/10.1111/j.1540-6237.2006.00392.x

Campbell, A., Converse, P. E., Miller, W. E., & Stokes, D. E. (1960). *The American voter.* John Wiley.

Castonguay, A. (2017). Victoire de Valérie Plante: des leçons pour les chefs à Québec. *L'Actualité,* 6 November.

Ceci, S. J., & Cain, E. L. (1982). Jumping on the bandwagon with the underdog: The impact of attitude polls on polling behavior. *Public Opinion Quarterly, 46*, 228–242. https://doi.org/10.1086/268715

Cloutier, E., Nadeau, R., & Guay, J.-H. (1989). Bandwagoning and underdoging on North American free-trade, a quasi-experimental panel study of opinion movement. *International Journal of Public Opinion Research, 1*, 206–220. https://doi.org/10.1093/ijpor/1.3.206

Cutler, F., & Matthews, S. (2005). The challenge of municipal voting: Vancouver 2002. *Canadian Journal of Political Science, 38*, 359–382. https:// doi.org/10.1017/S0008423905040151

Dabin, S., Daoust, J.-F., & Papillon, M. (2019). Indigenous peoples and affinity voting in Canada. *Canadian Journal of Political Science, 52*, 39–53. https:// doi.org/10.1017/S0008423918000574

Dahlgaard, J. O., Hansen, J. H., Hansen, K. M., & Larsen, M. V. (2016). How are voters influenced by opinion polls? The effect of polls on voting behavior and party sympathy. *World Political Science, 12*, 283–300. https:// doi.org/10.1515/wps-2016-0012

Daoust, J.-F., & Bol, D. (2020). Polarization, partisan preferences, and strategic voting. *Government and Opposition, 55*, 578–594. https://doi.org/10.1017 /gov.2018.42

Daoust, J.-F., Durand, C., & Blais, A. (2020). Are pre-election polls more helpful than harmful? Evidence from the Canadian case. *Canadian Public Policy, 46*, 175–186. https://doi.org/10.3138/cpp.2019-011

Dassonneville, R., Claes, E., & Lewis-Beck, M. S. (2016). Punishing local incumbents for the local economy: Economic voting in the 2012 Belgian municipal elections. *Italian Political Science Review, 46*, 3–22. https:// doi.org/10.1017/ipo.2015.26

Duch, R. M., & Stevenson, R. T. (2008). *The economic vote: How political and economic institutions condition election results.* Cambridge University Press.

Frankovic, K., Johnson, T., & Stavrakantonaki, M. (2018). *Freedom to conduct opinion polls, a 2017 worldwide update.* https://wapor.org/wp-content

/uploads/ESOMA-WAPOR_Freedom-to-Conduct-Opinion-Polls-Final
-incl-edits.pdf

Hardmeier, S. (2008). The effects of published polls on citizens. In D.
Traugott (Ed.), *Handbook of public opinion research* (pp. 504–515). Sage.

Lewis-Beck, M. S., & Stegmaier, M. (2000). Economic determinants of
electoral outcomes. *Annual Review of Political Science, 3*, 183–219. https://
doi.org/10.1146/annurev.polisci.3.1.183

Martellini, C. (2017). Victoire de Valérie Plante: retour sur la campagne
médiatique. *Infopresse*, 7 November.

Martins, R., & Veiga, F. J. (2013). Economic voting in Portuguese
municipal elections. *Public Choice, 155*, 317–334. https://doi.org/10.1007
/s11127-011-9849-0

Matson, M., & Fine, T. S. (2006). Gender, ethnicity, and ballot information:
Ballot cues in low-information elections. *State Politics and Policy Quarterly, 6*,
49–72. https://doi.org/10.1177/153244000600600103

Meffert, M. F., Huber, S., Gschwend, T., & Pappi, F. U. (2011). More than
wishful thinking: Causes and consequences of voters' electoral expectations
about parties and coalitions. *Electoral Studies, 30*, 804–815. https://doi.org
/10.1016/j.electstud.2011.08.001

Morton, R. B., Muller, D., Page, L., & Torgler, B. (2015). Exit polls, turnout,
and bandwagon voting: Evidence from a natural experiment. *European
Economic Review, 77*, 65–81. https://doi.org/10.1016/j.euroecorev
.2015.03.012

Nadeau, R., Cloutier, E., & Guay, J.-H. (1993). New evidence about the
existence of a bandwagon effect in the opinion formation process.
International Political Science Review, 14, 203–213. https://doi.org/10.1177
%2F019251219301400204

Nadeau, R., Lewis-Beck, M. S., & Bélanger, É. (2013). Economics and elections
revisited. *Comparative Political Studies, 46*, 551–573. https://doi.org/10.1177
%2F0010414012463877

Normandin, P.-A. (2017). Comment Projet Montréal a pris la mairie. *La
Presse+*, 7 November.

Tessier, C., & Blanchet, A. (2018). Ballot order in cueless elections:
A comparison of municipal and provincial elections in Québec.
Canadian Journal of Political Science, 51, 83–102. https://doi.org/10.1017
/S0008423917000701

van der Meer, T., Hakhverdian, A., & Aaldering, L. (2016). Off the fence, onto
the bandwagon? A large-scale survey experiment on effect of real-life poll
outcome on voting intention. *International Journal of Public Opinion Research,
28*, 46–72. https://doi.org/10.1093/ijpor/edu041

4 Quebec City

JÉRÔME COUTURE AND SANDRA BREUX

At the time of the 2017 municipal election in Quebec City, Régis Labeaume had been mayor for 10 years. After first being elected in 2007, following the untimely death of the previous mayor, Andrée Boucher,[1] Labeaume won his subsequent elections easily. He became well-known for "his direct and flamboyant style and his personal and centralized way of exercising power" (Belley, Quesnel, and Villeneuve, 2011, p. 164).[2]

Labeaume's time as mayor overlapped with a period of significant change to the municipal party landscape in Quebec City. No party has succeeded in breaking his hold on power. A look at the presence of political parties and their success in Quebec City over the past two elections reveals two main findings. First, elections are contested not by one or two, but by several noteworthy parties (four in 2009; three in 2013). Indeed, the creation of new parties ahead of elections is common in Quebec City. Second, Équipe Labeaume (the mayor's party) has controlled City Council since 2009 and enjoys a large majority. In 2009, Équipe Labeaume crushed Renouveau municipal de Québec, a party whose origins date back to 1977 and that had enjoyed a continuous (and often majority) presence on City Council between 1989 and 2005. The party collapsed in 2008 and was dissolved in 2010. In the 2013 election, Démocratie Québec[3] rose from the ashes of Renouveau Municipal de Québec and succeeded in getting 3 of its candidates (out of 21) elected. In 2017, some five parties were in the running: Équipe Labeaume, Démocratie Québec, Québec 21, Alliance citoyenne de Québec, and Option Capitale-nationale.[4] Through it all, the victory of the incumbent mayor seemed a foregone conclusion; as François Bourque (2017a) pointed out in September 2017: "No hurricane in sight on the radar of the race for mayor of Quebec City."[5] Given the result of the 2013 election, many expected that Démocratie Québec would once again be Labeaume's main challenger in 2017. However, the emergence of Québec 21, a party created just months before the election, turned the race upside down; it got two candidates elected (compared to Démocratie Québec's one) and came in second in the mayoral race.

How might we explain the success – albeit relative – of this new party? This question is relevant because, although changes to the city's party system are common (Collin, 2011), incumbents generally dominate, and Québec 21 was not made up of incumbent candidates at the municipal level. Moreover, the demise of Renouveau municipal meant the end of the so-called popular, programmatic, militant, left-leaning parties on the political spectrum, leaving this ideological space empty. For its part, Québec 21 did not conceal its right-wing ideological orientation, even though municipal political parties in Quebec City are generally known for their lack of clear ideological positioning (Bherer and Breux, 2012).

In this chapter, we will focus on the political dynamics of the 2017 municipal election in Quebec City. We will begin by describing the campaign, the issues, and the results. We will then explore the emergence of a third party – Québec 21 – with reference to a theory developed by Maurice Pinard (1971, 1973), who argues that there are specific conditions that are favourable to the emergence of a new party. In our analysis of the 2017 election in Quebec, we will suggest that the dominance of the governing party, combined with the perception of a weak opposition and some dissatisfaction with the incumbent party, may explain the emergence of Québec 21.[6]

Election Overview

The Mayoral Campaign

In September 2017, editorial writer François Bourque wrote that the people of Quebec City were highly satisfied with the incumbent mayor and speculated that it was likely that Labeaume would be re-elected despite the presence of a new party, Québec 21. Just after first being elected in a 2007 by-election with 59% support, Labeaume created his eponymous party in 2008 – Équipe Labeaume – a political group that he distinguished from the city's other parties by arguing that it was less partisan, in the traditional sense.[7] Labeaume's new Équipe was touted as a party of independents (Porter, 2009) and was ultimately composed of several incumbent municipal councillors (see Table 4.1). In 2009, Labeaume won the mayoral race with nearly 80% of the vote; the main opposition, Renouveau municipal de Québec, had not even run a candidate. At the time, the newspapers highlighted the rather predictable

Table 4.1. Number of candidates, by political party, 2009–2017

	Number of candidates	Number of incumbent candidates
Équipe Labeaume		
2009	27/27 (100%)	13/27 (48%)
2013	21/21 (100%)	9/21 (43%)
2017	20/21 (95%)	14/20 (70%)
Démocratie Québec		
2013	20/21 (95%)	4/21 (19%)
2017	21/21 (100%)	1/21 (4,8%)
Québec 21		
2017	21/21 (100%)	0/21 (0%)

victory of Labeaume, whose party took 25 of the 27 seats on the City Council (Belley, Quesnel, and Villeneuve, 2011).

By the time of the 2013 election, the political landscape had changed. The previous year, Anne Guérette, who had been elected as an independent councillor in 2007, founded Démocratie Québec, which soon merged with three other parties: Alternative Québec (Radio-Canada, 2013), Québec Autrement, and Défi Québec (Gaudreau, 2013; Belley, Lavigne, and Quesnel, 2014). Guérette then handed over the party leadership to David Lemelin. Another party in the running in 2013 was Alliance de Québec, led by David Beaulieu, which identified itself as the municipal branch of the provincial party Action démocratique du Québec. This party did not run a mayoral candidate in 2013 and did not win any seats on the municipal council.

The 2013 elections were disappointing for Démocratie Québec. The party had three councillors: Anne Guérette and Yvon Bussières (in the borough of Cité-Limoilou), who had been the role since 1993, and Paul Shoiry (in Sainte-Foy–Sillery–Cap-Rouge), former mayor of the city of Sillery, which was amalgamated with Quebec City in 2001. Mayoral candidate David Lemelin was not elected, nor was his co-candidate.[8] Lemelin subsequently left politics (Radio-Canada, 2014), and Paul Shoiry, who took over the leadership of Démocratie Québec in 2013, became leader of the official opposition, serving until November 2016. On 3 December 2016, the leadership race was fought between Anne Guérette and François Marchand, a former and well-known councillor (1985–89). Marchand lost, and then ran as an independent against Guérette in 2017. At the same time, Paul Shoiry, on bad terms with Guérette, left the party, accusing the leader of being disorganized and failing to properly recognize the work of her team (Bourque, 2017b). Two of Guérette's close employees also left the party in July 2017. Then Yvon Bussières also departed, on good terms with the leader but stating that he preferred to do politics in a "non-partisan" way (Moella, 2019). This internal crisis did considerable damage to the party's image, and even former leader David Lemelin hesitated to offer his support, given the party's most recent setbacks. The party's chances of victory in 2017 were slim, so conditions were favourable for the emergence of a new party: Québec 21.

Québec 21 was founded in June 2017 by Jean-François Gosselin, a former elected official from Action démocratique du Québec (a now defunct provincial party that merged with Coalition Avenir Québec in 2012). Presenting itself as the "commonsense" choice, the party ran candidates for all 21 of the city's council seats in 2017. The election also included Alliance citoyenne de Québec (formerly Alliance de Québec), which presented four candidates, and Option Capitale-Nationale, a municipal party created in conjunction with the provincial Option Nationale party. Despite this diversity of options available to voters, the political landscape on the eve of the 2017 election remained dominated by the incumbent mayor and his team; the official opposition was in a poor state, and the new party, Québec 21, had only just emerged.

Council Races

Before describing the various races for municipal council, it is important to briefly review the institutional architecture of Quebec City. The city's municipal council is composed of 22 elected members: the mayor and 21 councillors. The mayor is elected at large. The city is divided into six boroughs, each of which includes a number of districts based on the borough's population. Each borough also has a borough council, which is "made up of, depending on the borough's population, three to five councillors whose electoral district is located in the borough" (Ville de Québec, 2020).[9]

Given that it had won 18 of the 21 seats on the municipal council following the 2013 election, the 2017 race was not much of a challenge for Équipe Labeaume. The defection of the two Démocratie Québec councillors, Shoiry and Bussières, had contributed to weakening the opposition. Nevertheless, Équipe Labeaume did not put up a candidate to run against the independent Yvon Bussières in the Montcalm–Saint Sacrement district (borough of La Cité–Limoilou) in 2017, whereas Démocratie Québec did. Notably, in addition to the political parties in the running, independent candidates ran in the districts of Cap-aux-Diamants, Vanier–Duberger, Cap-Rouge–Laurentien, Louis XIV, and Sainte-Thérèse-de-Lisieux.

Table 4.1 shows that in 2017, 70% of Équipe Labeaume candidates were incumbents, whereas Démocratie Québec and Québec 21 had only one incumbent between them. This presence of incumbent candidates was significant, in that it reinforced the non-competitive character of the 2017 election.

Issues and Events

Labeaume's 2009 election campaign had focused on the idea of making Quebec City an attractive place to live and visit. In 2013, he had concentrated on public transit and on his relationships with the city's unions. Though Labeaume focused his 2017 campaign on improving the quality of life in Quebec City (Béland, 2017), the overall campaign was once again dominated by public transit, along with occasional questions about municipal debt. Immigration and the construction of a Muslim cemetery may also have influenced the election, though neither matter was publicly debated by the parties.

The public transit debate revolved around the idea of a new bus rapid transit (BRT) service, which had been developed in collaboration with the mayor of Lévis and announced in 2015. Régis Labeaume organized a public consultation to identify citizens' concerns, at the end of which he reiterated his support for the project (Radio-Canada, 2017b). Some local radio stations opposed the project (Grondin, 2017), and in April 2017, Démocratie Québec also announced its opposition, arguing that the service would not serve the entire city (Morin, 2017a). A few days later, the mayor of Lévis retracted his support.

On 20 April 2017, Labeaume abandoned the SRB (*service rapide par bus*) project and launched a new round of consultations. These revealed that opposition to the BRT project came not so much from ordinary Quebec City residents as from some radio hosts. Québec 21 also opposed the project; the party preferred privately operated vehicles and proposed the building of a third road linking Quebec City and Lévis. For Gosselin, one local columnist explained, "the current election is essentially a referendum on Mayor Labeaume's public transit project" (Porter, 2017). Alliance citoyenne de Québec, led by Daniel Beaulieu, shared this view: "There's not going to be any SRB, TGV, tramway or crazy project that will try to force drivers to take public transport," he insisted. "Our vision is to offer the best possible service and then leave it up to citizens whether to take public transit or their cars" (Gaudreau, 2017).

Démocratie Québec, for its part, sought to improve existing public transit services and to establish a tramway between Sainte-Foy and downtown Quebec (Démocratie Québec, 2017). Option Capitale-Nationale proposed a light rail system from the Quebec Bridge to the north of Charlesbourg, a bus lane on Pierre Laporte Bridge, and a bike-sharing system, in addition to a green belt and more elevators between the city's upper and lower towns (Radio-Canada, 2017a).

In addition to public transit, a number of other issues arose intermittently throughout the election. One of them was the city's debt. In May 2017, the mayor's team presented very positive figures, showing a surplus of $39.5 million and a debt reduction of $43.3 million. According to Démocratie Québec and its leader Anne Guérette, however, these figures were misleading, since Labeaume had failed to mention that the debt had increased by 43% since he took office. Candidates also debated the financing of the Vidéotron Centre, a large hockey arena that had been built in an attempt to lure an NHL team to the city (Martin, 2017).[10]

A final important issue during the 2017 election was the mayor's management style. Already a subject of debate in 2012, his management approach was often criticized: "The opposition to Mayor Labeaume comes from both inside and outside the municipal council. Inside, his party's municipal councillors are increasingly on the verge of pulling out. In December 2012, two of them jumped ship and joined forces with a councillor who had quit two years earlier. These three councillors deplored the mayor's authoritarian style and the difficulty of expressing different points of view at caucus meetings"[11] (Belley et al., 2014, 106). Thus, the mayor's management was less a new issue than a recurring line of attack for his opponents, both before and during the election campaign.

Figure 4.1 shows, on a scale of 1 to 10, the importance given by the CMES respondents to each of the issues mentioned above. It indicates that traffic (i.e., congestion) and economic development were the most important issues considered by respondents, with an average score of 8. Property taxes came next (7.5), followed by public transit (7.0). Labeaume's management style scored a 6.5 in importance, and immigration scored a 6.

The Election Result

The 2017 municipal election in Quebec ended with an overwhelming victory by the incumbent mayor and his team; but those results also underscore just how competitive the election was (see Table 4.2). Équipe Labeaume won 17 of the 21 seats on council, along with the mayor's office. Voter turnout was 50.9%, higher than the provincial average (44.8%), a particularly respectable figure considering that it was the mayor's third re-election and that he had won the previous elections by impressive margins (see Table 4.A2 in the appendix to this chapter) – factors that

Figure 4.1. Issue importance in the 2017 Quebec City election

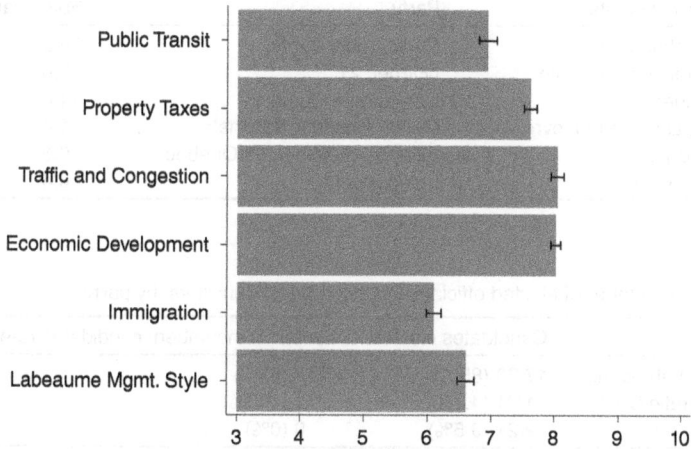

usually reduce turnout in Canadian municipalities (Breux, Couture, and Bherer, 2014; Breux, Couture, and Koop, 2017; Breux, Couture, and Goodman, 2017).

The incumbent candidates from Équipe Labeaume lost only one district that the party previously held, that of Sainte-Thérèse-de Lisieux. This was a narrow loss, by 69 votes (0.6%), to Québec 21, with Nancy Piuze winning against Marie-France Trudel of Équipe Labeaume. Piuze was the co-candidate of Jean-François Gosselin, which allowed him to take her spot on the council when he lost the mayoral election and thus to become leader of the opposition forces. Overall, Équipe Labeaume saw 93% of its incumbent candidates re-elected: 13 out of 14 resumed their positions (Table 4.3).

Notwithstanding Équipe Labeaume's commanding victory, the 2017 results also indicated some disruption to the city's power dynamics. First, Démocratie Québec had collapsed. The party's performance had already been disappointing in 2013, with only three candidates elected. Things were even worse in 2017: the party managed to elect just a one candidate, Jean Rousseau, in the borough of La Cité–Limoilou (Cap-aux-Diamants district). The party's internal crisis in 2016 seems to have been a fatal blow, especially considering that its former member Yvon Bussières, who ran this time as an independent, was elected over the Démocratie Québec candidate (borough of La Cité–Limoilou, district Montcalm–Saint-Sacrement). All told, Démocratie Québec ranked second in only 6 of the 21 districts (Table 4.4).

Table 4.2. Mayoral vote share

Mayoral candidate	Party	Vote share (%)
Régis Labeaume	Équipe Labeaume	55.3
Jean-François Gosselin	Québec 21	27.6
Anne Guérette	Démocratie Québec	14.6
Nicolas Lavigne-Lefebvre	Option Capitale-Nationale	1.4
Daniel Brisson	Alliance citoyenne de Québec	0.6
Claude Gagnon	Independent	0.4

Table 4.3. Number of elected officials and incumbent councillors, by party

	Candidates elected	Number of incumbent candidates re-elected
Équipe Labeaume	17/20 (85%)	13/14 (93%)
Démocratie Québec	1/21 (4.7%)	1/1 (100%)
Québec 21	2/21 (9.5%)	0 (0%)

By contrast, Québec 21 emerged as a relative winner in 2017. The party placed second in 12 of 21 districts, suggesting that it might become the city's new opposition. Two of its candidates were elected in the Beauport borough, where the party had only ever placed second before, and it won in the districts of Sainte-Thérèse-de Lisieux and Chute–Montmorency–Seigneurial (see Table 4.4). In a by-election on 9 December 2018, a third councillor from Québec 21 was elected. These results suggest that Démocratie Québec is no longer in a position to figure as the official opposition, whereas Québec 21 seems well poised to meet this challenge.

No other parties besides the three discussed so far elected candidates in 2017; these other parties were unimportant in this election, as shown by the "effective number of candidates" calculation of 2.48 (Laakso and Taagepera, 1979). In the end, the 2017 election was a race among three political parties – a dominant incumbent party and two distant challengers. Of the two challengers, the newly formed Québec 21 seems more likely to challenge Labeaume's dominance in the future.

In terms of the geographic distribution of the mayor's support, Figure 4.2 map shows the vote share obtained by Régis Labeaume in each of Quebec City's electoral districts. The incumbent mayor won the popular vote in all the electoral districts. His highest vote share – 61.7% – was in the Pointe-de-Sainte-Foy district, a suburb to the east of downtown Quebec City. His lowest vote share – 47.5% – was in the Val-Bélair district in the suburbs north of the city. Though there is some geographic variation, Labeaume was a dominant force throughout the city.

Figure 4.2. Vote share for Labeaume, by ward

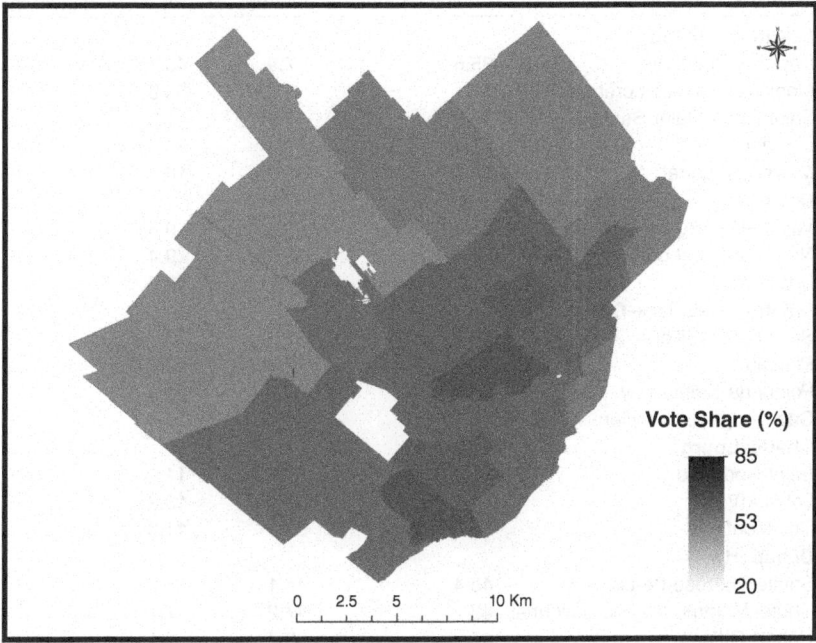

Table 4.4 shows the council vote shares obtained for the three major parties in each electoral district. Québec 21 received the most votes in most of the former towns that merged with Quebec City in 2001, with especially strong support in the eastern sector of the city, where the construction of a third mode of transit between Quebec City and Lévis, supported by Québec 21 during the election campaign, was planned. Démocratie Québec was stronger in the neighbourhoods comprising the former city of Quebec – that is, the city that existed prior to the municipal merger – as well as in some inner suburbs. The party won the Cap-aux-Diamants district by a margin of 4.1% over Équipe Labeaume and finished second in six districts. The candidates for Équipe Labeaume, meanwhile, won by margins that on average were slightly lower than Régis Labeaume's winning margin in the mayoral race, except in Val-Bélair, where Sylvain Légaré, another former member of Action démocratique du Québec, did better, obtaining 49.2% of the vote. This means that at the electoral district level, some voters voted for the incumbent mayor but not for his party. Labeaume's party still managed to get 17 out of 21 candidates elected, with winning margins ranging from 33.0% in the Pointe-de-Sainte-Foy district to 5.7% in the Haute-Saint-Charles district.

Table 4.4. City council vote share, by district (%)

Councillor vote share	Équipe Labeaume	Québec 21	Démocratie Québec
La Cité–Limoilou			
Cap-aux-Diamants	35.6	7.9	40.7
Montcalm–Saint-Sacrement*	–	6.7	33.9
Saint-Roch–Saint-Sauveur	46.9	15.9	31.3
Limoilou	51.6	18.3	24.7
Maizerets–Lairet	56.6	24.9	18.6
Des Rivières			
Vanier–Duberger	57.1	30.3	9.8
Neufchâtel–Lebourgneuf	55.0	32.9	9.4
Des Saules	51.2	34.1	13.2
Sainte-Foy–Sillery–Cap-rouge			
Saint-Louis–Sillery	46.4	17.5	33.7
Plateau	52.4	22.3	22.2
Pointe-de-Sainte-Foy	55.2	20.0	22.4
Cap-Rouge–Laurentien	42.7	27.0	16.4
Charlesbourg			
Saint-Rodrigue	54.4	30.8	11.2
Louis XIV	48.1	35.4	10.3
Des Monts	47.4	38.8	11.0
Beauport			
Sainte-Thérèse-de-Lisieux	45.4	46.1	6.6
Chute–Montmorency–Seigneurial	43.7	47.2	7.1
Robert-Giffard	48.9	38.7	8.1
La Haute-Saint-Charles			
Lac-Saint-Charles–Saint-Émile	46.7	41.0	10.3
Loretteville–Les Châtels	52.8	34.0	11.0
Val-Bélair	49.2	41.0	6.9

* Independent Yvon Bussières won this district with 53.2% of votes.

Finally, two independent candidates stand out: Yvon Bussières, elected in Montcalm–Saint-Sacrement (where Équipe Labeaume did not present any candidates) with 53.2% of votes, and François Marchand, defeated contender in the Démocratie Québec leadership race, who finished third in the Cap-aux-Diamants district with 9% of votes.

Vote Choice

As in the other chapters in this volume, we now present an analysis of the correlates of vote choice in the Quebec mayoral election. The CMES survey was completed by 1,309 respondents in Quebec. As part of that survey, respondents were asked to locate each of the candidates for mayor on a left–right axis (0–10). Anne Guérette of Démocratie Québec

Figure 4.3. Vote choice for Labeaume – marginal effects

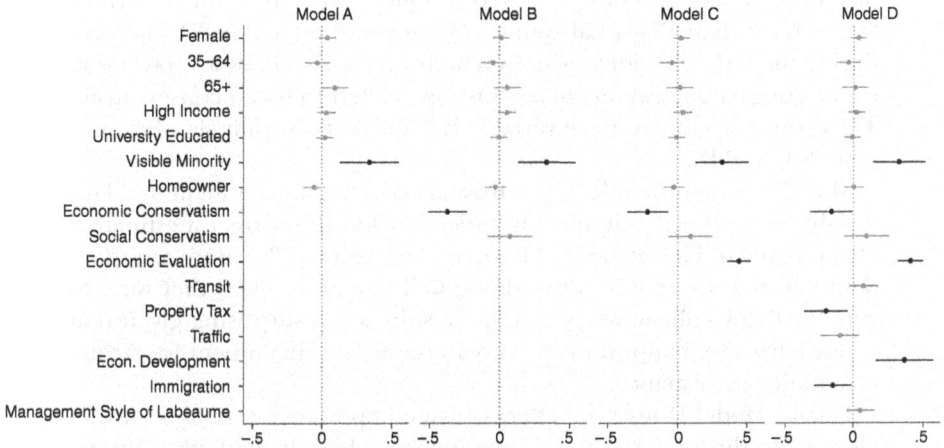

Notes: Entries report marginal effects and 95% confidence intervals. Coefficients in black are statistically significant at p < 0.1.

was positioned at 3.9, on the left of the axis; Jean-François Gosselin of Québec 21 and incumbent mayor Régis Labeaume were both on the right of the axis, at 6.9 and 5.6 respectively. It was thus the most centrist candidate who won the election.

Figure 4.3 shows the results of a series of logistic regression models (marginal effects shown) in which we introduce predictors in a step-wise fashion. The purpose is to identify factors that were related to voting for Labeaume as opposed to another mayoral candidate.

Model A focuses on socio-demographic factors. Only one such variable has a statistically significant relationship with vote choice: being a member of a visible minority increased the probability of voting for Régis Labeaume by 33 percentage points. This result can be explained in particular by the leadership shown by the mayor in his relationship with the Muslim community, especially in the days and weeks following the mosque attack in Quebec City in early 2017. Visible minority status is statistically significant in all four models.

Model B tests the impact of economic and social conservatism on the vote for Labeaume. The results show economic conservatism to be negatively linked to the vote for the incumbent mayor. In other words, the more economically conservative a respondent was, the less likely they were to have voted for Régis Labeaume. This result can be explained by the ideological position of Québec 21 and its mayoral candidate

Jean-François Gosselin, former ADQ member of the Assemblée nationale du Québec, who was perceived by Quebeckers to be much further to the right than Régis Labeaume. Moreover, the Québec 21 platform during the 2017 elections focused mainly on economic issues (tax, debt, traffic congestion) rather than on issues related to social conservatism. The economic conservatism variable is likewise statistically significant in models C and D.

Model C tested the effect of retrospective economic evaluations. This variable is statistically significant; indeed, it has the strongest estimated effect of any in Figure 4.3, at 41 percentage points. The more a respondent felt that the economy was doing well, the more likely they were to vote for Régis Labeaume. This relationship is not surprising given that voters have a well-known propensity to reward an incumbent for strong economic performance.

Finally, Model D tests the effect of issue importance variables on vote choice. On this subject, three issues appear to have had an effect on the vote for Régis Labeaume. First, respondents who prioritized economic development were more likely to vote for the incumbent mayor. Second, respondents who believed in the importance of property taxes were less likely to vote for him (it should be noted that this was one of the three main campaign issues of Québec 21). Issues therefore seem to have played a significant role in the outcome of the 2017 Quebec mayoral election.

Still, compared to the dynamics observed during the campaign, Model D leaves us somewhat perplexed. Transit was the main and seemingly the only issue for Québec 21. Démocratie Québec likewise focused a large part of its campaign on transit. However, these two issues were not negatively associated with the vote for Régis Labeaume, which could suggest that, even though the two opposition parties focused heavily on transit, the matter was no less important for Labeaume supporters than it was for their own. As well, even though the mayor's management style was debated in the media all year long and could have revealed whether the election was in fact a referendum on the incumbent mayor, this variable was not linked to a vote for Labeaume.

It is noteworthy that the Pseudo-R^2 of Model D is only 0.11, which makes this the model with the smallest amount of explained variance among all the eight cities studied in this book. This raises the question of whether there are any important missing variables that might explain the vote for Régis Labeaume. Among such variables, one stands out as potentially important, given the long-term dominance of Labeaume: satisfaction with the mayor's performance in office. When such a measure is added to Model D above, the Pseudo-R^2 increases to 0.44. The results of this updated model are shown in Figure 4.4.

Figure 4.4. Correlates of mayoral vote choice (with mayoral evaluation)

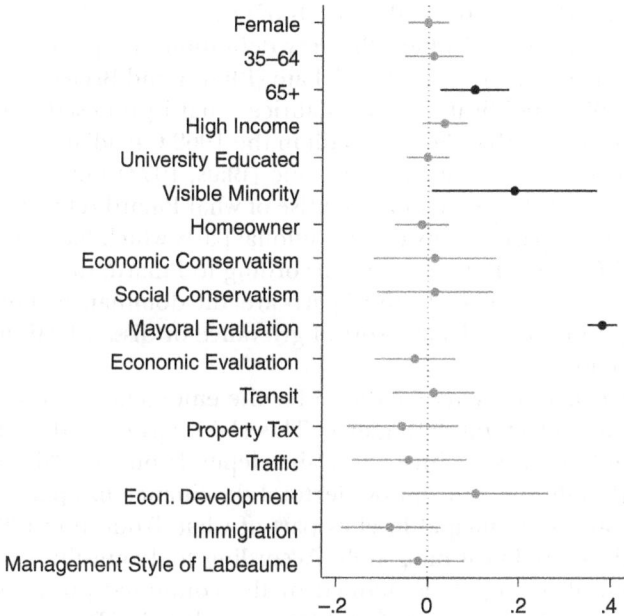

Figure 4.4 shows that the more satisfied a respondent was with Régis Labeaume, the more likely he or she was to vote for him. There is nothing surprising here, except that the effect of this variable is so substantial that several of the other variables shown as statistically significant in Model D no longer have an effect in the updated model. One way of interpreting this result is to conclude that the election was indeed a referendum on the incumbent mayor, with all of the other factors feeding into voters' satisfaction with the incumbent.

The Rise of a Third Party?

Thus far, we have emphasized that Quebec's elections have been dominated by Équipe Labeaume through several election cycles, with Québec 21 appearing as a new challenger in recent years. Such results suggest that Pinard's (1971) theory of third-party emergence could provide interesting insights here. However, we must apply this theory with some caution. First, we cannot simply take a theory designed to explain phenomena occurring at higher levels of government and apply it to the municipal level (Trounstine, 2009) without taking into account the specific characteristics of the municipal context. Second, a theory of political parties may well be inapplicable in a province where municipal governance is very distinct from other levels of government (Breux, Couture, and Bherer, 2014) and where the very definition of a political party in the municipal arena is subject to debate (Bherer and Breux 2012).

In the 1970s, political scientist Maurice Pinard proposed a theory to account for the birth of Social Credit in the 1962 Canadian federal election. This theory was criticized by some (Blais, 1973) but has nonetheless proven useful in explaining the rise of what Pinard refers to as third parties. A third party is "any non-traditional party which has not yet been in power" (Pinard, 1973, p. 455). According to Pinard, the three conditions for the emergence of a third party are: the dominance of one party, a weak opposition, and some sort of grievance or dissatisfaction among the electorate.

For Pinard, a necessary condition for the emergence of a third party is single-party electoral dominance. This claim has been the subject of considerable criticism, since the claim depends on how "dominance" is defined. Still, the concept of electoral dominance has particular significance at the municipal level as part of what Trounstine (2006) has described as a political monopoly. According to Trounstine, a (municipal) political monopoly is defined by the continued presence of the same elected official or team for at least one decade (Trounstine, 2006, p. 879). In Quebec, municipal political monopolies are not unusual. Incumbent candidates are likely to be re-elected, and several large cities have experienced or are still experiencing situations where elected officials have been in power for more than twenty years (Breux, Couture, and Bherer, 2014).

As noted earlier, in the case of the 2017 elections in Quebec City, the incumbent mayor had been in power for ten years. In addition, his team had clearly dominated City Council for the last two elections, winning 90% of council seats over this period. But while the dominance of the mayor and his team is indisputable in this instance, for Pinard, party dominance also must mean that the official opposition is not perceived by the electorate as a viable alternative (Pinard, 1973, p. 440). In other words, for there to be party dominance, the opposition must not be *perceived* as sufficiently credible in the eyes of a large part of the electorate.

What does it mean for an opposition party to lose credibility? Pinard provides some examples: "If the party has met repeatedly with resounding defeats in the past, or if, as a result of internal crises (leadership problems, internal conflict, etc.), the party is suddenly in a state of disarray, if (largely as a consequence of these) its organization is in very poor shape, if its cadres have been destroyed and have to be completely reconstituted, if voters find few of their relatives, friends, or acquaintances, at work, in their neighbourhood, or in other areas of participation ready to support that party, then a collective definition of this party as a hopeless contender is likely to develop, and a situation of one-party dominance prevails" (Pinard, 1973, p. 441). These descriptions certainly call to mind the troubles experienced by Démocratie Québec, which suffered disappointing electoral results in 2013, an internal crisis in 2016, and the departure of key figures like Yvon Bussières and Paul Shoiry.

CMES data suggest that both of Pinard's conditions were met in Quebec in 2017. When asked about each mayoral candidate's chances of winning, Labeaume received an average score of 76.4%. No other party leader came close – the closest competitor was Gosselin at 34.5%, while Guerette was given a 24.1% chance of winning (N = 700). By way of contrast, in Montreal – the only other partisan and incumbent mayoral race in the CMES study – the perceived gap between Coderre and Plante was just 2.2 points.

Pinard's final criterion for the emergence of a third party is some sort of widespread public grievance. "If [voters] perceive the main opposition to be weak, that is electorally dominated by the incumbent party, then they will turn en masse to a third party in order to express their grievances" (2004, p. 583). The dominance of one political party creates a situation in which not all voters are represented (Pinard, 1973, p. 442). In such a context, the emergence of a new party can serve as an outlet for dissatisfaction.

In Figure 4.5, we demonstrate the relevance of Pinard's theory to the 2017 Quebec election. The figure plots the predicted probability of a Gosselin vote (that is, a vote for the third-party candidate) conditional on respondents' assessments of the probability of victory for Anne Guérette (the second-party candidate). The dashed line plots these predicted probabilities for those who were satisfied with Mayor Labeaume's performance, while the dotted line plots the same probabilities for those who were unsatisfied. Pinard's theory would suggest that the probability of a third-party vote should increase among those who are dissatisfied with the mayor's performance as the perceived chances of the traditional challenger decrease. This is precisely what we see in the figure; as Guérette's perceived chances increase – as we move from left to right across the figure – the probability of supporting the third-party candidate declines rapidly among the unsatisfied respondents.

Taken separately, the variables in the figure (satisfaction, and probability of each mayoral candidate's success) are the most important factors for understanding who voted for the leader of Québec 21. Their interaction is even more revealing. Notice the marked difference between

Figure 4.5. Perceptions of likelihood of Guérette victory and support for Gosselin

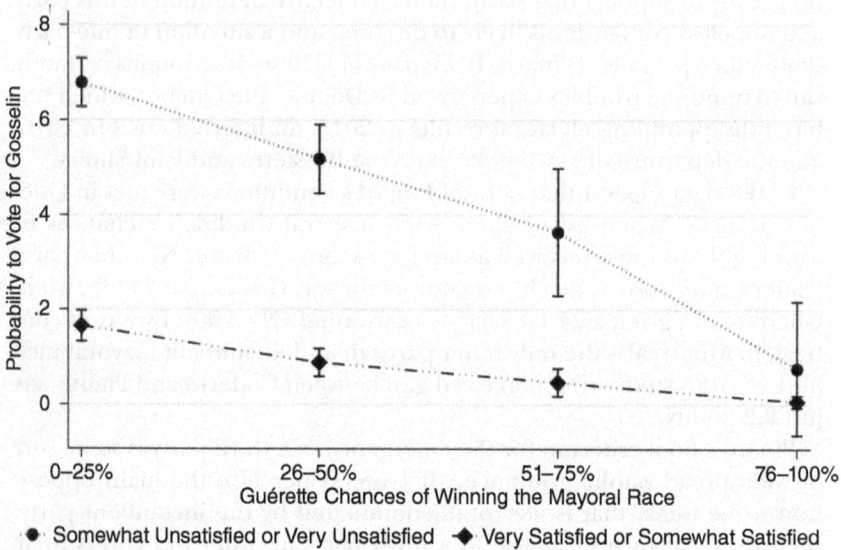

Note: Marginal effects predicted with 95% CIs.

respondents who were satisfied with the incumbent mayor (the dashed line) and those who were dissatisfied with him (the dotted line). And when the respondents believed that the leader of the official opposition, Anne Guérette, was unlikely to win the election, they were significantly more likely to vote for Jean-François Gosselin.

In his own presentation of his theory, Pinard focuses on economic grievances as the form of dissatisfaction that can lead to third-party emergence. However, this may not be applicable to the municipal level, where issues such as roads and transportation can be just as important as the economy (see Figure 4.1). In Quebec City, the transportation issue was salient because of debates about the third road link and public transit. Indeed, the issue of traffic may have constituted here what Pinard calls a "grievance" allowing a third party to emerge. However, we can only speculate on this, since the CMES survey did not include a specific question on this topic.

Pinard further distinguishes two types of third parties: protest parties and radical parties. In a nutshell, protest parties are those that rally voters around dissatisfaction rather than ideology. Radical parties, in contrast, are more organized around "long-term grievance against the social order, imbedded in an articulated ideology" (Pinard, 1973, p. 443). It is difficult to categorize Québec 21 in this distinction, especially since Pinard specifies that the distinction is one of degree rather than kind. However, in previous research, we showed that the 2017 election marked a change from the past: while municipal political parties often avoid positioning themselves on a left–right axis, Québec 21 has not tried to hide its position on the right of the political spectrum (Breux, Couture, and Mévellec, submitted).

In sum, our analysis reveals several important features of the 2017 election. The absence of any major issues in the election and the assured victory of the incumbent mayor were no obstacle to the emergence of a new political force. Nevertheless, Québec 21 emerged thanks to the convergence of specific favourable conditions, namely the perception that the official opposition had little chance of victory and the presence of dissatisfaction among some segments of the population. The problem for Québec 21 was that too few voters were dissatisfied with the mayor. Studying an election where the population is more dissatisfied with the mayor would be an important next step in examining the applicability of Pinard's theory to local elections. Nonetheless, Pinard's theory offers a useful lens through which to understand why Québec 21 was able to become the official opposition. Indeed, the dominance of incumbents at the local level could prove to be central to an explanation for the relative instability of local party systems in Canada.

APPENDIX TO CHAPTER 4

Table 4.A1. Date of creation of parties and name of leader

Name	Date of creation	Leader
Équipe Labeaume	2008	Régis Labeaume
Démocratie Québec	2013	Anne Guérette
Québec 21	2017	Jean-François Gosselin
Alliance citoyenne de Québec	2017	Daniel Beaulieu
Option Capitale-Nationale	2017	Nicolas Lavigne-Lefebvre

Table 4.A2. Labeaume vote share and margin of victory, 2007–2017

	2007	2009	2013	2017
Vote share (%)	59.0	79.9	74.1	55.3
Margin victory (%)	26.3	71.4	49.8	27.6

Sources: Breux, Couture, and Bherer (2014) and Données Québec (2017).

NOTES

1 Boucher died suddenly during her term. She was mayor of Sainte-Foy, a city that had merged with Quebec City, from 1985 to 2001. She campaigned against municipal mergers in 2000. In 2001, she ran for mayor of Quebec City as leader of the Action civique de Québec party, but was defeated by Jean-Paul L'Allier, mayor of Quebec City since 1989. In 2005, she ran as an independent candidate for mayor of Quebec City, winning the race with 46.2% of the vote.
2 Our translation.
3 For more information, see Belley, Lavigne, and Quesnel 2014.
4 See Table 4.A1 in the appendix for the dates of creation of the parties.
5 Our translation.
6 The objective of the final section of this chapter is to examine the emergence of one particular party (Québec 21). The ideological orientation of this party will not be the subject of specific attention here, but the relationship between party ideology and emergence patterns is certainly a topic worthy of future consideration.
7 This should be seen in the context of the first mandate of Régis Labeaume and the previous mayor, Andrée Boucher: "Andrée Boucher's victory in 2005 seems to have marked a turning point. During the twenty months or so of her time at city hall, she relentlessly attacked the official opposition, Renouveau municipal de Québec. She criticized the RMQ for unnecessarily blocking or delaying her projects, for making 'partisan' opposition

systematic and for abusing its majority – in short, for putting the interests of the party before those of citizens. Boucher's anti-partisan strategy, which consisted of attempting to convince voters that political parties no longer had a place on the municipal scene and that democracy would be better served by independent candidates, thus seems to have borne fruit and was again taken up in December 2007" (Belley, Quesnel, and Villeneuve, 2011, pp. 151–152; our translation).

8 Section 146 of the *Act respecting elections and referendums in municipalities* states: "Every eligible person may be nominated as a candidate for one office on the council of a municipality at a time, by filing a nomination paper with the returning officer. Notwithstanding the foregoing, a municipality having a population of 100,000 or over may, by a by-law of its council, allow double candidacies in accordance with this paragraph ... If such a by-law is in force 44 days before polling day, the candidate for the office of mayor of a party authorized under Chapter XIII may, jointly with another candidate of the party who is his co-candidate, also be candidate for the office of councillor in an electoral district."

9 Unlike the City of Montreal, these borough councils do not have a borough mayor. Section 17 of the Charter of Ville de Québec states that "the borough council shall designate a borough chair from among its members" (Charter of Ville de Québec, 2020). Moreover, unlike in the City of Montreal, all borough councillors shall sit on the Municipal Council.

10 Immigration was also an occasional topic of debate, although the issue does not fall under municipal jurisdiction. News of the arrival of immigrants in Lacolle, near Montreal, prompted the leader of Québec 21 to speak out against Quebec City becoming a "sanctuary city," as Montreal's City Council had recently done (Banerjee, 2017). Équipe Labeaume likewise announced that it did not want Quebec City to become such a city (Morin, 2017b). This issue therefore came onto the public agenda in Quebec only in reference to what was happening in Montreal. At the same time, two anti-immigrant demonstrations were held in August 2017, organized by La Meute and Atalante Québec. All leaders distanced themselves from the demonstrations.

11 Our translation.

REFERENCES

Banerjee, S. (2017). Montréal devient une ville sanctuaire pour les immigrants sans statut. *Le Soleil*, 20 February.

Béland, G. (2017). Le grand risque de Labeaume. *La Presse*, 24 September.

Belley, S., Lavigne, M.-A., & Quesnel, L. (2014). L'élection municipale de 2013 à Québec: la légitimation par les urnes d'un nouveau leadership local. *Canadian Journal of Urban Research*, *23*(2), 100–122.

Belley, S., Quesnel, L., & Villeneuve, P. (2011). Québec 2009: l'impact de la "fierté retrouvée" sur le pouvoir local. In S. Breux & L. Bherer (Eds.), *Les élections municipales au Québec: enjeux et perspectives* (pp. 145–172). Presses de l'Université Laval.

Blais, A. 1973. Third parties in Canadian provincial politics. *Canadian Journal of Political Science, 6*(3), 422–438. https://doi.org/10.1017 /S0008423900040014

Bourque, F. (2017a). Ça prendrait un ouragan. *Le Soleil,* 12 September.

Bourque, F. (2017b). Shoiry quitte, la crise s'amplifie chez Démocratie Québec. *Le Soleil.* https://www.lesoleil.com/chroniques/francois-bourque /shoiry-quitte-la-crise-samplifie-chez-democratie-quebec -535b435493a9e2d0bdcf8b7ca6b8e679

Breux, S., Couture, J., & Bherer, L. (2014). Les candidats sortants: atout ou obstacle à la participation électorale. *Canadian Journal of Urban Research, 23*(2), 59–78.

Breux, S., Couture, J., & Goodman, N. (2017). Fewer voters, higher stakes? The applicability of rational choice for voter turnout in Quebec municipalities. *Environment and Planning C: Politics and Space 35*(6), 990.

Breux, S., Couture, J., & Koop, R. (2017). Turnout in local elections: Evidence from Canadian cities. *Canadian Journal of Political Science, 50*(3), 699.

Breux, S., Couture, J., & Mévellec, A. (Forthcoming). Does the left–right axis matter in municipal elections? In É. Bélanger, C. Anderson, & R. M. McGregor (Eds.), *Voting in Quebec municipal elections: A tale of two cities.* University of Toronto Press.

Collin, J-P. (2011). Quel avenir. In S. Breux & L. Bherer (Eds.), *Les élections municipales au Québec: enjeux et perspectives* (pp. 311–351). Presses de l'Université Laval.

Démocratie Québec. (2017). Anne Guérette dévoile le plan de mobilité urbaine intégrée de Démocratie Québec. http://www.democratieqc.org /anne-guerette-devoile-le-plan-de-mobilite-urbaine-integree-de -democratie-quebec

Données Québec. (2020). Résultat des élections municipales générales. https://www.donneesquebec.ca/recherche/dataset/resultats-des -elections-municipales-generales

Gaudreau, V. (2013). Québec: les partis d'opposition fusionnent. *Le Soleil.* 2 mai 2013

Gaudreau, V. (2017). Un autre parti politique à la droite de Labeaume. *Le Soleil.* 10 May.

Grondin, M.-È. (2017). Nathalie Normandeau invite toutes les stations de radio à s'unir comme le SRB. *Le journal de Québec,* 12 April.

Laakso, M., Taagepera, R. (1979). Québec invite toutes les stations de radio à s'unir comme le SR. *Comparative Political Studies, 12*(1).

Martin, S. (2017). Situation financière de la ville: Guérette accuse Labeaume d'embellir les chiffres. *Le journal de Québec*. 19 May.

Moella, T. (2019). Deux autres départs au cabinet de Guérette. *Le journal de Québec*. 30 June.

Morin, A. (2017a). Guérette se positionne contre le SRB. *Le Soleil*. 12 April.

Morin, A. (2017b). Pas question que Québec devienne une ville sanctuaire, dit Québec 21. *Le Soleil*. 9 August.

Pinard, M. (1971). The rise of a third party: A study in crisis politics. Prentice-Hall.

Pinard, M. (1973). Third parties in Canada revisited: A rejoinder and elaboration of one-party dominance. *Canadian Journal of Political Science*, 6(3), 439–460. https://doi.org/10.1017/S0008423900040026

Porter, I. (2009). L'Équipe Labeaume: quelle équipe? *Le Devoir*, 30 May.

Porter, I. (2017). Jean-François Gosselin veut un pont pour stimuler l'économie de Québec. *Le Devoir*, 12 October.

Radio-Canada. (2013). Partis d'opposition à Québec: la tentative de fusion échoue. Radio-Canada. https://ici.radio-canada.ca/nouvelle/595729/fusion-partis-labeaume.

Radio-Canada. (2014). David Lemelin quitte la tête de Démocratie Québec. Radio-Canada. https://ici.radio-canada.ca/nouvelle/658735/david-lemelin-democratie-quebec-depart-chef

Radio-Canada. (2017a). Anne Guérette se rétracte au sujet d'Atalante Québec. https://ici.radio-canada.ca/nouvelle/1050681/anne-guerette-atalante-quebec-benefice-doute-anti-immigration

Radio-Canada. (2017b). Cimetière musulman: Québec vend un terrain à la communauté. https://ici.radio-canada.ca/nouvelle/1048805/cimetiere-musulman-quebec-vente-terrain

Trounstine, J. (2006). Dominant regimes and the demise of urban democracy. *The Journal of Politics*, 68(4), 879.

Trounstine, J. 2009. All politics is local: The reemergence of the study of city politics. *Perspectives on Politics*, 7(3), 611–618. https://doi.org/10.1017/S1537592709990892

Ville de Québec. (2000). Charter of Ville de Québec. http://legisquebec.gouv.qc.ca/en/ShowDoc/cs/C-11.5

5 Vancouver

ELINE A. DE ROOIJ, J. SCOTT MATTHEWS,
AND MARK PICKUP

In January 2018, Gregor Robertson announced that, after serving as mayor of Vancouver for ten years, he would not be seeking re-election in the upcoming municipal election. This, together with his party, Vision Vancouver (Vision), hitting an all-time low in popularity, meant that the race for mayoral and council candidates was wide open.

Vision had held the majority of council seats, as well as the position of mayor, since 2008. In previous elections, the party had run on a platform of fighting homelessness and promoting green policies. However, homelessness had not decreased and many citizens thought the city had gone too far with its signature green policy, arguing that there were now *too many* bike lanes. Even worse, Vision had gained a reputation for being in the pockets of developers and having made the city's housing affordability crisis even worse. The party failed to field a mayoral candidate, and none of its candidates for city council were elected in the October elections.

Although many candidates ran, the campaign for mayor ended up being a three-way race, with two independent candidates on the left of the political spectrum squaring off against a new face representing the major party on the right. Notwithstanding concerns about vote-splitting on the left, it was Kennedy Stewart, a former NDP Member of Parliament, who ultimately won the most votes.

In this chapter, we first discuss the mayoral and council races, which were both characterized by an atypically large number of candidates. We then focus on the issues and events that were central to the campaigns, identifying, among other things, the leading role played by the affordability crisis for candidates and voters. Following a summary of the election results, we examine a statistical model of mayoral vote choice. We also report on a unique survey experiment designed to uncover subtle effects of the affordability issue on voters' attitudes and behaviour. We conclude – consistent with previous research (Cutler and Matthews, 2005), and in spite of the complexities of the political context – that voters in Vancouver made up their minds in 2018 in much the same way they do in elections at more senior levels: they rely on a mixture of ideological and issue-centred considerations.

Election Overview

The Mayoral Campaign

By the nomination deadline of 14 September, an unprecedented 21 candidates had registered to run for mayor, including 15 independents. Just days before the nomination deadline, Vision's candidate, Squamish hereditary chief Ian Campbell, announced that he would not be running for personal reasons. Vision subsequently decided not to field any mayoral candidate, opening up space on the left of the political spectrum.

None of the other established parties on the left – the Coalition of Progressive Electors (COPE), the Green Party of Vancouver (Greens), and the more recently formed OneCity – nominated a mayoral candidate. In April 2018 these parties, together with Vision, were still exploring the possibility of uniting behind one mayoral candidate to ensure that the progressive vote would not be fragmented and to "foil the Non-Partisan Association's plan to take back city hall" (Howell, 2018). By May, having failed to rally behind one candidate, this possibility was off the table. By early June, Vision had chosen its candidate, Ian Campbell, and long-time city councillor Adriane Carr decided after months of deliberation not to run as the candidate for the Greens; concerned about vote-splitting, she opted to run again for City Council instead (Fumano, 2018a). Her decision prompted Patrick Condon to seek COPE's nomination for mayoral candidate (Fumano, 2018b), but in July, Condon decided against running after suffering a stroke. Because of all this, along with a need to create distance from the unpopular Vision, the progressive left was represented mainly by independent candidates. Among them, the two most high-profile candidates were Kennedy Stewart and Shauna Sylvester.

Between 2011 and 2018, Kennedy Stewart had been on leave from his position as an associate professor at Simon Fraser University (SFU) to represent Burnaby as an NDP MP (first in the riding of Burnaby-Douglas, then in the newly formed riding of Burnaby-South). He gained important visibility after being arrested in March 2018 while protesting the Trans Mountain Pipeline, and in early May of that year he announced he was resigning as an MP to run for mayor of Vancouver. He stated that he was motivated to run as an independent by the need to "bring together progressives and keep the NPA out of City Hall" (Stewart in Fumano,

2018c). Like many other candidates, Stewart identified affordable housing as his number one priority (Stewart, 2018). His candidacy was endorsed by OneCity and the Vancouver and District Labour Council.

Shauna Sylvester, director of SFU's Morris J. Wosk Centre for Dialogue, announced in early April her decision to run for mayor, hoping to unite the progressive left behind her (McElroy, 2018a). Although she was running as an independent, she had close ties with Vision as a former board member and, notably, as a lead facilitator on Gregor Robertson's Task Force on Affordable Housing. She had no experience running for elected office but had a long record of community engagement, having been involved in public debates on a range of issues and having gathered extensive experience as a board member for the Vancity credit union, Mountain Equipment Co-op (MEC; a Vancouver-based cooperative selling outdoor gear), and BC's property assessment authority. Sylvester, too, identified affordable housing as Vancouver's number one priority, but she also provided a detailed policy platform covering a range of issues. Like Stewart, she was viewed as an environmentalist: she was the founding executive director of Carbon Talks and Renewable Cities and had the endorsement of David Suzuki (among others). If elected, Sylvester would be Vancouver's first female mayor.

Among progressive voters there were concerns that Stewart and Sylvester would split the vote. This is broadly reflected in our data, which indicates that voters viewed Stewart as slightly more left-wing than Sylvester on a 0–10 scale of ideological (left–right) perceptions, the former scoring 4.2 and the latter 4.5.[1] And indeed, many of these two candidates' proposed policies were similar.

On the right of the political spectrum, the space was also crowded. The Non-Partisan Association (NPA), Vancouver's long-standing party of the right, struggled to settle on a mayoral candidate who would help overcome the party's image as one of "greying, white men" (Tanner, 2018). Controversy surrounded the nomination process. Hector Bremner was initially seen as the front-runner after winning a council seat for the NPA in a 2017 by-election, but the NPA Board of Directors barred him from standing for the nomination. Bremner's rejection generated dissatisfaction among a subgroup of NPA members and caused several potential NPA council candidates to withdraw their bids for nomination (Little, 2018; Pablo 2018a). After being barred, Bremner started his own party, YES Vancouver.

Another mayoral candidate on the right, Wai Young, considered running for the NPA nomination. After being rebuffed by the NPA, she too formed her own party, Coalition Vancouver. In the beginning of June, NPA members voted for Ken Sim to be their mayoral candidate over John Coupar and Glen Chernen, the only other two candidates approved by the party (Chernen ended up running for City Council as a candidate for Coalition Vancouver). Although in the preceding year the NPA had recruited many new members, with Bremner alone claiming to have recruited more than 2,000 (Pablo, 2018a), only 1,960 members cast a ballot in the nomination contest (NPA Vancouver, 2018a).

Sim, a local businessman with no political experience, provided a much-needed fresh face for the NPA. He was born and raised in Vancouver and came from a humble background. After earning a business degree from the University of British Columbia (UBC), he co-founded both a successful home-care nursing service and a chain of bagel bakeries. As a relatively young (47) family man of Chinese heritage, experienced in running large companies but without obvious ties to developers, he was viewed as the ideal NPA candidate to shed the party's stodgy image. Sim's platform focused on housing and the local economy; it suggested ways to increase housing supply (rather than suppress demand), emphasized the need for neighbourhood consultations on densification (NPA Vancouver, 2018b), and made specific policy proposals aimed at promoting small businesses (NPA Vancouver, 2018c).

Neither Young nor Bremner nor any other of the non-NPA candidates on the right were expected to win the election, which led to concerns that they would split the right-wing vote. Young, a former Conservative MP for Vancouver South with extensive experience in community service and politics, became best-known for her strong opposition to bike lanes, although her platform also focused on housing and other issues. Bremner, a young, up-and-coming politician with experience working for the BC Liberals, was expected to do well with millennials. His campaign focused heavily on housing, taking a pro-development and pro-density stance. Probably because of his proposal to substantially increase the supply in housing, voters viewed Bremner as significantly less right-wing than Sim (5.7 versus 6.4 on the 0–10 left–right scale, according to our data).

The polls showed Stewart consistently in the lead in the four weeks preceding the election (Research Co, 2018a, 2018b, 2018c). This is supported by the CMES data, which indicate that about 22% of voters said they would vote for Stewart at the start of the campaign, falling to 19% in the final week (see Figure 5.1).[2] Sim's support also remained fairly stable, with about 10% of voters indicating they would vote for him. Sylvester consistently polled third, a few percentage points behind Sim, followed by Bremner and Young. Importantly, though, many voters remained undecided until the election: in the week before the election, as many as 38% indicated they did not know whom they would vote for.

To gain a deeper sense of how Vancouverites felt about the top mayoral candidates, respondents in the CMES were asked to indicate on a scale from 0 to 100 how they felt about each candidate, with 0 meaning

Figure 5.1. Vote intention for the top five candidates, and 90% confidence intervals

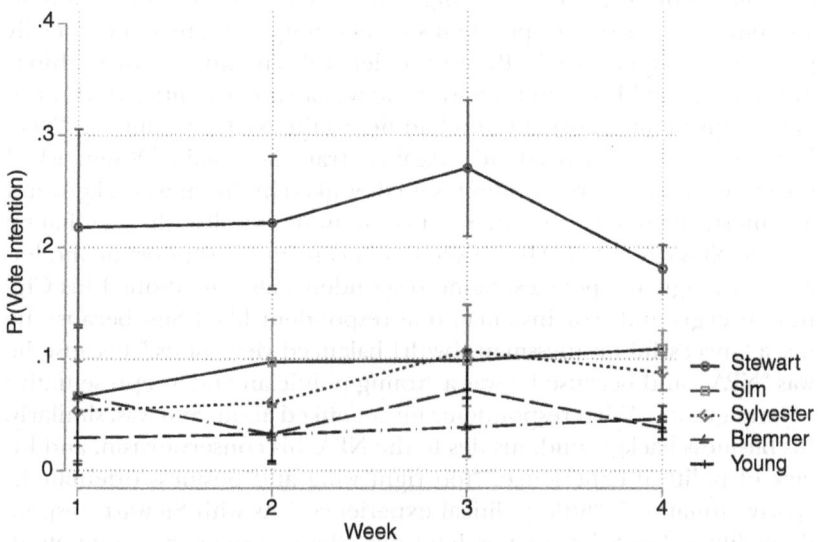

Note: Other/don't know included in the estimation model but not shown in the plot.

"really dislike" and 100 meaning "really like." Of the four leading candidates (the question was not asked for Young), respondents liked Sylvester the most (a mean of 54.9), closely followed by Stewart (53.5). Sim scored an average of 45.2. Of the four candidates, Bremner was liked the least with an average of 43.4.[3]

The choice between Stewart and Sylvester, on the one hand, and Sim, on the other, seemed to mostly reflect a choice between the political left and right. Progressive voters' rationale for preferring Stewart over Sylvester, or vice versa, is less easy to pinpoint. To get a picture of what Vancouverites specifically liked or disliked about the top three candidates we can look at the open-ended responses from respondents about what they (dis)liked about each. After rating the candidates, respondents were asked what they particularly liked about each. They could list up to three things or simply indicate there was nothing they liked about the candidate. Respondents were then asked what they disliked about each candidate. Caution is required in interpreting these data, as more than 70% of the respondents chose not to list anything, and those who did perhaps held especially strong views.

Respondents said they liked Stewart's political experience, his left-wing/progressive politics, and his ties to the NDP. They also mentioned his policies on affordable housing and his stance on the environment and pipelines. As one respondent summed it up: "anti-pipeline, socially progressive, experienced." But respondents also mentioned these things as what they *dis*liked about Stewart: he was a career politician who formerly represented Burnaby and had ties to the NDP and unions: "NDP hack, not Vancouver resident"; "Against Trans Mountain." When asked the same about Sim, respondents said they liked his business background and his strong ties in the Vancouver community as well as the fact that he was the NPA candidate. He was seen as sincere and as supporting moderate and pragmatic policies. Some respondents also mentioned his Chinese background. For instance, one respondent liked Sim because he was a "successful businessman, [with] balanced viewpoints," because he was "NPA," and because he was a "young politician and a representative of immigrants." What respondents most *dis*liked about Sim was, similarly, his business background, his ties to the NPA, his conservativism, and his lack of political experience: "too right wing and business orientated," "party affiliation"; "little political experience." As with Stewart, respondents liked that Sylvester was left-wing. She was seen as a competent, progressive candidate with good policies, especially on transit, housing, and the environment. Many respondents also mentioned her gender as a positive: "She is a woman. She is articulate and she knows the issues." However, where Stewart was disliked for his ties to the NDP, Sylvester was seen as "too close to Vision." Some respondents also felt that Sylvester lacked experience. Finally, some respondents pointed to her more centrist positions (compared to those of Stewart) as something they disliked: "Her policies are more centrist than I would like."

Council Races

Alone among the cities included in the CMES, Vancouver uses an at-large electoral system. That is, there is only one city-wide electoral district; voters select up to ten of their preferred candidates for the ten-seat City Council from a list of all candidates running. The 2018 election was the first in twenty-five years in which the list of candidates on the ballot was not alphabetical, but randomly determined; however, all voters were still presented with the same ordering – likely still benefiting those listed higher up on the ballot (see De Rooij and Henderson, 2020).

Like the mayoral race, the election for City Council featured a record number of candidates.[4] In total, 71 candidates ran for city councillor, even though the established parties on the left (COPE, the Greens, OneCity) had decided to limit the number of candidates they

Table 5.1. Candidates running and elected for city council, by party affiliation

Party affiliation	Number of candidates	Vote intention (% votes)[†]	% votes (intention) per candidate	% votes	% votes per candidate	Elected
Coalition Vancouver	7	6.40	0.91	7.06	1.01	0
COPE	3	8.94	2.98	8.86	2.95	1
Green Party	4(2*)	15.86	3.97	15.61	3.90	3(2*)
NPA	8(3*)	21.16	2.64	24.89	3.11	5(3*)
OneCity	2	4.77	2.39	5.84	2.92	1
ProVancouver	4	2.83	0.71	2.11	0.53	0
Vancouver 1st	7	8.37	1.20	5.78	0.83	0
Vision Vancouver	5(2*)	10.47	2.09	9.85	1.97	0
YES Vancouver	5	3.82	0.76	4.63	0.93	0
Independent	26(2*)	17.39	0.67	15.37	0.59	0
TOTAL	71	100.00	1.41	100.00	1.41	10

* Number of incumbents (City Councillor, Park Commissioner, or School Trustee between 2014 and 2018).

[†] Of 6,286 votes; data are unweighted and no answer/don't know/won't vote excluded (total number of possible votes was 1,648 respondents x 10 votes = 16,480).

ran to avoid splitting the vote (Oen, 2018). Between them, the established left parties ran nine candidates. Although Vision did not field a mayoral candidate, it did support five candidates for council – far fewer than in previous elections.

Together, the parties on the (centre-)right fielded a far greater number of candidates, a total of 31. Among these parties, the new, centrist ProVancouver fielded the fewest, with only four, and the NPA fielded the most, with eight. In addition, 26 candidates (37%) ran as independents. The percentage of independent candidates was the highest it had been since 2008, but it was certainly not out of the ordinary in the recent history of Vancouver municipal elections.[5]

Before the election, respondents in the CMES were asked which City Council candidates they thought they would vote for. They could list up to ten candidates each. To assess vote intention, we added up the votes by party and calculated the percentage of votes each party received out of a total of 6,286 votes (Table 5.1, column 3). The result: 40% of respondents did not name any candidate. Because parties fielded different numbers of candidates, we subsequently calculated the average percentage of votes per candidate for each party (column four).

Candidates affiliated with the established parties – COPE (2.98%), the Greens (3.97%), the NPA (2.64%), and the somewhat newer OneCity (2.39%) – attracted the most votes on average among respondents who expressed a vote intention. Candidates for Vision followed not too far behind, with 2.09% of all votes. Vancouver 1st candidates attracted just over 1% of the vote, while candidates affiliated with all other parties, as well as independent candidates, attracted on average less than 1% of all votes. Given the strong focus on the mayoral campaign, a general disenchantment with Vision,[6] and the handful of incumbents running for established parties (or as independents)[7], it is perhaps not surprising that candidates affiliated with those established parties attracted most voter attention.[8]

Issues and Events

The number one issue in the election was housing affordability for renters and owners. Most candidates made affordability the central issue of their campaign, and voters likewise indicated it was their most important issue. We asked respondents to indicate the importance of six different issues on a scale from 0 (not at all important) to 10 (extremely important). By far the most important issue for Vancouverites was affordability, which achieved an average importance score of 8.4 (see Figure 5.2) – a significantly higher score than for the other issues. Public transit was also deemed important, with a mean score of 7.5, followed by traffic and congestion (7.4), homelessness (7.4), and economic development (7.3). Out of the six issues that were asked about, property taxes was considered least important, although clearly still important, with an average score of 6.9.[9]

Although there was widespread agreement on the importance of affordability, policy approaches differed between candidates and parties. In part, policies differed depending on whether they emphasized increasing the housing supply or suppressing demand, particularly by discouraging foreign investment and restricting short-term rentals (such as through Airbnb) (Davidoff, as cited in Bula, 2018c). Coalition Vancouver, Vancouver 1st, and the NPA proposed little change to the status quo and/or abolishing the existing empty-homes tax, a demand-suppressing measure (Bula, 2018c; O'Connor, 2018). The NPA mainly committed to increasing consultation in developing neighbourhood-specific plans and pledged to allow two rental suites in detached homes (O'Connor, 2018). Bremner and his party, YES Vancouver, distinguished themselves from the NPA by proposing to substantially increase the supply in housing through city-wide rezoning for duplexes, rowhomes, and apartments (Bula, 2018c). In contrast, both COPE and ProVancouver's policies were aimed mainly at reducing demand through taxation, although both also favoured increased protections for renters and an increase in social housing (Bula, 2018c; O'Connor, 2018). The Greens, OneCity, Vision, and the independent mayoral candidates, Stewart and

Figure 5.2. Issue importance in the 2018 Vancouver election (0–10 scale)

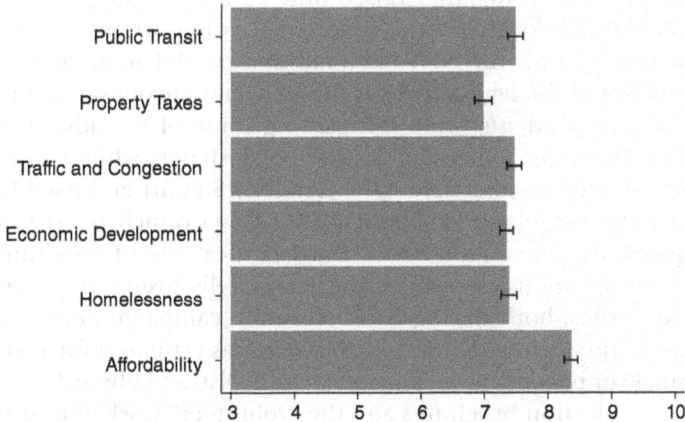

Sylvester, favoured a combination of increasing housing supply through zoning and building affordable rental housing on undeveloped city land and temporary modular housing for homeless individuals; they would also address demand by maintaining the empty-homes tax and increasing or adding additional taxes (Bula, 2018c; O'Connor, 2018). Among this latter group, the Greens took the most moderate stance, having in the past blocked densification efforts by voting against proposals to allow duplexes in single-family zones (O'Connor, 2018).

The second issue of importance during the campaign centred on the need for more investment in public transit. One major issue was the extension of the proposed new SkyTrain line all the way to the UBC main campus, on Vancouver's western edge. Most major mayoral candidates and political parties expressed clear support for this, with only Sim and the Greens being more cautious in their support (Bula, 2018a). Wai Young set herself apart by taking a strong position against the construction of new bike lanes and promising to review and/or cancel existing bike routes (McElroy, 2018b).

A major development that affected all candidates and parties was a change in campaign financing laws. Before the 2018 election, the provincial NDP government had banned donations from corporations and unions and capped individual donations at $1,200 per candidate or group of candidates affiliated with a political party (City of Vancouver, Independent Elections Task Force, 2019, p. 8). This was intended to decrease the influence of corporations and unions in politics and restore voter confidence. As a result, COPE, the Greens, the NPA, OneCity, and Vision together raised only 29% of the money they had raised in the previous election; however, it is important to note that of these parties, only the NPA ran a mayoral candidate in 2018 (p. 8). One criticism of the legislation was that it would encourage candidates to run as independents while still gaining some of the advantages of parties by endorsing other candidates. For instance, while running as an independent mayoral candidate, Kennedy Stewart endorsed OneCity's Christine Boyle and Brandon Yan for City Council (p. 10). Moreover, questions were raised about third parties' use of own funds or in-kind contributions, as well as the lack of disclosure requirements for third parties, both during and before the campaign period. As an example of the former, Stewart's campaign was criticized for receiving substantial support from the Vancouver and District Labour Council in the form of election brochures and the "volunteer" work of four union employees (p. 10; Bula, 2018b). Ultimately though, this does not seem to have affected his popularity much.

In contrast, the lack of disclosure may have affected Hector Bremner's campaign. Before the election campaign officially began on 22 September, billboards sponsored by a group called Vancouverites for Affordable Housing appeared promoting Bremner and his party. On 21 September, the *Globe and Mail* reported that Peter Wall, a major Vancouver developer and long-time funder of Vision, had paid $85,000 for the billboards (Bula & Mason, 2018). Bremner, who ran on a platform of increasing the housing supply through new development, claimed he did not know anything about the billboards; however, given voters' aversion to developers' influence in municipal politics, it is unlikely that this news helped his campaign.

The Election Result

Turnout in the Vancouver municipal election was 39.36% of 448,322 eligible voters. This was lower than in the 2014 election, which saw exceptionally high turnout at 43.4%, but still substantially higher than the turnout in 2011 and 2008.

Although the polls, as well as our survey data, put Stewart in the lead in the mayoral race throughout the month preceding the election, ultimately the election turned out to be close, with Stewart winning 28.71% and Sim winning 28.16% of the vote – that is, he won by fewer than 1,000 votes (Table 5.2). Shauna Sylvester placed third, with 20.48% of all votes. Further behind were the two other candidates on

Table 5.2. Election results for city council and mayor

City Council candidates[†]	Party affiliation	% votes	Mayoral candidates	Party affiliation	% votes
Carr, Adriane*	Green	4.99	**Stewart, Kennedy**	–	28.71
Fry, Pete	Green	4.42	Sim, Ken	NPA	28.16
De Genova, Melissa*	NPA	3.81	Sylvester, Shauna	–	20.48
Swanson, Jean	COPE	3.50	Young, Wai	Coalition Vancouver	6.86
Hardwick, Colleen	NPA	3.42	Bremner, Hector	YES Vancouver	5.73
Wiebe, Michael	Green	3.26	Harding, Fred	Vancouver 1st	3.26
Boyle, Christine	OneCity	3.25	Chen, David	ProVancouver	2.06
Dominato, Lisa	NPA	3.20	Cassidy, Sean	–	0.89
Bligh, Rebecca	NPA	3.15	Fogal, Connie	IDEA Vancouver	0.83
Kirby-Yng, Sarah	NPA	3.12	Hansen, Mike	–	0.55
Grewal, David	NPA	3.00	Lamarche, Jason	–	0.40
Wong, David HT	Green	2.93	Rollergirl	–	0.40
Deal, Heather*	Vision	2.83	Chan, Ping	–	0.38
O'Keefe, Derrick	COPE	2.74	Yano, John	–	0.29
Goodrich, Justin P	NPA	2.71	Ly, Tim	–	0.20
Roberts, Anne	COPE	2.62	Kaiser, Sophia Cherryes Kaur	–	0.19
Yan, Brandon	OneCity	2.59	Shottha, Satie	–	0.19
Quimpo, Jojo	NPA	2.48	Massey, Lawrence	–	0.13
Blyth, Sarah		2.11	Le Rougetel, Katy	–	0.10
Paz, Tanya	Vision	2.06	Buday, Gölök Z.	–	0.10
Cardona, Diego	Vision	1.96	Aubichon, Maynard	–	0.08
Evans, Catherine	Vision	1.80		–	

Source: *City of Vancouver (2019c)*.

Note: Winning candidates in bold.

* Incumbent councillors (those on City Council between 2014 and 2018).

† Only city council candidates who received more than 25,000 votes are shown (22 out of 71).

the ideological right: Wai Young just eking out ahead of Hector Bremner with 6.86% compared to 5.73% of the vote. With Stewart's election, Vancouver had elected its first independent candidate as mayor in 30 years.

It came as no surprise that none of the seats on City Council were won by Vision candidates. Still, the five candidates from that party together managed to win 9.85% of the votes, which placed them, in terms of average votes per candidate, behind the other major established parties (COPE, the Greens, the NPA, and OneCity) but ahead of the newer parties and independent candidates (Table 5.1, columns 5 and 6). The ten council seats ended up being split among these established parties, as well as being neatly divided between left and right (Table 5.2).[10] Five of the eight NPA candidates won seats on City Council, including former councillor Melissa De Genova, former school trustee Lisa Dominato, and former park commissioner Sarah Kirby-Yung. They were joined by newcomers Colleen Hardwick and Rebecca Bligh. The Greens won three seats: incumbent Adriane Carr, who won the most votes (as she had in the 2014 election), was joined by Pete Fry, who came in second place, and former park commissioner Michael Wiebe. In addition, COPE's Jean Swanson, who had placed second in the 2017 by-election after Hector Bremner, won a seat, as did OneCity's Christine Boyle. These results are mirrored in those for the park board (three seats for the Greens, two for the NPA, and two for COPE) and the school board (three seats for the Greens, three for the NPA, one for COPE, one for OneCity, and one for Vision's incumbent candidate). It seems that, as our vote intention data suggested, with little else to go on voters might have been deciding whom to vote for based mainly on incumbency and/or name recognition, as well as established party labels.[11]

A final thing to note about the election result for City Council is that eight of the ten councillors elected were women. Of the cities included in the CMES, the only other city where women are the majority of councillors is Mississauga (6/11). On the other hand, given Vancouver's demographic make-up – according to the 2016 Census, 48.9% of Vancouverites are visible minorities (Statistics Canada, 2019) – it is problematic that only one of the city councillors is non-white, describing himself as a "person of mixed race" (Fry, as cited in Pablo, 2018b). This substantial underrepresentation of visible minorities may be due in part to Vancouver's at-large electoral system, which has been shown to systematically disadvantage minority candidates (under certain conditions), while being marginally beneficial for women candidates (see Trounstine and Valdini, 2008, and the literature quoted therein). It remains to be seen whether the electoral system will be replaced by a ward system during the mayoralty of Kennedy Stewart, who is a well-known critic of Vancouver's at-large system (Bailey, 2018).

Vote Choice

Given the mixture of issues and candidate characteristics potentially in play during the election, what factors drove voters' decisions? To answer this question, we turn to statistical models of vote choice. Figure 5.3

Figure 5.3. Vote choice for Stewart – marginal effects

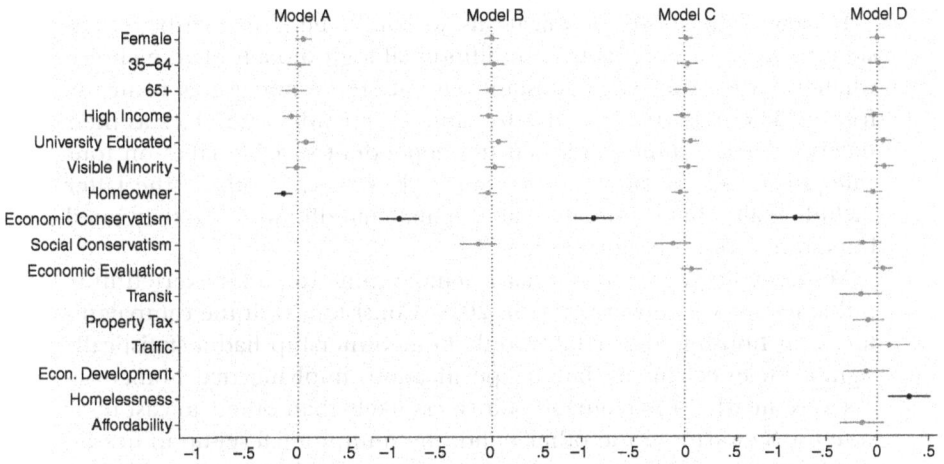

Notes: Entries report marginal effects and 95% confidence intervals. Coefficients in black are statistically significant at p < 0.1.

presents the average marginal effects estimates derived from a series of logistic regression models. These indicate the percentage point change in the probability of voting for a candidate due to a one unit change in a variable, while holding the other variables at their observed values. Successive models add variables that are, in theory, more causally proximal to the vote (see Miller and Shanks, 1996).

As in other chapters, the dependent variable in these models is always a dichotomy that separates those supporting the winner of the mayoral election, Kennedy Stewart in this case, from all other candidates on the ballot. While a sensible simplification for other cities, this approach at times poses interpretive challenges for the Vancouver case. For one thing, given the final vote totals (see Table 5.2), it is clear the choice of mayor was not even approximately a binary one for voters. More importantly, as noted, two major candidates (Stewart and Sylvester) placed themselves on the left side of the political spectrum and, furthermore, were seen by voters as occupying relatively similar positions (see above). Consequently, these regression estimates may fail to identify effects of variables that depend on perceived differences between candidates that are correlated with ideological placements. More generally, to the extent that any of the "non-Stewart" candidates are not approximate substitutes for one another with respect to some criterion of vote choice, these models may underestimate the effect of that criterion.

In view of the above complications, we supplement the logistic regression results with insights from multinomial logit models of vote choice whenever the latter yield substantively different conclusions from the former. These models contain the same independent variables as their binary logistic counterparts, but the dependent variable takes on four categories – specifically, Stewart, Sim, Sylvester, and "other," the latter including all other candidates and the small handful who said they voted but did not indicate their choice.[12]

Model A suggests that standard demographic variables exerted little influence on Vancouver voters in 2018. Consistent with the campaign's focus on housing affordability, only homeownership had a statistically significant effect in the binary specification, implying that homeowners were nearly 14 percentage points less likely than others to cast their vote for Stewart. On the other hand, the multinomial set-up indicates, in addition to a homeownership effect, significant differences according to gender, age, and income. On these estimates, women were 7 points more likely to vote for Sylvester than those identifying otherwise; women were also 11 points less likely than others to choose a non-major candidate. Middle-aged and senior voters were less likely than those under 35 to choose a non-major candidate (by 16 and 24 points, respectively), as well as – coinciding with the NPA's "greying" image – much more likely to support Sim (by 20 and 36 points, respectively). High-income voters (i.e., those earning more than $75,000 per year) were also more likely to back Sim (by 14 points). Regarding the homeownership effect, the multinomial model estimate adds the subtlety that, in addition to reducing support for Stewart (by 14 points), the variable increased the likelihood of voting for a non-major candidate by nearly 14 points.

Model B adds measures of economic and social conservatism to the demographic variables in Model A. The binary set-up indicates that economic conservatism had a massive effect on voters: economic conservatives were less likely to back Stewart, with the difference across the range of the scale a stunning 89 points. Social conservatism, however, has no effect here. The multinomial specification adds nuance to the economic conservatism finding, indicating that, relative to those at the bottom of the scale, those at the top of this measure were 81 points less likely to vote for Stewart and 38 and 40 points more likely to choose a non-major candidate and Sim, respectively. As regards social conservatism, the multinomial set-up reveals a positive effect with respect to non-major candidates – extreme social conservatives, on this measure, were 25 points more likely to choose a non-major candidate than extreme social liberals.

The addition of ideological measures facilitates interpretation of the demographic effects in Model A. The homeownership effect is not significant in Model B, reflecting a positive correlation between this variable and economic conservatism ($r = .23$). Homeowners, then, were repelled by Stewart largely for ideological reasons rather than for reasons unique to homeownership; the comparable multinomial logit estimates yield the same conclusion. As regards the other demographic effects in the multinomial set-up, they are not attributable to ideology – the relevant coefficients are largely undisturbed by the addition to the model of the economic and social conservatism scales.

Model C adds a measure of retrospective economic evaluation to the model. Given that no incumbent was on the ballot, the 2018 election was a challenging context for Vancouverites seeking to discipline economic performance. And the binary set-up implies that they did not try to do so – the effect estimate is not significant. Estimates of the comparable multinomial logit model, however, indicate that the economy *did* matter. Specifically, those who thought the economy had improved over the previous year were 10 points less likely to support Sim. At the same time, although not to a statistically significant degree, those with favourable economic evaluations would seem to have been more likely to back Stewart (by about 9 points; $p = .147$). This pattern suggests that antecedent partisan connections between Robertson and Stewart – both of whom had historic affiliations with the NDP – may have saddled the latter with responsibility for economic performance, which the average voter in our study saw as flagging over the preceding year.

Model D, finally, adds measures of issue importance attitudes. In the binary set-up, just one issue variable exerts a significant effect: those who thought homelessness an "extremely important" issue were 31 points more likely to support Stewart than those who were not at all concerned about the issue. The multinomial estimate yields essentially the same inference for the homelessness issue (specifically, an increase of 32 points in the probability of supporting Stewart across the range of the measure) and also indicates that the transit issue affected vote decisions: those who thought transit "extremely important" were 17 points less likely to support Sim than those who thought the issue "not at all important." In terms of the interpretation of effects entering in earlier stages, the addition of issue variables shrinks somewhat the effect of economic conservatism, in both the binary and multinomial specifications. This reflects, in part, economic conservatism's negative correlations with the measures of both transit ($r = -.28$) and homelessness ($r = -.46$) importance. In the multinomial model, the inclusion of issue attitudes also drives the effect of economic evaluations to insignificance.

The effects of attitudes on transit and homelessness are consistent with the account of the campaign presented in the previous section. The non-effect of views on housing affordability is surprising, however, given the prominence of the issue in the campaign and the high level of importance attached to the issue by voters. One possible explanation is that the level of importance attached to the affordability issue did not effectively discriminate between the major candidates, at least in the minds of voters. Certainly all the major candidates prioritized housing affordability to some degree. The critical differences between candidates on this issue, however, were the proposed remedies, with some candidates (e.g., Stewart) placing relatively more emphasis than others (e.g., Sim) on containing demand through targeted taxation. Our conclusions about this issue, therefore, might well have been different had we been able to access different measures, particularly those that better captured positional – as opposed to valence – attitudes in this domain.[13]

In any event, overall, the vote models indicate that Vancouver voters made up their minds in 2018 in a way that was consistent with the content of the election campaign and in much the same way as do voters in other contexts. Issues and ideology, especially, exerted considerable influence on voters' decisions. Age and income also had notable net effects on voters, at least in models that treat the vote as a multinomial outcome. Even with numerous political attitudes controlled, these demographic characteristics, especially age, exerted sizable effects. This would seem to imply that Vancouverites had important group-related associations with the candidates – in the realm of interests or of identity – over and above those captured by ideology and short-term political issues.

Housing Affordability and Social Pressure

Housing affordability was certainly a prominent issue in the Vancouver election, both in the content of candidates' appeals and in voters' stated issue priorities. Indeed, the issue was significantly more important for Vancouver voters than for those in Mississauga and Toronto, the two other cities in the CMES with expensive housing markets. Yet for reasons discussed in the previous section, indications of the issue's importance do not emerge clearly from the vote models. In this section we approach affordability's political significance in an entirely different way, asking whether the salient political identities generated social pressures on voters.

Up to this point, consistent with a long research tradition (e.g., Converse, 1964), we have been treating ideology as a set of interrelated policy preferences (e.g., economic and social conservatism). There is increasing evidence, however, that ideology can – and perhaps should – also be understood as a social identity, akin to party identification (Kinder and Kalmoe, 2017; Mason, 2018). A social identity is "that part of an individual's self-concept which derives from his [*sic*] knowledge of his membership in a social group (or groups) together with the value and emotional significance attached to that membership" (Tajfel 1978, p. 63). Understood in this way, seeing oneself as "progressive" or "conservative" is less about certain policy commitments and more about one's attachment to an ideologically defined social group.

Seeing oneself as part of a social group has consequences for what individuals are willing to say and do. As social identities, ideological identities may come with expectations of behaviour – ways in which identifiers believe they and others in their identity group should behave (Cooper et al., 2001; Suhay, 2015). Such expectations are also called *injunctive norms* (Akerlof and Kranton, 2000, 2001; Bicchieri, 2016): shared rules of behaviour that people expect group members (e.g., fellow progressives) to follow and believe other group members expect them to follow. Research has shown that individuals may be willing to pay a cost, be it financial or in the form of psychological discomfort, in order to comply with these norms (Pickup et al., 2020). This can have important implications for political issues that individuals support, such as housing affordability. If a political identity, such as an ideology, is made salient (as it might be during an election campaign), the desire to comport with expectations of that identity may affect individual decision-making, according more weight to group expectations and less to other preferences individuals might hold. This is particularly true if the group expectations run counter to these other preferences.

In Vancouver, an example of an issue where group expectations may be in conflict with other preferences is housing. On the one hand, many Vancouverites believe that housing affordability (high rents and housing prices) is a problem. On the other hand, many Vancouverites personally benefit from high rental and housing prices. Individuals who identify as left-wing or progressive may believe that others who identify themselves as such expect them to support lowering rental and housing prices to address this issue, even if it means lowering the price of their own properties. We designed a survey experiment to investigate this expectation, in the first test of the impact of ideological injunctive norms in a municipal election.

The survey experiment consisted of three questions embedded in the CMES Vancouver survey, the second of which was an experimental intervention (treatment) randomly assigned to be seen by only half the respondents, and the third of which was our outcome measure. We tested the impact of our intervention on our outcome measure. Understanding the role of political identities and the norms attached to them in altering people's political preferences can help us understand, for instance, how campaign rhetoric – even at the municipal level – has the potential to sharpen divisions between groups of voters differentially placed on the political spectrum. We now describe the design in more detail.

Experimental Design

In a first question, all respondents were asked their ideological identity: "When it comes to (municipal) politics, do you think of yourself as (choose the one that best applies)?" The eight response options were: liberal; left-wing; progressive; libertarian; right-wing; conservative; none of the above, and don't know. Although some labels suggested similar political stances (e.g., progressive and left-wing), we wanted to give respondents the opportunity to choose the political label they most closely identified with, if any. Half the respondents were then assigned to the treatment group and asked this second question: "How do you think other [insert ideological identity] Vancouverites like you would approve if you said you opposed lowering rental and housing prices in your neighbourhood in order to combat housing affordability?" They were provided with a 0–10 scale to respond, with 0 labelled as "strongly disapprove" and 10 labelled as "strongly approve."[14] By asking individuals how others in their group would view their actions (approve or disapprove), we were asking and therefore priming the individual's normative expectations regarding this action. That is, we made the respondent's political group and specifically the group's expectations salient before asking the third question. The other half of the respondents, the control group, were not asked this norm question. To measure our outcome, we then asked all respondents this final question: "As part of this study we are going to give $500 to the campaign of one of the mayoral candidates in the upcoming municipal election. We will choose the candidate at random but you get to vote on whether or not we include the following statement with the donation: 'With this contribution, we ask that if elected you enact policies to lower rental and housing prices in my neighbourhood.' The statement will be included with the donation if a majority of 1,000 survey respondents vote for it. Would you like this statement included or not?" (Response options were "Yes", "No," or "Don't know.")

Results

Table 5.3 indicates that, in our data, the most common identity as indicated by our first question was liberal (25%), followed by conservative (17%),

Table 5.3. Ideological identities and associated norm of opposing lowering rental and housing prices in one's neighbourhood in order to combat housing affordability

Ideological identity	%	Norm, 0–10*	Standard deviation	Norm direction
Liberal	25.40	5.18	(3.09)	Approve
Left-wing	13.46	3.60	(3.42)	Disapprove
Progressive	15.47	4.45	(3.10)	Disapprove
Libertarian	3.59	5.23	(2.37)	Approve
Right-wing	3.29	5.64	(2.57)	Approve
Conservative	17.42	4.89	(2.68)	Neither approve nor disapprove
None of the above	9.44	–		
Don't know	11.94	–		
N	1,642	633		

* Strongly disapprove to strongly approve.

progressive (15%), and left-wing (13%). Less than 4% each identified as libertarian or right-wing, and 21% indicated "none of the above" or that they did not know.[15]

What was the nature of the injunctive norms in these ideological groups? That is, what did the identifiers think others in their identity group would expect of them? Based on the answers to our second question, right-wing, libertarian, and liberal identifiers on average expected approval for opposing "lowering rental and housing prices in your neighbourhood in order to combat housing affordability" (Table 5.3, column 3). All three groups of respondents scored between 5.2 and 5.6 on the 0–10 scale, with higher numbers indicating more approval. In contrast, left-wing and progressive identifiers on average expected disapproval for opposing lowering rental and housing prices, with scores of 3.6 and 4.5. The fact that liberal identifiers were included with right-wing and libertarian identifiers in their expectation of approval suggests that many individuals who identify as liberal may do so because they identify with the centre-right BC Liberal Party. The average expectation for conservative identifiers was 4.9, indicating neither approval nor disapproval. Note, though, that there is a fair bit of variance in the responses within all groups, indicating the consensuses are not clear. This suggests that the norm for each group, to the extent that it exists, is not strong.

Figure 5.4 presents the results of priming the norm for those identities that expect approval for opposing lowering rental and housing prices to combat housing affordability (right-wing, libertarian, and liberal), those identities that expect disapproval (left-wing and progressive), and the group that expects neither (conservative). The first thing to note is that most individuals were willing to include the statement "With this

Figure 5.4. Treatment effects of group-norm prime on willingness to include a statement, by expected approval of one's ideological identity group for opposing lowering rental and housing prices

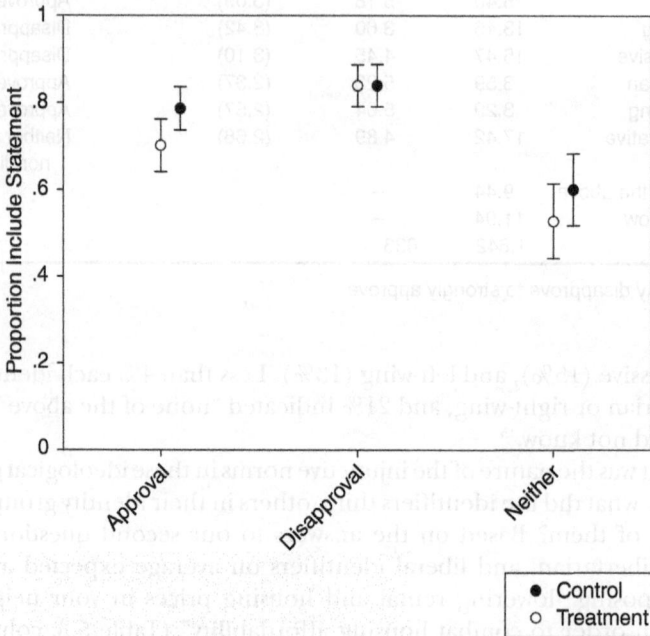

Note: 95% confidence intervals shown.

contribution, we ask that if elected you enact policies to lower rental and housing prices in my neighbourhood." Also, 79% of liberal, libertarian, and right-wing identifiers voted to include the statement when not primed with the group norm, and 84% of unprimed left-wing and progressive identifiers and 60% of unprimed conservative identifiers did so.

When those groups that expected *approval* for opposing the inclusion of the statement (right-wing, libertarian, and liberal) were primed with their group norm in the treatment, they were 8.5 percentage points less likely to vote to include a statement (*p*-value: 0.032). That is, they behaved in a way more consistent with the group norm. Conversely, among those groups that expected *disapproval* for opposing the statement's inclusion (left-wing and progressive), priming the norm did not change the behaviour (*p*-value: 0.996). This null effect may partly be due to a ceiling effect: as noted, even without priming, 84% of these individuals voted for the statement to be included. Finally, as we would expect, the priming effect for the group that expected *neither* approval nor disapproval is not statistically significant (*p*-value: 0.233).

To summarize, the results of the experiment suggest that many Vancouver voters did experience social pressure to conform to injunctive norms regarding the housing affordability issue. Those who perceived a neutral norm within their group, appropriately, were not moved by the priming of group norms. Likewise, those already very likely to conform with group norms were unaffected by the treatment.

Conclusion

From the perspective of electoral studies, the Vancouver election of 2018 had several notable features. The record number of candidates – for both mayor and council – obviously stands out. The mayoral electorate was remarkably fractionalized: on Election Day, only three candidates captured more than 20% of the vote and no single candidate captured as much as one third of the vote on their own. The field was especially congested on the left, where two major candidates were seen by voters as highly similar in ideological terms. A host of issues were in play during the campaign, although one – housing affordability – captured the lion's share of candidate and voter attention.

Our analysis suggests that, notwithstanding the complex political circumstances, Vancouver's citizens decided in much the same fashion as voters do in other elections. In reasoning their way to vote choice, Vancouverites relied, like voters in federal and provincial elections, mainly on their ideological commitments and issue attitudes. We also uncovered traces of the social pressure voters experienced to conform with the expectations of their identity groups – in this case, the pressure felt by voters on the broad political right to adapt their political behaviour on the affordability issue. Summing these and other forces together, the election delivered a veritable rout to the incumbent party, the narrowest of victories to its new mayor, and a patchwork of parties to the new city council.

NOTES

1 Throughout this chapter, unless otherwise indicated, estimates from the survey data are weighted to reflect census proportions by age and gender. We report as significant any differences that are significant with a p-value ≤ 0.05.

2 The plot is based on a pre-election vote intention model, adjusting for features of the sample that may vary over time in the campaign. In particular, we estimate a multinomial probit model of vote choice, including indicators for interview week, demographic variables (those included in Model A, section 2, below) and a control for whether the respondent was recruited from the panel or via interactive voice response interviewing. *Per* endnote 1, the estimation sample is weighted for age and gender.

3 Only the ratings between Sylvester and Stewart do not significantly differ.

4 In fact, a total of 158 candidates ran for mayor, city councillor, park commissioner, and school trustee, "resulting in a longer than usual ballot which caused paper jams in the vote counting machines at some locations" (City of Vancouver, 2019a).

5 In 1999 and 2005 respectively, 40% and 39% of candidates ran as independents. In the 2008, 2011 and 2014 elections, 25%, 29% and 20%, respectively, of candidates were independents (City of Vancouver, 2019b).

6 Our data show that in Vancouver before the election only 41% of respondents indicated they were satisfied with the performance of the current City Council; this is the lowest percentage of all cities included in the CMES.

7 Adriane Carr of the Green Party, Melissa de Genova of the NPA, and Heather Deal of Vision had been elected as councillors in 2014, and an additional six candidates had recently been Park Commissioner or School Trustee.

8 Also, the highest percentage among all cities, 29% of respondents only finalized their council vote decision on Election Day. Although part of this relatively high percentage might be explained by the fact that voters could vote for up to ten candidates, in contrast to other cities where they voted for only one city councillor, it bears noting that the percentage of respondents who finalized their decision for mayor on Election Day, 17%, was also one of the highest among all cities, only topped by Mississauga.

9 The average scores on affordability and on property taxes differ significantly from those on the other issues. The average scores on public transit, traffic, homelessness, and economic development do not differ significantly from one another. The survey did not ask about two other potentially important issues in the campaign: the Trans Mountain Pipeline and the opioid crisis.

10 Voters could cast votes for up to ten candidates each. In total, 1,396,928 votes were cast. The mean number of votes cast for a candidate was 19,675 (1.41% of all votes), the minimum was 1,946 (0.14%) and the maximum was 69,730 (4.99%).

11 It is notable that together the independent candidates won 15% of the votes. This is a substantially higher percentage compared to the 2002 to 2014 elections, in which independents won 3 to 7% of the votes; however,

it is not unique for Vancouver – for instance, in 1999, independents won 21% of the votes (City of Vancouver, 2019b). Moreover, as far back as the 1996 election, no independent candidate has been elected to City Council (idem). So, although with the waning of Vision, the party system in Vancouver might be in upheaval, it does not seem to be disappearing.

12 In what follows, we report marginal effects that are significant at the 95% level or better.

13 If this analysis is correct, it seems likely that the strong effect of attitudes toward homelessness may reflect, in part, confounding with the effect of affordability attitudes. This would be the case if those least concerned about homelessness were also least inclined to support demand-side (i.e., taxation-based) measures to respond to housing affordability concerns.

14 No answer was recorded for respondents assigned to treatment who indicated "none of the above" or "don't know" in the first question (a total of 190). All other respondents assigned to treatment provided an answer.

15 Estimates from the survey data reported in this Special Topics section are not weighted as we are interested in comparing the outcome between respondents in the treatment and the control groups.

REFERENCES

Akerlof, G. A., & Kranton, R. E. (2000). Economics and identity. *Quarterly Journal of Economics, 115*(3), 715–753. https://doi.org/10.1162/003355300554881

Akerlof, G. A., & Kranton, R. E. (2001). Identity and the economics of organizations. *Journal of Economic Perspectives, 19*(1), 9–32. https://doi.org/10.1257/0895330053147930

Bailey, I. (2018). Newly elected mayor Kennedy Stewart makes case for ward system in Vancouver. *The Globe and Mail.* 22 October. https://www.theglobeandmail.com/canada/british-columbia/article-newly-elected-mayor-kennedy-stewart-makes-case-for-ward-system-in

Bicchieri, C. (2016). *Norms in the wild: How to diagnose, measure, and change social norms.* Oxford University Press.

Bula, F. (2018a). Metro Vancouver politicians divided in support of different regional transit plans. *The Globe and Mail.* 30 September. https://www.theglobeandmail.com/canada/british-columbia/article-metro-vancouver-politicians-divided-in-support-of-different-regional

Bula, F. (2018b). Union electioneering sparks legal controversy in Vancouver mayoral race. *The Globe and Mail.* 12 October. https://www.theglobeandmail.com/canada/british-columbia/article-union-electioneering-sparks-legal-controversy-in-vancouver-manyoral

Bula, F. (2018c). In the Vancouver election, it's all about housing. *The Globe and Mail.* 13 October. https://www.theglobeandmail.com/canada

/british-columbia/article-all-vancouver-candidates-are-talking-of-more
-housinyg-in-some-form-or

Bula, F., & Mason, G. (2018). Vancouver developer's money paid for billboards supporting mayoral candidate. *The Globe and Mail*. 21 September. https://www.theglobeandmail.com/canada/british-columbia/article-vancouver -developers-money-paid-for-billboards-supporting-mayoral/

City of Vancouver. (2019a). *Legacy open data catalogue. Anonymous ballot marking*. https://data.vancouver.ca/datacatalogue/anonymousBallotMarking.htm

City of Vancouver. (2019b). *Open data portal. Municipal election results*. https://opendata.vancouver.ca/explore/dataset/municipal-election -results/information

City of Vancouver. (2019c). *Election results 2018 – table*. https://vancouver.ca /your-government/election-results-2018-table.aspx

City of Vancouver, Independent Election Task Force. (2019). *A review of campaign financing by third parties and independent candidates in municipal elections*. https://vancouver.ca/files/cov/independent-election-task-force -report-on-campaign-financing-june-2019.pdf

Converse, P. E. (1964). The nature of belief systems in mass publics. In D. E. Apter (Ed.), *Ideology and discontent*. Free Press.

Cooper, J., Kelly, K. A., & Weaver, K. 2001. Attitudes, norms, and social groups. In M. A. Hogg and S. Tyndale (Eds.), *Blackwell handbook of social psychology: Group processes*. Oxford: Blackwell.

Cutler, F., & Matthews, J. S. (2005). The challenge of municipal voting: Vancouver 2002. *Canadian Journal of Political Science, 38*(2), 359–382.

de Rooij, E. A., & Henderson, C. (2020). Election ballot order effects in Vancouver municipal elections (Appendix C). In City of Vancouver, *Report back on the random order ballot model used in the 2018 Vancouver Election*. https://council.vancouver.ca/20210119/documents/p2.pdf

Fumano, D. (2018a). Dan Fumano: This won't be the year for Vancouver's first Green mayor, after all. *Vancouver Sun*. 9 June. https://vancouversun.com /news/politics/dan-fumano-this-wont-be-the-year-for-vancouvers-first -green-mayor-after-all

Fumano, D. (2018b). Dan Fumano: The reason Patrick Condon is doing what he earlier said "would be a nightmare." *Vancouver Sun*. 12 June. https:// vancouversun.com/news/local-news/dan-fumano-the-reason-patrick -condon-is-doing-what-he-earlier-said-would-be-a-nightmare

Fumano, D. (2018c). Burnaby MP Kennedy Stewart to run as independent for mayor of Vancouver. *Vancouver Sun*. 11 May. https://vancouversun.com/news /local-news/burnaby-mp-kennedy-stewart-to-run-for-mayor-of-vancouver

Howell, M. (2018). Shauna Sylvester is running for mayor of Vancouver. *Vancouver Courier*. 5 April. https://www.vancourier.com/news/shauna -sylvester-is-running-for-mayor-of-vancouver-1.23256028

Kinder, D., & Kalmoe, N. (2017). *Neither liberal nor conservative: Ideological innocence in the American public.* University of Chicago Press.

Little, S. (2018). NPA faces defections over decision to drop Hector Bremner from mayoral race. *Global News.* 10 May. https://globalnews.ca/news/4201523/npa-defections-hector-bremner

Mason, L. (2018). *Uncivil agreement: How politics became our identity.* University of Chicago Press.

McElroy, J. (2018a). Shauna Sylvester wants to become mayor of Vancouver. Here's what she needs to have happen. *CBC News.* 5 April. https://www.cbc.ca/news/canada/british-columbia/shauna-sylvester-vancouver-mayor-announcement-1.4605291

McElroy, J. (2018b, June 21). "Free the Roads": Wai Young joins Vancouver's race for mayor on anti-bike lane platform. *CBC News.* 21 June. https://www.cbc.ca/news/canada/british-columbia/wai-young-vancouver-mayor-1.4717309

Miller, W., & Shanks, J. (1996). *The new American voter.* Harvard University Press.

NPA Vancouver. (2018a). NPA Vancouver members nominate Ken Sim to be their mayoral candidate for the October 2018 municipal election. *NPA Vancouver.* 3 June. https://npavancouver.ca/latest-news/npa-vancouver-members-nominate-ken-sim-to-be-their-mayoral-candidate-for-the-october-2018-municipal-election

NPA Vancouver. (2018b). Housing plan. https://npavancouver.ca/housing-plan

NPA Vancouver. (2018c). Economic Plan. *NPA Vancouver.* https://npavancouver.ca/economic-plan

O'Connor, N. (2018). Where do the candidates stand on housing in Vancouver? *Vancouver Courier.* 18 October. https://www.vancourier.com/real-estate/where-do-the-candidates-stand-on-housing-in-vancouver-1.23468589

Oen, C. (2018). Can union-brokered deal prevent vote-splitting in Vancouver election? *The Tyee.* 31 July. https://thetyee.ca/Analysis/2018/07/31/Union-Brokered-Deal-Prevent-Vote-Splitting-Vancouver

Pablo, C. (2018a). Board members, Vancouver Council hopefuls bolt NPA following foiled nomination of Hector Bremner. *Georgia Straight.* 16 May. https://www.straight.com/news/1076221/board-members-vancouver-council-hopefuls-bolt-npa-following-foiled-nomination-hector

Pablo, C. (2018b). Mixed-race heritage stirs Vancouver councillor-elect Pete Fry to champion city's diversity. *Georgia Straight.* 24 October. https://www.straight.com/news/1155111/mixed-race-heritage-stirs-vancouver-councillor-elect-pete-fry-champion-citys-diversity

Pickup, M. A., Kimbrough, E. O., & de Rooij, E. A. (2020). Identity and the self-reinforcing effects of norm compliance. *Southern Economic Journal, 86*(3), 1222–1240. https://doi.org/10.1002/soej.12410

Research Co. (2018a). Stewart holds the upper hand in Vancouver mayoral race. [Press release]. 19 September. https://researchco.ca/wp-content /uploads/2018/09/Release_VanPoli_19Sep2018.pdf

Research Co. (2018b). Stewart remains ahead in Vancouver mayoral race. [Press release]. 9 October. https://researchco.ca/wp-content/uploads /2018/10/Release_VanPoli_09Oct2018.pdf

Research Co. (2018c). Stewart keeps lead as Vancouver mayoral election looms. [Press release]. 16 October. https://researchco.ca/wp-content /uploads/2018/10/Release_VanPoli_16Oct2018.pdf

Statistics Canada. (2019). *Census profile, 2016 census.* https://www12 .statcan.gc.ca/census-recensement/2016/dp-pd/prof/details/page .cfm?Lang=E&Geo1=CMACA&Code1=933&Geo2=PR&Code2=59 &SearchText=vancouver&SearchType=Begins&SearchPR=01&B1=Visible %20minority&TABID=1&type=1

Stewart, K. (2018). *Kennedy Stewart platform 2018.* http://d3n8a8pro7vhmx .cloudfront.net/themes/5bbe435745de94b12e192717/attachments /original/1539972364/KennedyStewartPlatform2018.pdf

Suhay, E. (2015). Explaining group influence: The role of identity and emotion in political conformity and polarization. *Political Behavior, 37,* 221–251.

Tajfel, H. (1978). Social categorization, social identity, and social comparisons. In H. Tajfel (Ed.), *Differentiation between social groups.* Academic Press.

Tanner, A. (2018). Ken Sim is a catch for the non-partisan association. *The Globe and Mail.* 8 June. https://www.theglobeandmail.com/canada/british -columbia/article-ken-sim-is-a-catch-for-the-non-partisan-association

Trounstine, J., & Valdini, M. E. (2008). The context matters: The effects of single-member versus at-large districts on city council diversity. *American Journal of Political Science, 52*(3), 554–569. https://doi.org/10.1111 /j.1540-5907.2008.00329.x

6 London

CAMERON D. ANDERSON AND LAURA B. STEPHENSON

When Londoners went to the polls in 2018 they faced a ballot different than any other in Ontario – one that allowed them to rank up to three candidates for the mayoral and councillor offices. All Ontario municipalities could have used ranked ballots, but only London took advantage of the 2016 change to the *Municipal Elections Act* and made it happen.[1] This meant that ballots allowed voters to indicate their first, second, and third preferences for mayor and local councillor.[2] In a ranked ballot system, second and third preferences are important; if a voter's first-choice candidate receives the fewest votes in the race, that candidate is eliminated and their votes are redistributed to the other ranked candidates on the eliminated candidate's ballots. Votes continue to be redistributed as candidates are eliminated until one candidate passes the vote threshold (50% of votes plus one) or there are no votes left to be redistributed.

Aside from the new electoral system, which brought considerable media attention to the city, London's election was also notable because of the individuals who were and were not running. The mayoral race was an open contest because the sitting mayor, Matt Brown, had decided not to run after a scandal erupted over an extra-marital affair he conducted during his only term in office. Several candidates emerged to compete for his office, ranging from well-known politicians (Ed Holder, the eventual winner and former area MP) to first-time candidates (such as David Millie). In the 14 city councillor races, eleven incumbents ran again. Some races were between just two candidates while one had nine different names on the ballot. Across all campaigns, the candidates distinguished themselves from one another on the issue of transit (specifically, bus rapid transit; BRT) and fought to appeal to voters with their plans to make London a more vibrant and economically successful community.

While the campaign did not have any dramatic moments or pivotal scandals, it did energize the community and divide Londoners in specific ways. In this chapter, we discuss the campaigns, issues, and candidates, explore the factors that affected mayoral vote choice, and analyse the impact of the switch to ranked ballot voting. Two elements of particular interest in this election were the role of partisanship in the mayoral race and the impact of the ranked ballot electoral system on the outcome.

Election Overview

The Mayoral Campaign

The roots of the 2018 mayoral campaign can be found in the 2014 election. In that race, London City Council underwent a dramatic facelift after a scandalous period with Joe Fontana as mayor. During his tenure, Fontana was accused and ultimately convicted of fraud-related offences stemming from actions while he was a federal cabinet minister, and City Council was twice investigated for inappropriate backroom meetings[3] between Fontana and his supporters (Fontana eventually resigned in June 2014). Voters sent a clear message by soundly electing Matt Brown, a former London city councillor and a clear contrast in style and substance to Fontana, and by blocking any of the so-called "Fontana 8" from returning to council (including one who ran for mayor).[4] However, Brown found himself in a similarly scandalous position when his extramarital affair with councillor Maureen Cassidy was revealed in 2016. After taking a leave, he returned to his position and finished his term, but he chose not to run for re-election in 2018. That left the field open for a new crop of competitors.

There were four front-runners in the race for mayor in 2018: Ed Holder, Paul Cheng, Paul Paolatto, and Tanya Park. Together, these candidates received about 95% of first-preference votes. There were ten other candidates in the race: Vahide Bahramporian, Ali Hamadi, Dan Lenart, Nina McCutcheon, David Millie, Jordan Minter, Mohamed Moussa, Carlos Murray, Sean M. O'Connell, and Jonas White. Some candidates had run for mayor in the past (Paul Cheng, Dan Lenart, and Carlos Murray), while others were known for other political positions they had held. Most importantly, Ed Holder, who emerged as the early front-runner, was a former federal Conservative Member of Parliament and cabinet minister and was thus well-known to many Londoners. He had entered politics in 2008 running as a Conservative candidate for the London West riding, eventually serving as the Minister of State (Science and Technology) in the Harper government. Paul Paolatto was also a familiar name, as he was executive director of Western Research Parks at Western University and a former member of the London Police Services Board. Paul Cheng had run for the mayor's chair previously with a well-publicized campaign, so many voters would have remembered him from 2014. Finally, Tanya Park had been the councillor for Ward 13 since 2014. All of the front-running candidates were therefore familiar to some degree among London's electorate.

Among the four front-runners, there was an interesting ideological spread. Holder, Paolatto, and Cheng were all perceived as small-c conservatives, or right-wing candidates, compared to Park, who was viewed as being on the left. This was confirmed by CMES data: respondents placed Park at 3.2 on a 0–10 left–right ideological scale (where 10 is the most right-wing), compared to Paolatto (6.1), Cheng (6.5), and Holder (6.8).

We can also use CMES data to see whether the four front-runners were perceived in a partisan light. As noted in this volume's chapter on Calgary and in McGregor et al. (2016), if voters perceive candidates to be affiliated with parties, then those perceptions, combined with their own partisan leanings, can influence their vote choice. The CMES asked respondents to indicate whether they thought the candidates were associated with a federal party. The results, shown in Table 6.1, confirm our earlier findings about ideology in that Cheng, Holder, and Paolatto were all seen as affiliated with the Conservative Party, while Park was associated with the NDP. Even more interesting is that a majority of respondents identified Holder as a Conservative, whereas the numbers for the other candidates were far lower. In fact, between 42% and 51% of respondents didn't know how Cheng, Holder, and Park were affiliated. This reinforces the idea that Holder was well-identified in the electorate because of his past political life as an MP for London West.

The abundance of right-wing candidates seems consistent with London's reputation as a conservative southwestern Ontario city. However, Park's candidacy should not be seen as an anomaly. A closer look at London's recent federal and provincial legislators suggests that the city's conservative reputation is not based on elections at other levels of government (see Table 6.2). At the federal level, the 2015 election brought two Liberals, one NDP and one Conservative MP to office (four seats in total). In no year since 2000 has the Conservative Party held every seat – in fact, the only time that a party has held all of London's seats was in 2000, when they were held by the Liberal Party. At the provincial level there has been similar diversity, although in 2003 and 2007 the Liberals swept all of the offices.

Table 6.1. Impressions of partisan associations of mayoral candidates (%)

Federal parties	Cheng	Holder	Paolatto	Park
Conservative	30.1	58.3	26.5	2.3
Liberal	7.8	7.4	12.6	10.2
NDP	2.3	2.1	3.1	36.2
Green	0.6	0.6	0.9	4.4
Don't know	47.3	28.6	51.0	42.3
None/other	11.8	3.0	6.0	4.6

Table 6.2. Recent history of London's federal and provincial ridings

	London Fanshawe	London North Centre	London West	Elgin–Middlesex–London
Federal				
2015	Irene Mathyssen (NDP)	Peter Fragiskatos (Liberal)	Kate Young (Liberal)	Karen Vecchio (Conservative)
2011	Irene Mathyssen (NDP)	Susan Truppe (Conservative)	Ed Holder (Conservative)	Joe Preston (Conservative)
2008	Irene Mathyssen (NDP)	Glen Pearson (Liberal)	Ed Holder (Conservative)	Joe Preston (Conservative)
2006	Irene Mathyssen (NDP)	Joe Fontana (Liberal)	Sue Barnes (Liberal)	Joe Preston (Conservative)
2004	Pat O'Brien (Liberal)	Joe Fontana (Liberal)	Sue Barnes (Liberal)	Joe Preston (Conservative)
Provincial				
2018	Teresa Armstrong (NDP)	Terence Kernaghan (NDP)	Peggy Sattler (NDP)	Jeff Yurek (Progressive Conservative)
2014	Teresa Armstrong (NDP)	Deb Matthews (Liberal)	Peggy Sattler (NDP)	Jeff Yurek (Progressive Conservative)
2011	Teresa Armstrong (NDP)	Deb Matthews (Liberal)	Christopher Bentley (Liberal) 2013: Peggy Sattler (NDP)	Jeff Yurek (Progressive Conservative)
2007	Khalil Ramal (Liberal)	Deb Matthews (Liberal)	Christopher Bentley (Liberal)	Steve Peters (Liberal)
2003	Khalil Ramal (Liberal	Deb Matthews (Liberal)	Christopher Bentley (Liberal)	Steve Peters (Liberal)
1999	Frank Mazzilli (Progressive Conservative)	Dianne Cunningham (Progressive Conservative)	Bob Wood (Progressive Conservative)	Steve Peters (Liberal)

Council Races

The contests for council seats were less contentious in 2018 than they had been in 2014, when the drama of the Fontana council and accusations of inappropriate meetings drove a widespread desire for change. In 2018, by contrast, there was no such imperative. In 11 of the 14 wards, incumbents were running again; in one case, a former councillor (Paul Van Meerbergen) who had been part of the "Fontana 8" decided to run once more (successfully, as it turned out). The number of candidates running in each ward ranged from two (three wards) to nine (Ward 8). Of the 66 candidates who ran for city councillor, only 17 (26%) were women. Ultimately, four women were elected to London's council, among them the first visible minority woman elected in the city's history (Arielle Kayabaga).

Issues and Events

During the campaign, there was a single major issue – bus rapid transit (BRT).[5] That issue had a considerable history in the city and remained controversial. The focus of this particular debate was that, given London's size and transportation requirements (including a large student presence), a rapid transit system was long overdue. The plans for the BRT system had begun in earnest when the city passed *The London Plan* in June 2016, which called for the integration of rapid transit into the community. That plan was the culmination of years of study, including the Smart Moves 2030 Transportation Plan (begun in 2009 and finished in 2013), which recommended two rapid transit routes. A Rapid Transit Master Plan was approved in July 2017, providing details about where the system would run. In May 2018, City Council officially approved the BRT plans, but public debate on the matter was far from over. The sources of public disagreement were many: the expected costs, which were well into the hundreds of millions of dollars; the routes that had been proposed, which upset both homeowners and businesses; and, finally, the appropriate form of transportation (light rail versus bus-only) (Maloney, 2017b). Given the range of ongoing public disagreement and the fact that the BRT's development would involve numerous stages and considerable consultation and assessment, it was going to continue to be a major issue after the 2018 election. So it made sense for candidates to make known their positions on this issue. The BRT became a major point of division for more than just the candidates. Interested third parties also campaigned to make BRT a deciding factor in the election by placing For and Against signs around the city.[6]

The candidates put forward their positions on a number of other issues, both in their platforms and during organized debates. Economic concerns, such as taxes and development, were important for all the candidates. Various promises were made: to attract tourism events to London (Cheng), to increase apprenticeships (Park), to fight for fair shares of money from other levels of government (Holder). Social issues were also important to all the candidates: addiction, mental illness, food security, and housing were all discussed. But no other issue approached the BRT in intensity and degree of polarization.

Voters had their own views on which issues were important to them. Figure 6.1 shows the importance of different issues as indicated by CMES respondents in London in response to the following question: "How important are each of the following issues to you in this election? Please indicate each issue's importance on a 0–10 scale, where 0 means not at all important and 10 means extremely important." It is interesting that BRT ranked lowest among all the issues, albeit with the highest standard deviation (not shown); in other words, that issue brought the greatest variation in responses, with people thinking either that it was very important or that it was not. For some voters, it was *the* issue on which they would be basing their vote choice; for others it was irrelevant. Not all Londoners were affected by traffic or by the planned development of BRT lines (which would involve considerable construction throughout the downtown core), which is likely why the issue was polarizing. Among the other issues, traffic and congestion and economic development emerged as most important. In the next section we will revisit these in terms of how they affected vote choice.

Regarding the campaigns themselves, there was more negativity than expected given the incentives that ranked ballots provide for candidates to try to appeal to other candidates' supporters for second- and third-rank votes. For example, there were several reports of election sign interference: some signs were reported missing, and others were vandalized (Stacey, 2018b). There was even a report of signs being pushed over and urinated upon (Stacey, 2018c). In a CBC news story, political scientist Jacquetta Newman contended that candidates were still acting as if they were in a first-past-the-post election, where all that matters is winning first-place votes (Dubinski, 2018b). Indeed, three of the four mayoral front-runners indicated they would only rank one candidate on their ballot (only Park indicated she would support other candidates with her second and third votes) (Dubinski, 2018a). In terms of the signals sent to voters by the candidates, this may have discouraged voters from using the ballot to its full potential and negated one of the potential benefits of the ranked-ballot system.

Figure 6.1. Issue importance in the 2018 London election

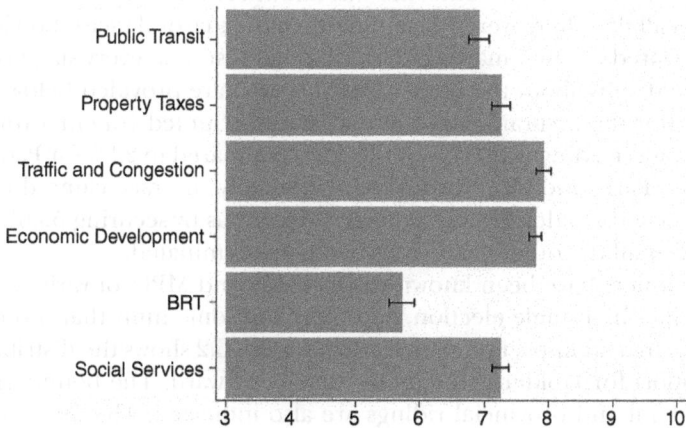

More strikingly, but perhaps not surprisingly given recent election events elsewhere, negative campaigns were launched against two female incumbents, Maureen Cassidy in Ward 5 and Virginia Ridley in Ward 10. In Cassidy's case, the campaign involved lawn signs and a fake campaign website that questioned her stances on transit, the "sanctuary city" label, and her integrity (in relation to her affair with former mayor Matt Brown). The campaign against Ridley was also a website, which raised the idea of child abuse in relation to bringing her child to a City Council meeting. These negative websites were also notable for expressing gender stereotypes (Stacey, 2018a).

The Election Result

The outcome of the election took longer to communicate than in previous years due to the shift to ranked ballots (which can entail a much longer vote-counting process). As Andrew Lupton of the CBC tweeted, "Depending on how you look at it, this round-by-round release of results is either suspense-building or annoyingly long." Christopher Wynder tweeted: "Is there a reason that they do not do 1 big 'cut' down to those that still have a viable chance? The line between possible and impossible seems pretty clear. You could get down to Park, Cheung [*sic*], Paolatto, Holder. Im [*sic*] all for completeness but this defies logic." Because each of the minor candidates had to be eliminated one-by-one, getting down to the race between the four front-runners took a long time.

Nonetheless, about 18 hours after the polls closed all of the races had been tabulated and the outcome was known. After 14 rounds of counting (recall that there were 14 candidates in the mayoral race), Ed Holder was declared the new mayor after having led results at every stage (more specific details about the ranked-ballot system are provided below). Initially, after the first-ranked preferences were counted (the first round), Holder was leading with 34% of the votes compared to 22% for Paolatto, 20% for Park, and 20% for Cheng. Ultimately the race came down to Paolatto and Holder. Holder emerged victorious by securing 59.6% support after all the other candidates had been eliminated.

Londoners have been known to elect MPs and MPPs of various partisan stripes in a single election, and there are some hints that those tendencies had an impact on the election. Figure 6.2 shows the distribution of support for Holder throughout the city by ward. The boundaries of the federal and provincial ridings are also indicated. The figure shows that Holder's first-round support on Election Day ranged from 23% in Ward 13 to 43% in Ward 9. Not surprisingly, Wards 7, 8, 9, and 10 showed the strongest support for him, as they overlap with Holder's former federal riding of London West. However, we do not see a similar pattern of cross-level vote similarity with support for Park, whom many associated with the NDP. The riding of London-Fanshawe, to the east of the city, was the seat of an NDP MP in 2018, but Park's highest support came from downtown ridings (Wards 11 and 13).

Table 6.3 displays the election results for each of the 14 wards. In this table, we include a range of information about the ward race (including the number of candidates running for office, the number of female candidates, whether there was an incumbent running, who won, the number of rounds of counting, and the final vote share). Additionally, we show the Round 1 support for the eventual winner of the mayoral race (Ed Holder) and the primary left-wing challenger (Tanya Park).

Six of the council races required more than one round of counting to find a majority winner under the new ranked-ballot procedure. Eight incumbents were returned to office; three were defeated by either newcomers (such as Bill Armstrong's defeat by Shawn Lewis in Ward 2) or former councillors (Virginia Ridley's defeat by "Fontana 8" member Paul Van Meerbergen in Ward 10). The nature of ranked ballots is such that the eventual winner has the support of a majority of voters at some rank. In eight races, this occurred after the first count of ballots. The vote shares of the winners ranged from just over 50% (Wards 1 and 4) to over 75% (Ward 7). However, there can be situations in which a winner is declared because there are no ballots left to be redistributed (this can happen when voters do not rank three candidates or support candidates

Figure 6.2. First preference vote share for Holder, by ward

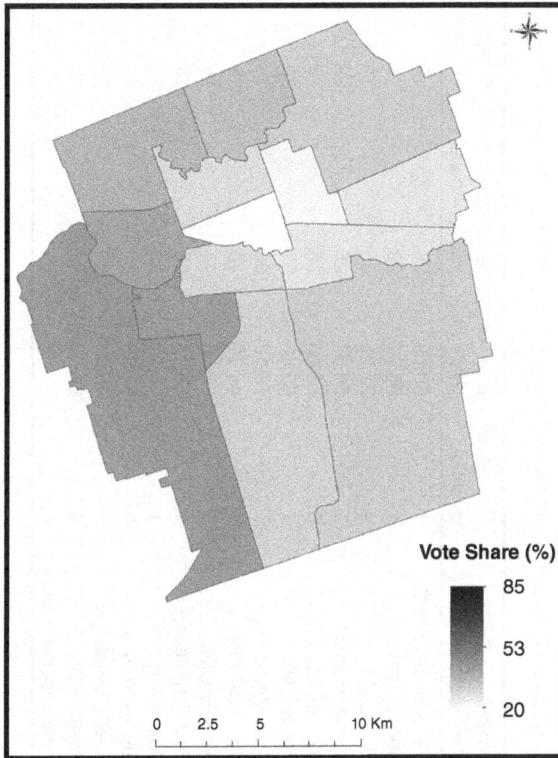

who have been eliminated). This occurred in two wards (8 and 13), each of which had many candidates (9 and 8, respectively) and required many rounds of counting to determine a winner (9 and 8, respectively).

Another interesting aspect of this election is the turnout. One argument in favour of ranked ballots – and indeed many proposed electoral changes – is that it inspires voters to make their voices heard. That does not seem to have occurred in London, as turnout was lower in 2018 than in 2014 (39.46% compared to 43%). One interpretation of this drop in participation is that, although the city engaged in an education campaign to make the ranked-ballot process easy to understand, many were still confused as Election Day neared. An alternative interpretation, which is also quite likely, is that the change in turnout reflected the more contentious nature of the 2014 election, when many voters were motivated to prevent the Fontana 8 from being returned to office.[7] So it may be inappropriate to blame the new electoral system for the decline in turnout.

Table 6.3. Election results, by ward

Ward	# candidates	# women	Incumbent candidate	Winner (* = incumbent)	Rounds of counting	End vote share (%)	% support for Holder (round 1)	% support for Park (round 1)
1	3	1	Yes	Michael Van Holst*	1	50.69	29	18
2	3	3	Yes	Shawn Lewis	1	63.97	29	14
3	2	0	Yes	Mo Sali*	1	72.76	33	16
4	5	2	Yes	Jesse Helmer*	1	50.54	25	28
5	6	6	Yes	Maureen Cassidy*	6	52.65	36	18
6	2	0	Yes	Phil Squire*	1	69.49	29	29
7	2	0	Yes	Josh Morgan*	1	75.18	38	18
8	9	3	No	Steve Lehman	9	48.79	40	18
9	5	2	Yes	Anna Hopkins*	3	52.55	43	15
10	5	0	Yes	Paul Van Meerbergen	1	53.14	42	18
11	6	2	Yes	Stephen Turner*	1	54.09	30	35
12	6	0	No	Elizabeth Peloza	5	51.99	32	16
13	8	1	No	Arielle Kayabaga	8	49.07	23	38
14	4	4	Yes	Steve Hillier	4	64.45	32	15
Summary	66	17	11	8 incumbents, 6 new				

Vote Choice

The big story of any election is the outcome and why voters voted the way they did. We provide some insight into the decisions of Londoners in this section. Figure 6.3 shows the marginal effects of several different vote models. Using CMES data, we ran logistic regressions with several sets of variables. The dependent variable in each model is support for Holder compared to all other candidates, so the models essentially show which factors contributed to his vote share. The independent variables are included in the model in stages, which allows us to see whether values and issue preferences had an independent impact on vote choice. In some ways, this type of analysis is similar to what has been done in previous examinations of Canadian elections using something called a bloc recursive approach (see, for example, Gidengil et al., 2012), which is based on the idea that vote choice is the product of a "funnel of causality" (Campbell et al., 1960). This approach was first developed in Miller and Shanks (1996). Marginal effects, shown in black, are statistically significant.

Model A shows how demographics related to support for Holder. Men, those over 65, and homeowners were more likely to support him. Those who had a university education were slightly less likely to cast a ballot in his favour. Model B adds two measures of conservatism as indicators of values. Not surprisingly given his background, economic conservatives were more likely to support Holder. Adding an evaluation of the economy in Model C does little to affect the findings. While the state of the economy is often a strong predictor of vote choice, it is more relevant when an incumbent is running for re-election and voters are able to decide whether to allow that person another term.

Model D adds issue importance measures to the model. Recall that the most important issues for Londoners were traffic and economic development and that BRT was somewhat polarizing. The results in Figure 6.3 suggest that Holder gained support from those who felt that the property tax was an important issue in the election and those who prioritized economic development. By contrast, those who considered BRT to be important were significantly less likely to support Holder, which is unsurprising given his anti-BRT stance. When we factor in issue importance, homeownership no longer has a significant effect on Holder's support. This is not surprising given that homeowners are likely to be the same people as those who feel property taxes are an important issue.

The constellation of factors that emerge as relevant for supporting Holder are perhaps not surprising given his ideological image as a right-wing candidate. Indeed, when we reran Model D with support for Park as the dependent variable (results not shown), we found that young

Figure 6.3. Vote choice for Holder (first choice votes) – marginal effects

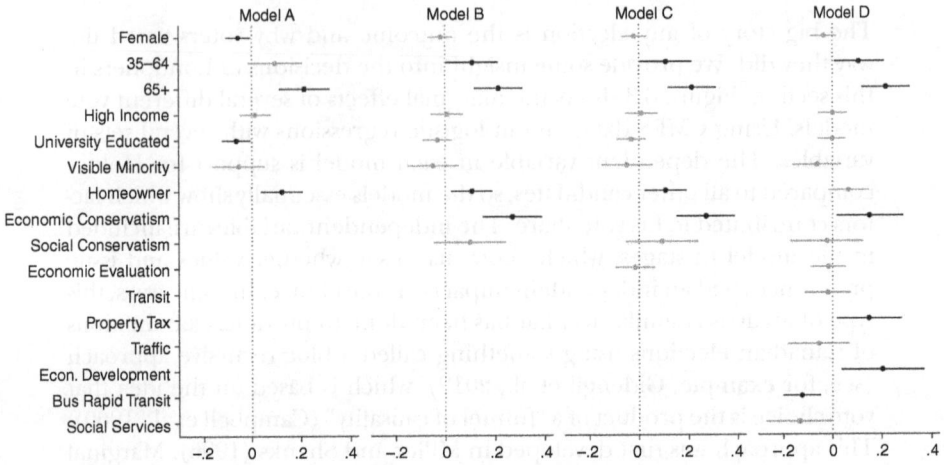

Notes: Entries report marginal effects and 95% confidence intervals. Coefficients in black are statistically significant at p < 0.1.

people, those with higher incomes, homeowners, economic and social liberals, and those who thought BRT and social services were important issues supported her. Those who indicated that traffic and/or economic development were important issues were less likely to vote for her than for the other candidates. These factors make sense for a typical left-wing candidate. It seems, then, that some typical ideological divisions were at play during the campaign.

However, it is important to remember that Holder was competing against two other viable right-wing candidates. It is interesting, then, that his support base (which should be understood as significantly different from those of the other candidates) was so stereotypically conservative. This suggests that Holder was able to set himself apart from those competitors, possibly due to his background as a well-known Conservative MP. To investigate this, we looked at support for the mayoral candidates among Conservative partisans. Conservative partisans supported Holder far more than any other candidate, with 43% ranking him in first place, compared to 15% for Cheng and 19% for Paolatto. Holder was clearly seen as *the* choice of Conservatives. It is perhaps unsurprising, then, that the demographics of his supporters look so similar to those of traditional conservative support bases.

Ranked Ballots

Given the novelty of London's experience with ranked ballots in 2018, we delve deeper to understand the consequences of the electoral system change for voters. We do so in three ways: first, we consider the outcome of the election. Second, we consider whether voters' behaviour changed when they were able to rank candidates. Finally, we approach the issue from a more theoretical position, assessing whether ranked ballots led voters to feel differently about the election result.

The Outcome

As the election results rolled in, many commentators were quick to notice that even though people were glued to their screens awaiting announcements about subsequent rounds of vote tallies, there were no indications that the change in electoral system affected results. Indeed, not a single council race, nor the mayoral race, saw a change from what would have been the outcome had only the first count (of first-choice rankings) been considered. Some, following the returns, commented on this at the time, such as *London Free Press* reporter Megan Stacey, who remarked on the results on Twitter: "seems to suggest ranked ballots did very little in 2018 race." As noted earlier, some council races were decided after one round of counting (by definition, all of the two-candidate races were), while others continued as each candidate was eliminated individually.

This was an unexpected outcome for the election, given that ranked ballots have the potential to change outcomes substantially when lower-ranked preferences are taken into consideration. For example, if all of the followers of Cheng had thrown their support behind Holder, their combined ballots (first rank for each) would have been 33,043 (for Holder) + 19,192 (for Cheng) or 52,205 – greater than the threshold for winning of 48,324. Instead, Cheng's supporters were distributed to all three of his main competitors, with most going to Holder (46%), 37% going to Paolatto, and 17% going to Park. When Park was eliminated, her support was almost evenly distributed between Holder and Paolatto (53% and 47%, respectively).

Another element that contributed to the outcome was the number of individuals who did not indicate second- and third-ranked candidates. There were 97,947 ballots cast for mayor. Of those, less than 0.5% (442) were blank. Only 46% of ballots were clearly marked with first, second, and third preferences, perhaps indicating that the mayoral candidate's declarations that they were not going to rank other candidates had some effect.

Considerable numbers of ballots ranked fewer candidates than allowed: only 1 candidate (30%), or only 2 candidates (22%). Also, a number of ballots were marked incorrectly. Some voters indicated the same candidate in all three ranks (2%). Others indicated more than one candidate in the first rank (859, or less than 1% of ballots), second rank (166) or third rank (42).[8]

Voter Behaviour

One of the major challenges of analysing changes in voter behaviour from election returns is that we cannot assume that voters would make the same choices under different rules. Blais et al. (2012) ran an experiment during the 2011 Ontario election in which they asked respondents to indicate how they would vote under three different electoral rules. They found that there were significant differences in the choices individuals would make under different electoral systems – in other words, when they held constant the true preferences of voters in a real election campaign, and when those voters were faced with indicating support for real candidates, they indicated different support depending on the rules. Mindful of this, we asked respondents in the CMES survey not only how they ranked the candidates on their ballot but also how they would have voted had they only had one choice. While this is not as good as actually observing a vote, it at least holds constant the preferences of the respondents for each question and enables us to make comparisons. Ranked ballots, by enabling voters to have their second and third preferences continue to affect the outcome if their first choice is eliminated, provide an incentive to indicate support for candidates even when they are unlikely to be successful. This essentially removes most strategic considerations from the vote calculus.

Table 6.4 shows how respondents said they would have voted if they had had to choose a single candidate.[9] Here, 89% of voters indicated they would have voted the same way. However, there is a considerable difference depending on whether the candidate was a strong contender. Among the four front-runners, at least 90% of voters who supported each of Cheng, Holder, Paolatto, and Park indicated they would have supported the same candidate under both sets of rules. The situation is quite different for minor candidates. Very few of our respondents indicated support for the other ten candidates, but far fewer (a candidate average of 45%) indicated that they would have voted the same way. This suggests that voters did understand the incentives provided by the ranked-ballot rules and voted accordingly.

Table 6.4. Comparisons of actual ranked ballot first preference to hypothetical first-past-the-post vote

	Who would you rank first? (%)													
	1	2	3	4	5	6	7	8	9	10	11	12	13	14
Who would you vote for if you had only one choice? Bahramporian (1)	16	0	0	0	0	0	0	0	0	0	0	0	0	0
Cheng (2)	19	95	0	2	0	0	0	0	14	0	0	0	0	0
Hamadi (3)	14	0	56	1	0	0	0	0	0	0	0	3	0	0
Holder (4)	0	1	44	93	12	0	0	40	16	0	0	2	1	0
Lenart (5)	17	0	0	0	24	0	0	0	0	0	0	0	0	0
McCutcheon (6)	0	0	0	0	12	35	0	0	6	0	0	0	0	0
Millie (7)	4	0	0	0	0	0	68	0	0	0	0	0	0	0
Minter (8)	0	0	0	0	0	0	0	36	0	0	0	0	0	0
Moussa (9)	8	0	0	0	0	9	0	24	48	0	0	0	0	0
Murray (10)	0	0	0	0	0	0	0	0	0	50	0	0	0	0
O'Connell (11)	8	0	0	0	0	22	0	0	0	13	87	0	0	0
Paolatto (12)	5	2	0	0	0	0	7	0	8	0	0	90	0	0
Park (13)	0	1	0	0	52	0	0	0	0	0	0	0	98	0
White (14)	9	0	0	0	0	0	0	0	8	0	0	1	0	100
Don't know	0	1	0	4	0	35	26	0	0	50	0	2	1	0
N	23	213	7	285	7	11	8	5	13	4	12	157	284	2

Notes: Total N = 697. Data are weighted for age and gender to match the 2016 census. Due to weighting, column percentages are based upon a denominator which is a non-integer value (though rounded integers are shown in the "N" row). Carlos Murray was not listed by any respondents for either question, so is not included here. Column numbers indicate corresponding candidate listed in rows.

Voter Attitudes

The change to ranked ballots was not universally popular. Using CMES data, we can evaluate how Londoners felt about the change and whether it affected opinions of the quality of democracy in the city. First, having a chance to experience a ranked-ballot election did not convince a majority of Londoners that the change was positive. When asked their opinion of the change in electoral system, only 38% thought the change was a good one, while 23% thought it was bad. Most telling is that many either did not have an opinion (responding "don't know") or thought the change did not matter: 20% and 18%, respectively. It seems that the experience was not particularly negative for voters, but many remained unconvinced that the change was a positive step for the city.

However, it is still possible that moving to ranked ballots could improve how voters feel about their municipal democracy. For example, one of the most frequent comments about first-past-the-post elections is that so few voters actually supported the winner. In a typical Canadian election, less than 40% of voters will have voted in support of a majority government. In 2015, for example, Justin Trudeau's Liberals received 39.5% of the vote. A benefit of ranked-ballot elections is that the eventual winner usually has majority support from voters. Would thinking about the election outcome in this way affect how voters felt about the winner?

To test this, we ran a question wording experiment in the post-election wave of the CMES survey. The respondents were asked whether the new mayor, Ed Holder, "has a mandate to govern London." Half of the respondents were told the vote share he received during the first round of counting (34.2%), and the other half were told his vote share in the final round of counting (in which he received a majority of the vote). This framing had a significant effect on attitudes toward Holder's legitimacy. When told the first-round vote shares, 57% indicated they thought the mayor had a mandate. When told the final-round share, however, that number rose to 79%, a difference of more than 20 points. Whereas 21% of respondents were unsure of how to respond in the first scenario, only 11% were unsure in the second. This suggests that the idea of a winner having greater support in the electorate can positively affect the perceived legitimacy of elected officials. Interestingly, effects were not found only among Holder supporters. Those who cast a first-place ballot for him were more likely to believe he had a mandate (85% and 100% in the two respective experimental conditions). Even among those who did not support him, knowing that the mayor eventually received a majority of support among Londoners had a positive effect on their views of the legitimacy of the election outcome.

Conclusion

Reflecting on the 2018 London election results, one sees considerable continuity and only slight change from previous years. Continuity is evident in terms of whom voters elected as mayor (a former federal MP) and the number of incumbents re-elected to council. Ed Holder was the choice of most of the city's conservative voters, and his support was greatest in the part of the city that had elected him as an MP in the past. Incumbents also fared well in most wards, where they had name recognition and a track record. Another point of continuity was the BRT issue, which had structured debates in the city for years. Indeed, even the factors that affected voting for Holder were typical of what one would expect for a conservative candidate.

The changes observed were both structural (the ranked ballot) and in the composition of the council. London's first ranked-ballot election brought a lot of attention to the city, as it was the first to take advantage of the change in the *Municipal Elections Act* (two other municipalities, Cambridge and Kingston, had referendums on the issue during the election). It also set up some significant expectations as to how the campaign would unfold – some of which were realized while others were not. Importantly, supporters of ranked ballots had touted the likelihood of more diversity in the candidate pool and more civility in the campaign. On the first count, ranked ballots could be judged as successful, as the city's first black and first openly gay councillors were elected. On the second, however, the electoral system had no discernable effect. Ward 6 councillor Phil Squire was quoted in the *London Free Press* as saying: "This is probably the most uncivil campaign. From the point of view of personal attacks (on social media) and (disappearing) signs, this is the worst it has been" (Rivers, 2018). The fake campaign websites that targeted Maureen Cassidy and Virginia Ridley were unprecedented for the city and suggest a negative change. It is too early, of course, to make a final judgment on ranked ballots in London. More elections and experience would be needed to determine whether Londoners would have realized the full potential of the new electoral system. Unfortunately, the change back to first-past-the-post instigated by the province makes that unlikely.

NOTES

1 Interested municipalities had to pass a by-law by 1 May 2017 in order to run a ranked ballot election in 2018. By a 9–5 margin, London City Council voted on 1 May 2017 in favour of change to a ranked ballot electoral system

(Maloney, 2017a). While some thought the change had the potential to lessen negative campaigning and provide for a more diverse candidate pool, concerns were expressed over the added cost (close to $500,000, according to city manager Martin Hayward) for conducting elections. City administrators recommended against the change. Beyond the discussion within London City Council, the topic failed to capture public imagination among Londoners more generally.

2 School board races continued to be first-past-the-post, with voters asked to indicate support for a single candidate.

3 The Ontario Ombudsman found that a 2013 meeting was illegal, although a 2012 meeting under similar circumstances was not found to be illegal.

4 The "Fontana 8" was a name given to a collection of city councillors (including Fontana himself) who acted as a voting block on City Council in support of Fontana's policy initiatives.

5 Bus Rapid Transit is the term used for policy proposals designed to chart a new course for public transportation in the city.

6 A group of downtown merchants, calling themselves "Down Shift," opposed BRT route plans that would impact the core of the city. They expressed concerns about project costs, unknown ridership levels, and expropriation of lands needed for construction (Maloney, 2017b). Another group, called "Shift Happens," favoured the BRT plan passed by City Council, arguing that London needed to do something to reduce congestion, improve mobility, and make London a more sustainable city (Maloney, 2017b).

7 For comparison, turnout in the previous four municipal elections from 2000 averaged 37.9%.

8 These details can be found in the 2018 Municipal Election staff report provided to the authors by the city clerk. Note that some values reported here were determined by dividing the raw number of votes by the total number of votes cast.

9 Table 6.4 includes first ranked from the post-election survey and vote intent if only one choice from the campaign survey. This removes the possibility that respondents' answers to this question were influenced by the election outcome.

REFERENCES

Blais, A., Héroux-Legault, M., Stephenson, L., Cross, W., & Gidengil, E. (2012). Assessing the psychological and mechanical impact of electoral rules: A quasi-experiment. *Electoral Studies*, *31*, 829–837. https://doi.org /10.1016/j.electstud.2012.05.009

Campbell, A., Converse, P., Miller, W., & Stokes, D. (1960). *The American voter.* University of Chicago Press.

Dubinski, K. (2018a). Here's how the top mayoral candidates will rank their ballots. *CBC News*. 18 October. https://www.cbc.ca/news/canada/london /london-ontario-votes-ranked-ballots-mayoral-candidates-1.4863220

Dubinski, K. (2018b). How did London's municipal election campaign turn so nasty? *CBC News*. 19 October. https://www.cbc.ca/news/canada/london /london-ontario-votes-nasty-campaign-1.4867210

Gidengil, E., Nevitte, N., Blais, A., Everitt, J., & Fournier, P. (2012). *Dominance and decline*. University of Toronto Press.

Maloney, P. (2017a). Electoral reform: City council votes 9–5 to scrap first-past-the-post voting and make London a Canadian trailblazer. *London Free Press*. 1 May. https://lfpress.com/2017/05/01/electoral-reform-city -council-votes-9-5-to-scrap-first-past-the-post-voting-and-make-london-a -canadian-trailblazer

Maloney, P. (2017b). Bus Rapid Transit 101: Everything you need and want to know about BRT in London. *London Free Press*. 28 April. https://lfpress.com /2017/04/28/bus-rapid-transit-101-everything-you-need-and-want-to-know -about-brt-in-london/wcm/bce4d8bb-d41c-bf70-44d4-a83aa07d2cdd

McGregor, R. M., Moore, A., & Stephenson, L. (2016). Political attitudes and behaviour in a non-partisan environment. *Canadian Journal of Political Science, 49*(2), 311–333. https://doi.org/10.1017/S0008423916000573

Miller, W. E., & Shanks, J. M. (1996). *The new American voter*. Harvard University Press.

Rivers, H. (2018). Analysis: Did London see a difference with ranked ballot voting? *London Free Press*. 23 October. https://lfpress.com/news/local-news /analysis-did-london-see-a-difference-with-ranked-ballot-voting

Stacey, M. (2018a). Election sign attacks on the rise, candidates say. *London Free Press*. 24 September. https://lfpress.com/news/local-news /election-sign-attacks-on-the-rise-candidates-say

Stacey, M. (2018b). Candidate loses 40 signs as City Hall election vandalism continues. *London Free Press*. 1 October. https://lfpress.com/news /local-news/candidate-loses-40-signs-as-city-hall-election-vandalism -continues

Stacey, M. (2018c). Digital dirty tricks sandbag a second female London politician. *London Free Press*. 3 October. https://lfpress.com/news/local -news/digital-dirty-tricks-sandbag-a-second-london-woman-politician

7 Mississauga

ERIN TOLLEY AND ERICA RAYMENT

With a population of more than 721,000, Mississauga is Canada's sixth-largest city, yet in the minds of many, it is simply another suburb in the sprawling Greater Toronto Area. Mississauga, just west of Toronto, was once known as Toronto Township. The city's origins are a tract of land acquired from the Mississaugas in 1805. In 1820, several villages were incorporated and settled by newcomers. Many of these European settlers were Loyalists whom the government had provided with land; those settlers eventually displaced many of the Mississaugas.

By the 1920s, the town's farms and orchards had given way to new developments, including the Queen Elizabeth Way (QEW), an expressway that crosses Mississauga east to west and extends all the way to the American border in the Niagara Region. Although less than half (46%) of Mississaugans commute to work beyond the city limits (compared to 80% and higher in Ajax and Pickering), the QEW is one of the city's main arteries (Statistics Canada, 2016).

Mississauga has witnessed tremendous change over the past century, much of it in the past 40 years. As housing prices increased in Toronto, Mississauga developed into an attractive "edge city" (Garreau, 1991). As it grew, it became more multiracial, as shown in Figure 7.1. Between 2006 and 2016, the city's population increased by 33%. It also became more diverse: its visible minority[1] population rose from 34% to 57% of the city's population. Meanwhile, Indigenous peoples make up less than 1% of the city's population.

In many ways, Mississauga is a community of contradictions. It is a stand-alone city with its own governance, by-laws, and infrastructure, but it is also embedded in the larger Peel Region. It shares some services and a regional governance structure with Brampton and Caledon. Peel's regional chair is appointed by the 24 regional councillors who represent their respective cities on the regional board; half of these regional

Figure 7.1. Demographic diversity in Mississauga, 2006–2016

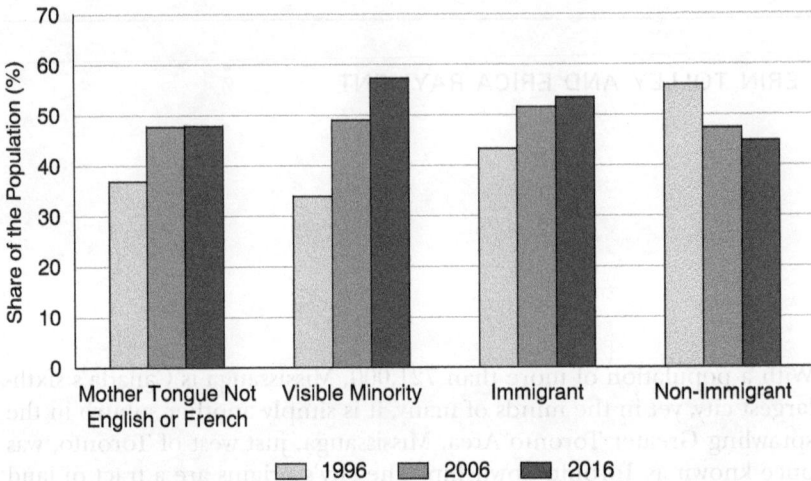

Source: Compiled by authors with data from Statistics Canada's 1996, 2006, and 2016.
Censuses of Population.

councillors are from Mississauga, the remainder from Caledon and
Brampton. Peel Regional Council is responsible for policing, ambulance
services, garbage collection, public health, child care, housing, social
services, water, and regional roads, while the City of Mississauga looks
after property taxes, city planning, building permits, by-laws, transit, fire
services, libraries, snow clearing, community centres, arts and culture,
city parks, and local roads and sidewalks.

Mississauga is integrated into Peel Region but is often viewed more as an
extension of Toronto. The two cities are interconnected, but not as seamlessly
as one might imagine. For example, there are two separate transit networks:
the TTC in Toronto and MiWay in Mississauga. Although transit riders may
transfer between the two networks, they pay a separate fare for each.

The city's together-but-separate nature is also evident in the media
landscape. There is no Mississauga-specific daily print newspaper or tele-
vision newscast. A talk radio station, two online newspapers, and various
neighbourhood weeklies serve the city, but much of the daily news is
delivered by stations in Toronto, whether online or in traditional formats. Yet the Toronto outlets pay little attention to Mississauga issues
or local politics. Mississauga's municipal elections reflect the usual low-
information context – a lack of partisan labels, less attention from voters –
and these features are exacerbated by the limited local media.

Voter turnout in the city's municipal elections has historically been low, often hovering around 25% of eligible voters (Rosella, 2010), and the style of municipal campaigns is remarkably low-key, particularly when compared to the frenetic pace of elections in neighbouring Toronto. Even in 2014, when there was an open mayoral race with two credible front-runners, voter turnout was just 36%. Tom Urbaniak, a long-time observer of Mississauga politics, suggests "there isn't a culture of civic engagement in Mississauga ... It's as if politics is someone else's business" (qtd in Rosella, 2010). The city's fifth mayor, Hazel McCallion, held the post for 36 years, and for the 20 years between 1991 and 2010, she ran without so much as a platform (Urbaniak, 2009). As we note later, this complacency was a feature of the 2018 campaign.

A final contradiction, and the focus of this chapter, is the mismatch between the city's diverse population and the relative absence of diversity on its council. While racialized candidates came forward in large numbers in the 2018 election, only one was elected. We argue that some features of the campaign – including the large number of incumbents and a context that made it more difficult for newcomers to break in – helps explain the lack of diversity on council. However, as we also show, low voter turnout among racialized minorities could also be factor. To make our case, we begin by examining the election campaign, its key issues and events, and the results. We then use data from the Canadian Municipal Election Study (CMES) to understand voters' preferences and how these influenced the outcome. In a rather sleepy election campaign, one of the few noteworthy features was the city's paradoxical diversity dynamics.

Election Overview

Mayoral Campaign

The 2018 mayoral campaign officially launched on 1 May, when Bonnie Crombie announced her intention to seek another term and became the first registered candidate. Crombie had first been elected as mayor four years prior, when Hazel McCallion, Mississauga's long-time doyenne, retired from office at the age of 93. Mississauga is not a city where a woman mayor is an oddity. In 2014, McCallion had endorsed Crombie, who went on to defeat Steve Mahoney, a former city councillor, MPP, MP, and federal cabinet minister. Despite going up against a well-known competitor in 2014, Crombie finished with 64% of the vote. Prior to this, Crombie herself was the MP for Mississauga-Streetsville, having previously served as municipal and regional councillor.

In 2018, Crombie went unchallenged until mid-June, when Scott Chapman entered the race. Chapman had run against Crombie in 2014 but finished with less than 1% of the vote. In total, there were eight mayoral candidates in 2018, but six of these contenders did not register until the final days of the registration period. Crombie was viewed as the front-runner for the duration of the campaign and was widely expected to win (Kan, 2018c). Most of the candidates ran relatively low-key campaigns, some with hardly even an online presence.

The only candidate besides Crombie to attract much attention was her closest competitor, Kevin Johnston. In addition to his electoral pursuits, he is the proprietor of an alt-right website and has had videos removed from YouTube because they violated the site's policy on hate speech (Gordon, 2017). At the time of the 2018 election, Johnston was facing a criminal charge for willful promotion of hatred after he made comments targeting Muslims. Johnston was not invited to the campaign's only scheduled mayoral candidate forum, which was organized by the Students' Union at the University of Toronto Mississauga. He nonetheless showed up at the event, but was denied entry when he attempted to register (Aflaki, 2018).

Much of the 2018 campaign was uneventful, save for a brief moment of suspense when the newly elected Ontario provincial government announced that instead of allowing voters to directly elect Peel's regional chair – a change brought in by the previous Liberal government – the Conservatives would be reverting to the old process of appointing a chair. Prior to the election's cancellation, Patrick Brown had been among the front-runner candidates. Brown is the former leader of the Progressive Conservative Party; he resigned abruptly amid allegations of sexual misconduct, and Doug Ford succeeded him as leader. When the election for regional chair was quashed – a move many interpreted as an attempt by Premier Ford to shun Brown – Brown began looking at electoral opportunities elsewhere. He reportedly eyed Mississauga's mayoral race but ultimately decided his chances would be better in Brampton, where he squared off against the incumbent, Linda Jeffrey. His wager was sound. Brown ultimately defeated Jeffrey, thus allowing Brampton to turn the page on the most exciting chapter in Mississauga's electoral campaign.

Council Races

Patrick Brown's many political lives would not have been out of place in Mississauga, where politicians have turned political longevity into an art form. There is ample crossover between local, provincial, and federal politics, with candidates defeated at one level often turning around to run at another. Moreover, many councillors go on to serve multiple terms in office, and this election was hardly different. The large number of incumbents who sought re-election was one of the main stories to emerge from the 11 council races.

There were open seats in just two wards, and these were among the most hotly contested. In Ward 7, following the retirement of councillor Nando Iannicca after 30 years in office, there were 12 candidates. The contenders included Dipika Damerla, who had served in Kathleen Wynne's provincial cabinet and had just recently lost her seat as MPP for Mississauga-Cooksville. Meanwhile, there was jostling between Wards 1 and 6, a result of the uncertainty over the regional chair election. Former MP Brad Butt initially announced his intention to run in Ward 6, which was to be vacated by sitting councillor Ron Starr, who planned to run for regional chair. When the regional chair elections were shelved, Starr entered the Ward 6 race, and Butt shuffled over to Ward 1, which had been vacated following the death of councillor Jim Tovey a few months prior. In total, eight candidates came forward in Ward 1. Meanwhile, over in Ward 6, which initially looked like it would be up for grabs with the departure of Starr, several competitors threw their hats into the ring; most remained even when Starr opted to run again, and he squared off against 10 candidates. Outside of these wards, most races had comparatively fewer candidates – the average number of candidates in the city's eight other wards was just over five.

Given the number of long-time councillors returning as candidates, it is perhaps not surprising that most ran largely on their records and name recognition. One commentator reported there was just one ward with an active roster of candidate forums or debates, which exacerbated the challenges faced by new candidates seeking to make a name for themselves with voters (Stewart, 2018).

The combination of long-time incumbents and a low-information context makes Mississauga a decidedly inhospitable place for political newcomers to break through. These factors may help explain why Mississauga's council has not, for some time, reflected the city's demographics. Prior to 2018, no racialized candidate had ever been elected to serve on Mississauga's council. Council's persistent homogeneity is not because racialized Canadians are not running for office. As Table 7.1 shows, more than half the candidates who came forward in 2018 had racialized backgrounds, a proportion almost on par with the broader population. The lack of racial diversity is therefore not a function of limited supply: racialized candidates come forward, but, as we discuss below, voters do not elect them.

By contrast, the proportion of women candidates in 2018 – 24% – was well below their share of the population. This figure suggests that the blockage in the political pipeline for women differs from that for racialized

Table 7.1. Candidate demographics, by ward

	Number of candidates	Women candidates		Racialized candidates		Incumbent running
		n	%	n	%	
Mayoral	8	2	25	5	63	Yes
Ward 1	8	2	25	2	25	No
Ward 2	3	1	33	2	67	Yes
Ward 3	4	1	25	2	50	Yes
Ward 4	9	4	44	7	78	Yes
Ward 5	6	2	33	5	83	Yes
Ward 6	11	0	0	7	64	Yes
Ward 7	12	3	25	6	50	No
Ward 8	6	1	17	2	33	Yes
Ward 9	5	1	20	2	40	Yes
Ward 10	3	2	67	2	67	Yes
Ward 11	3	0	0	2	67	Yes
Total	78	19	24	44	56	10

Source: Compiled by authors.

minorities. This being said, the proportion of women candidates in Mississauga in 2018 was broadly consistent with that of other Ontario municipalities, where women made up, on average, 27% of all candidates (Association of Municipalities of Ontario, 2018). Still, it is somewhat surprising that in a city with a long history of political leadership by women, there are not more women entering the electoral arena. Even with role models like McCallion and Crombie, it appears Mississauga has not managed to convince more women to enter municipal politics.

Issues and Events

Which issues dominated the campaign? The CMES asked Mississauga respondents to gauge the importance of six policy issues: public transit, property taxes, traffic and congestion, economic development, crime and community safety, and housing affordability.[2] Respondents assessed each issue on a 10-point scale, with 0 indicating the issue was not at all important and 10 indicating the issue was extremely important. Figure 7.2 shows the mean response for each issue.

The policy issue garnering the lowest rating was public transit. Overall, respondents rated public transit at an average score of 6.8. The lukewarm response is somewhat surprising, given the candidates sparred over the proposed Hurontario light rail transit project, which would run through Mississauga and connect it to neighbouring Brampton. This was one of Mayor Crombie's pet issues, and it is slated to be built and running by

Figure 7.2. Issue importance in the 2018 Mississauga election

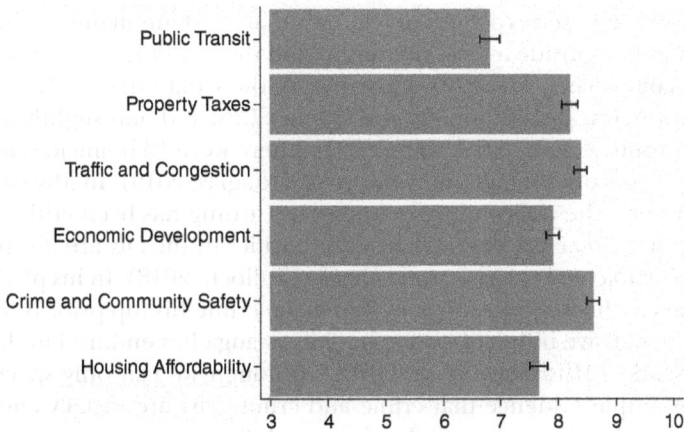

2024, with funding provided entirely by the provincial government. The rail line has been controversial, however, with some expressing a preference for below-ground subways over above-ground trains, and with the city of Brampton having decided to opt out of the funding package rather than have the rail run through its downtown. Notwithstanding respondents' tepid feelings toward public transit, they cited traffic and congestion as their second most important policy issue, with an average score of 8.4.

Housing affordability received the second-lowest rating overall, with an average score of 7.7. This was somewhat out of step with at least the mayoral candidates' assessment of the key policy issues. According to one media report, housing affordability was one of the issues most often mentioned by those running for mayor (Knope, 2018). Mississauga has long been a city of single-family homes, and under McCallion's watch, densification was largely shunned. Development was horizontal, with neighbourhoods spreading out rather than up, with the result that the number of single-family homes built on the city's green space ballooned. Development fees kept the city prosperous – property taxes were frozen from 1994 to 2002 – but with vacant land now in short supply, Mississauga is today a different city than the one McCallion oversaw. Torontonians priced out of the city's housing market have been venturing farther afield, into the surrounding cities, in their search for homes. As mayor, Crombie has pushed for what she called a "complete community" mindset, envisioning the city as more than an outpost of Toronto. Most of her competitors in the mayoral race presented a similar vision, although Andrew Lee suggested a "village-spirit in a mega-city" (Knope, 2018).

Crime and community safety emerged as the issue of greatest importance to respondents; just 2% said it was unimportant. This emphasis on safety followed a series of high-profile criminal incidents in the city, including a bombing inside a local restaurant and the stabbing of a teenager at a graduation party. The city's crime rate is lower than that of Vancouver, Edmonton, Calgary, Winnipeg, and Quebec City, and only slightly higher than Toronto's (Kan, 2019), but in 2018, there were 13 homicides in Mississauga, up from nine the previous year (Douglas, 2019). In Mississauga, as elsewhere, the police practice known as carding has been criticized; it was reported recently that racialized minorities in the city are disproportionately subjected to these street checks (Tulloch, 2018). In his platform, mayoral candidate Johnston vowed to make crime his top priority and to "stop the massive influx of crime that Mississauga has endured in the last three years" (*Mississauga News*, 2018). Although we can only speculate, there is ample evidence that crime and criminality are racially encoded and that racial biases often underpin appeals for safer communities (Bhatia et al., 2018). The prioritization of this policy issue may be indicative of respondents' anxieties about race and the city's growing diversity.

Respondents' specific views on the city's approach to diversity were not probed in the battery of policy issue questions, but the topic did arise during the campaign in other ways, beginning with the registration of a mayoral candidate with white supremacist views who was facing a hate crime charge. Johnston's candidacy ignited some discussion about prejudice in the city, but the issue also arose after Nikki Clarke, a Black woman, was removed from the candidate list because of irregularities on her nomination forms; these included incorrect postal codes for some of the individuals whom she had included as endorsers. One of the signatories was contacted by Carolyn Parrish, the councillor in the ward where Clarke was set to run, and Parrish asked the signatory to confirm her identity. Sometime after this, the city clerk's office contacted Clarke about errors on her forms. With just three hours remaining before nominations closed, Clarke was unable to comply with the requested revisions and was dropped from the list. Parrish denies there was any racial motivation behind her inquiry and argues that Clarke should have been more diligent. Clarke's supporters, however, insisted that she had been purposefully overscrutinized (Kan, 2018b); her disqualification left one less racialized candidate on the ballot.

Election Results

Apart from these events, Mississauga's election offered very few surprises. The campaign lacked the drama in Toronto, where incumbent councillors squared off against one another, or the suspense in Brampton, where the incumbent mayor went down to defeat against a

Table 7.2. Election results, by ward

Ward	Council winner	Margin	Mayoral winner	Margin
1	Stephen Dasko	24.4	Bonnie Crombie*	70.4
2	Karen Ras*	88.3	Bonnie Crombie*	73.6
3	Chris Fonseca*	55.1	Bonnie Crombie*	63.9
4	John Kovac*	31.7	Bonnie Crombie*	61.0
5	Carolyn Parrish*	53.0	Bonnie Crombie*	68.1
6	Ron Starr*	2.3	Bonnie Crombie*	55.1
7	Dipika Damerla	25.3	Bonnie Crombie*	65.3
8	Matt Mahoney*	74.0	Bonnie Crombie*	67.1
9	Pat Saito*	69.6	Bonnie Crombie*	53.1
10	Sue McFadden*	85.0	Bonnie Crombie*	60.4
11	George Carlson*	46.9	Bonnie Crombie*	60.8
Overall			Bonnie Crombie*	63.2

Source: Compiled by authors using Mississauga election returns.

* = incumbent.

polarizing opponent. In Mississauga, by contrast, not a single incumbent was defeated, and the sitting mayor was returned to office with a majority of votes in every single ward.

As Table 7.2 makes clear, other victories were equally decisive. In Ward 2, incumbent Karen Ras won with 92% of the vote, while over in Ward 10, council veteran Sue McFadden garnered 90%. In Ward 4, incumbent John Kovac faced a field of nine competitors and still won a majority of the votes (53%). The tightest race was in Ward 6, where incumbent Ron Starr squeaked by Joe Horneck in a field of 11 candidates. Even in Ward 7, the race with the most candidates, Dipika Damerla bested the field of 12 candidates with a 25% margin of victory over her closest competitor.

Crombie's win was decisive and city-wide; she received the highest number of votes in every single ward, and by a substantial margin, as the uniformly dark colour in Figure 7.3 plainly shows. Although her support was highest in the northern and southern parts of the city (Ward 5 and Wards 1 and 2, respectively), it was strong throughout the city. This geographic consistency in support for Crombie was much more pronounced than in other races with incumbent mayors, including Calgary and Winnipeg, where there was wider variation across the city.

The one surprise, perhaps, was the number of votes Kevin Johnston garnered in the mayoral race. When he ran in the previous election, he garnered less than 1% of mayoral votes, but in 2018 he improved his vote share to nearly 14% even though he was facing a hate crime charge. Mississauga is a diverse, multicultural city, and that so many Mississaugans would favour Johnston seems somewhat peculiar. It is, however, emblematic of the city's inaction on multiculturalism policy

Figure 7.3. Vote share for Crombie, by ward

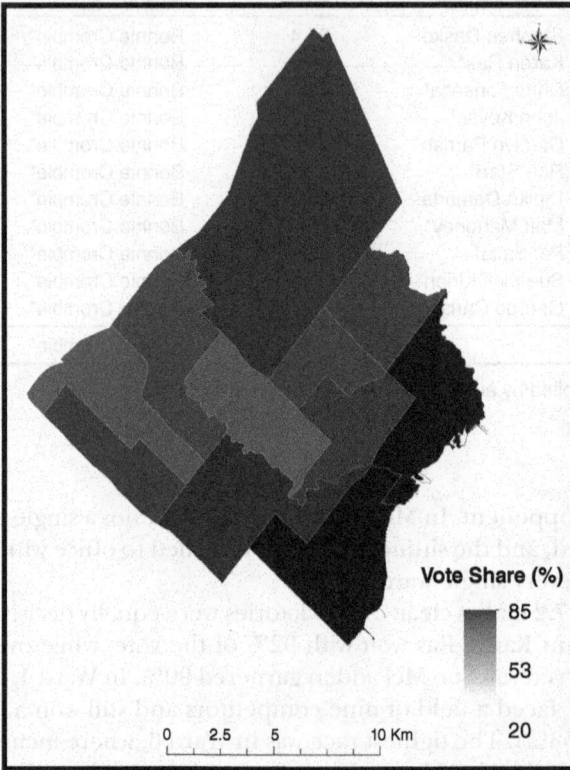

Vote Share (%)

85

53

20

0   2.5   5   10 Km

as well as its stance toward the concerns of immigrants and ethnocultural minorities, which Kristin Good (2009) succinctly calls "unresponsive."[3] As we discuss below, public attitudes suggest the city's white and racialized residents harbour some antipathy toward minority groups – Muslims in particular – and Johnston's anti-Muslim politics likely appealed to them. But this election, in one of the country's most racially diverse cities, was also the one in which Mississaugans finally elected the first racialized councillor in the city's history. What factors help explain the somewhat paradoxical diversity dynamics in Mississauga municipal politics?

Vote Choice

At just 27%, voter turnout in Mississauga was the lowest of all eight cities examined in this volume. We suggest this low level of engagement reflects,

Figure 7.4. Vote choice for Crombie – marginal effects

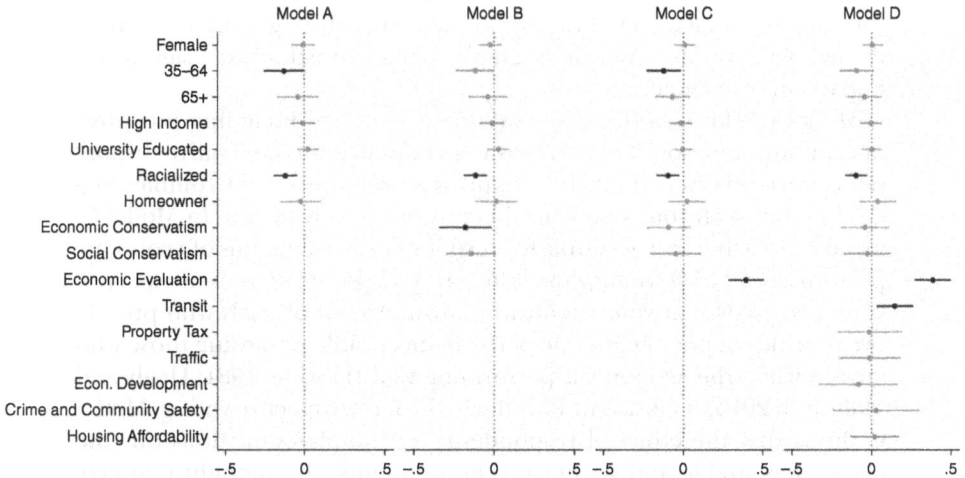

Notes: Entries report marginal effects and 95% confidence intervals. Coefficients in black are statistically significant at p < 0.1.

in part, the city's lacklustre municipal campaign and the limited competitiveness of most races. But it also is a function of the city's demographics. In Mississauga, racialized minorities are a large proportion of the population and have vote preferences that diverge somewhat from those of other residents, but they vote in relatively small numbers. To build this case, we look first at the factors that explained mayoral vote choice.

Mississauga's incumbent mayor faced very little opposition, and the effective number of candidates in the mayoral race – just 1.64 – was the lowest of any of the cities included in this volume (see the concluding chapter). Respondents evaluated Crombie as remarkably centrist, with a score of 5.1 on a left-to-right ideological scale ranging from 0 to 10. Squarely in the middle, Crombie could appeal to a large number of voters, or at least avoid alienating them. Interpreted against the backdrop of the advantage incumbents typically wield, the relative ease with which Crombie won re-election is hardly surprising.

To understand the impact of various factors on the probability of a vote for Crombie, we estimated four logistic regression models with blocs of variables added incrementally to each successive model; Figure 7.4 summarizes the results. Model A estimates the effect of key demographic characteristics on vote choice. The model includes variables for gender, income, educational attainment, and homeownership, but only age and racialized status are statistically significant. Racialized respondents and those between the ages of 35 and 64 were less likely to vote for Crombie, with the marginal effect of racialized status slightly larger than the effect of age. None of the other demographic characteristics had a significant impact on vote choice.

Model B adds controls for respondent ideology, including measures of economic and social conservatism. Economically conservative respondents were relatively unlikely to express a preference for Crombie, suggesting that such voters perceived her as too fiscally liberal. In Model C, we add a variable that accounts for respondents' evaluations of economic performance in Mississauga over the past year. Research on retrospective voting suggests that voters tend to punish elected officials who preside over periods of poor economic performance, while rewarding those who govern when the economy is performing well (Fiorina, 1981; Healy and Malhotra, 2013). Consistent with the logic of retrospective voting, Model C shows that the effect of respondents' economic evaluations on vote choice was sizable and significant. Respondents who thought that economic conditions had improved over the past year were 38 points more likely to say they would vote for Crombie than respondents who thought the economy had deteriorated.

Model D is the final model and includes measures that account for respondents' assessments of the importance of seven different municipal policy issues. Given the low-information environment and the absence of a credible challenger to the incumbent, the Mississauga election was not positioned to be one in which competing policy preferences and approaches would be a decisive factor in vote choice. The results from Model D confirm this expectation. Only one of the six policy issue variables emerged as statistically significant. Respondents who identified transit as an important issue were 15 points more likely to vote for Crombie than voters who were not concerned about transit. Support for Crombie among voters who saw transit as an important issue is unsurprising, given the Hurontario light rail project was one of the issues she championed during her first term as mayor.

In both Mississauga and Toronto, survey respondents were asked about the importance of housing affordability and crime and community safety, allowing us to compare policy preferences in proximate municipalities. Notably, these issues were not statistically significant predictors of vote choice in Mississauga's mayoral race but *were* key predictors in Toronto (see chapter 8 of this volume). In Toronto, respondents who thought that housing affordability was an important issue were comparatively unlikely to vote for incumbent mayor John Tory, while respondents who were concerned about crime and community safety were more likely to support Tory. The same issues in two adjacent municipalities thus had very different levels of political salience, an observation that counters the notion Mississauga is simply a suburban version of its closest neighbour.

In the final model, there are only three statistically significant predictors of vote choice: racialized status, evaluation of the economy, and the identification of transit as an important issue. Respondents who thought the economy had improved and who identified transit as an important issue were more likely to vote for Crombie than voters who thought otherwise, by 38 and 15 points respectively. By contrast, racialized respondents were 10 points less likely than white voters to vote for Crombie.

Perhaps the most notable finding, however, is the robustness of the effect of racialized status across all four models. The significance of the effects of age and economic conservatism fluctuated with the addition of further controls to the model. Despite the instability of these variables, the effect of racialized status remained consistent across all four models. Racialized respondents were consistently less likely to vote for Crombie than white respondents. This finding raises important questions about the participation and turnout of racialized citizens in the Mississauga election. The vote choice models show that racialized respondents were consistently less likely than white respondents to vote for Crombie, yet Crombie won the mayoral election by a landslide – this, even though racialized minorities make up more than half the population of Mississauga. This pattern suggests that racialized respondents' engagement in the election may have differed markedly from that of white respondents, a scenario that we examine below.

Diversity Dynamics

One clear outcome of the election was an increase in the council's racial diversity. Council moved from having *no* racialized councillors to having one, and more than half the new council members – 58% – were women. Women came forward as candidates in proportions well under their presence in the population, but all five female incumbents were re-elected. Meanwhile, racialized minorities came forward as candidates in proportions on par with their presence in the population, but their election rate was dismal; only 2% of racialized candidates were elected. What structural and attitudinal features help explain the limited success that racialized minorities have had in Mississauga politics? In the sections that follow, we examine these factors, beginning with the large number of white incumbent candidates who dominated the polls on Election Day. We suggest that low levels of legislative turnover narrowed the opportunities available for new, racialized political entrants and contributed to a rather lacklustre campaign that did little to spark voter interest. In 2018, voters mostly did not turn out, but racialized voters were especially likely to stay home, and this may have diminished the electoral prospects of the racialized candidates who put themselves forward. We say this because racialized candidates drew the bulk of their support from racialized voters. Thus, although diversity and inclusion have been issues on the municipal agenda, that agenda has been shaped by a white council. We argue that if (white) incumbents continue to reoffer and voter turnout among racialized voters remains low, survey respondents' aspirations for a more representative council are unlikely to be realized.

Limited Legislative Turnover

Legislative turnover tends to be very low in municipal politics, and incumbents are rarely defeated (Hajnal et al., 2002). Mississauga is no exception, and the city has a history of long-serving representatives. Hazel McCallion exemplifies this phenomenon, but councillor Pat Saito is not far behind, having served on council for more than 27 years. Over in Ward 8, Matt Mahoney had just one term under his belt when he ran in 2018, but he was running in a ward that has been held by a member of his family for most of the past 40 years; both his father and his mother previously served on council. Collectively, the incumbent candidates who ran in 2018 had a combined total of 84 years of council experience. The fact that two-thirds of racialized candidates ran against incumbents helps us understand why Mississauga's City Council remains so white.

All 10 incumbents who ran for re-election were victorious. This left just two seats – in Wards 1 and 7 – where political hopefuls would be spared the challenge of competing against a well-known and -resourced incumbent, and in both races, there was tight competition. In Ward 1, 2 of the 8 candidates were racialized, and Stephen Dasko, who is white, was victorious. In Ward 7, 6 of the 12 candidates were racialized, and it was here that Dipika Damerla, the city's first councillor of colour, was ultimately elected.

The number of incumbents who chose to reoffer in Mississauga does seem quite high, but their relative success is hardly surprising. Incumbency is an advantage at all levels of government, with incumbents accruing the benefit of name recognition, a known track record, and familiarity with constituents and the political process (Krebs, 1998). Incumbents can also benefit from electoral finance laws that allow them to carry over some of the funds raised in the prior election, whereas newcomers start from zero (Spicer et al., 2017). At the municipal level, many scholars also attribute the strong incumbency effect to the absence of political parties, which prompts voters to rely on a candidate's electoral experience as a means of arriving at their voting decisions (Schaffner et al., 2001; Trounstine, 2011). The low-information environment in which municipal elections are conducted may have exacerbated this effect. Not only are party cues typically absent, but there is less media attention and platforms are often minimal. Moreover, candidates kept a relatively low profile during the campaign. For example, on 26 September, less than four weeks before Election Day, Ali Raza, a journalist with the *Mississauga Guardian*, tweeted that of the five racialized candidates running for mayor, just one had responded to his request for an interview. In other wards, incumbents (all of whom were white) faced little opposition. This was the case in Ward 2, where incumbent Karen Ras won decisively. She was the only declared candidate for months, until two late entrants, Naser Ansari and Mohammad Azam, registered to run.

In the mayoral race, the conventional wisdom was that incumbent Crombie faced no real opposition and that she would likely be re-elected (Kan, 2018c). Qualitative responses from the voter survey reflected this sense of resigned complacency about the election outcome. For example, when asked what they liked about Crombie, many of the responses referred to the fact she seemed to be "doing a good job," suggesting there was no compelling reason to make a change. Respondents also saw Crombie as the heir apparent to Hazel McCallion's decades-long tenure as mayor, basing their approval of Crombie on McCallion's endorsement and on her not having deviated in any significant way from McCallion's agenda. For many voters, there seemed to be a sense of "same old, same old." The sleepy campaign benefited incumbents, and as we point out below, a general lack of voter engagement probably solidified their positions.

Political Engagement

CMES respondents were asked whether they had voted. Overall, nearly three quarters (73%) of respondents reported voting in the 2018 municipal election, a rate much higher than the observed voter turnout, which was 27%. This gap between reported and actual voter turnout is common in most survey research. There is social pressure to claim that one has voted, and besides, voters are more likely to participate in opinion polls. With this caveat, we nonetheless find that turnout was significantly lower among racialized respondents than among white respondents. Whereas 79% of white respondents said they had cast a ballot in the 2018 municipal election, only 63% of racialized respondents said the same (p < 0.01).

Table 7.3. Political engagement, by respondent race

	Made a political donation			Displayed a campaign sign		
	Federal % (n)	Provincial	Municipal	Federal % (n)	Provincial	Municipal
White	17 (91)	16 (86)	5 (24)	22 (119)	20 (103)	16 (82)
Racialized	15 (34)	11 (24)	4 (9)	21 (48)	20 (45)	19 (43)

Source: Canadian Municipal Election Study, Mississauga respondents.

The survey also asked respondents whether they had voted in the 2015 federal election. Reported rates of voting were higher at the federal level across the board: 92% of white respondents and 75% of racialized respondents reported voting in the 2015 election. Notably, though, the size of the turnout gap for white and racialized respondents was about the same at the municipal and federal levels (16% and 17%, respectively).

Thus, we found little evidence that racialized minorities are uniquely less likely to vote at the municipal level; rather, they are less likely to vote than their white counterparts, and by a similar margin, regardless of the level of government. This finding offers an instructive contrast to some other research, which indicates that *foreign-born* Canadians are particularly less likely to vote at the municipal level (Wallace et al., 2019). Although there are overlaps between the racialized and foreign-born categories, and they are often used interchangeably, our results suggest there is some utility in distinguishing them because racialized Canadians, as a group, seem less likely to vote, regardless of level of government.

The lack of engagement at the ballot box does not translate into other areas of political involvement. As Table 7.3 shows, respondents in general were less likely to donate to a political party or candidate or to display a campaign sign than they were to vote, but there were no significant differences between white and racialized respondents on either of these measures at any level of government. There thus appears to be something distinctive about voting that makes racialized Canadians less likely to participate than their white neighbours.

Diversity and Inclusion

It is not that diversity issues are unimportant in Mississauga. The city's demographic complexion has changed significantly even in the past 10 years, and there have been growing pains in the process. At a mayoral debate during the 2014 Mississauga election, Bonnie Crombie countered critics of a proposed mosque – who included Pat Saito, the ward's councillor – by stating that "anybody who says [the mosque] doesn't fit the character of the neighbourhood is a racist" (Vincent, 2016). Saito says the accusation of racism "caused a rift" between her and Crombie (Vincent, 2016).

Survey responses on residents' attitudes toward various minority groups confirm some of the tensions underlying this incident. Respondents in all eight cities were asked how they felt about several groups, including racial minorities, immigrants, and Muslims, with a score of 100 indicating that the respondent really liked the group and a score of 0 indicating that they really disliked the group. Figure 7.5 shows the average score for attitudes toward racial minorities, immigrants, and Muslims for each city included in the study.

Respondents in Mississauga did not have the most negative attitudes toward these three groups, and Mississauga's scores were not wildly out of line with those in other cities. However, interpreted alongside the consistently more positive attitudes toward racialized minorities, immigrants, and Muslims among respondents in neighbouring Toronto – a city characterized by a similar level of racial diversity and a shared media environment – the attitudes toward these groups among respondents in Mississauga are somewhat surprising.

One potential explanation is that Mississauga's long-time white residents are struggling to adapt to the city's shifting demographics and that this is driving hostility toward minority groups. Yet when we look at the data, this hypothesis does not fully hold. Specifically, differences between white and racialized respondents' attitudes toward minorities and immigrants were small and not statistically significant. Notably though, racialized respondents reported more negative attitudes toward Muslims more frequently than white respondents (with the difference significant at the 99% confidence level). In other words, antipathy toward minority groups, and Muslims in particular, is partly driven by racialized respondents, a finding that suggests cleavages in the city are deeper and more complex than explanations centred on white anxiety.

Even so, there is some appetite for more diversity in elected institutions. When asked about the gender and racial composition of City Council, 54% of CMES respondents agreed that its racial composition should reflect that of the population, and 57% said the same with regard to gender. However, although more than half of respondents agreed that City Council should be racially diverse, in 2018, only one elected city councillor was a racialized minority. Meanwhile, women occupied 7 of the council's 12 seats, with a woman at the helm. In other words, while respondents broadly expressed a preference for a council that reflected

Figure 7.5. Attitudes toward minority groups, by city

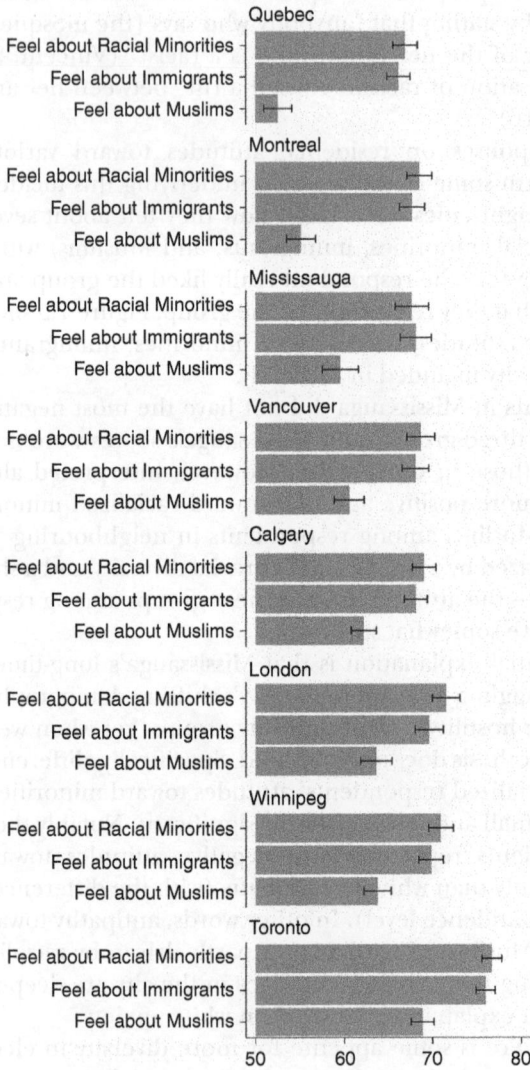

the gender and racial composition of the city, the population delivered on the former but not the latter in 2018.

Perhaps an explanation for the council's skewed demographic composition can be found by looking not just at who votes, but also at who votes for whom. Our analysis found that racialized Canadians were less likely to vote overall. When we examined which candidates they tended to support, we found that racialized respondents were significantly more likely to vote for racialized council candidates than their white counterparts. Specifically, only 12% of white respondents (N = 46) cast ballots for racialized council candidates, compared to 27% of racialized respondents (N = 35) who did so, a difference that is statistically significant (p < 0.01).[4] In other words, racialized voters were more likely than white voters to select racialized candidates but were also less likely to turn out. To be sure, a clear majority of both white and racialized respondents voted more frequently for white candidates, but the stronger propensity for racialized respondents to vote for racialized candidates suggests that if more racialized Canadians voted, they might alter the council's racial composition. This gap helps explain the lack of diversity on Mississauga's council.

In a move designed in part to compensate for the lack of racial diversity on council, Mayor Crombie appointed a Diversity and Inclusion Advisory Committee shortly after her election in 2014 (Grewal, 2015). The committee includes citizen members who are tasked with providing input on policies "to promote awareness of ethno-cultural relations and diversity matters with an emphasis on improving diversity and fostering greater inclusion of all residents and stakeholders" (City of Mississauga, 2019). Carolyn Parrish was one of the councillors who expressed support for that committee. In 2018, she suggested that a Peel Region police officer had been promoted because she was "Black and female." As a result of this comment, Parrish was found to have violated the Peel Region code of conduct. Her pay was docked, and she was ordered to undergo sensitivity training (Kan, 2018a). She was nonetheless re-elected in 2018. Her victory suggests that some of the city's residents are willing to support councillors who engage in such transgressions. If those who are opposed do not turn out, then Mississauga's efforts to foster greater inclusion are unlikely to bear fruit.

Conclusion

Across the country in Vancouver, when the city elected a council with just one mixed-race representative, citizens took to Twitter, coining the hashtag #CouncilSoWhite to criticize the lack of diversity. Two days later, Mississaugans similarly returned a council with just one racialized representative. But unlike in Vancouver, there was little outcry, even though Mississauga is one of the most racially diverse cities in the country.

The absence of diversity is not a pipeline problem: in Mississauga, racialized Canadians run for office in large numbers. However, their chances are stymied by a large number of incumbents who are nearly always re-elected; it is also clear that those who appear to be most supportive of racialized candidates – racialized voters – opt not to come out on Election Day. Racialized citizens engage in the political process in other ways, but they do not vote in large numbers.

Mississaugans are not opposed to diversity. Many survey respondents expressed a preference for a more racially inclusive council, and attitudes toward minorities are not considerably more negative than elsewhere. However, diversity issues have been a source of some tension, and navigating these challenges has fallen on a mostly white council. Some remedial action has been taken – namely, the creation of a parallel advisory committee – and in this regard, efforts to increase voter turnout, particularly among racialized populations, could be an important piece of the puzzle.

NOTES

1　The Census and many surveys use the term "visible minority" to refer to individuals who are non-Indigenous and non-white and non-Caucasian in race and colour, but this term is increasingly falling out of favour because it presents racial background as a static, biological entity instead of the outcome of a socially constructed process. It also centres whiteness as the standard against which other racialized groups are compared. Because of this, we mostly use "racialized" in this chapter except when we draw on data sources that specifically employed "visible minority" (or "racial minority") as the category.

2　Respondents were given a 10-point scale. Responses ranging from 0–3 were coded as "not important," those ranging from 4–6 were coded as "neutral," and those ranging from 7–10 were coded as important.

3　For example, under Hazel McCallion's direction, and despite requests from ethnocultural groups, Mississauga adopted a firm stance against the translation of municipal documents into languages other than English, a move that was out of step with other multicultural municipalities. In McCallion's view, if immigrants come to Canada, "they should adopt the Canadian way" (qtd in Good, 2009, p. 84). The city's webpage now includes a link to Google Translate, but it does not appear that official documents, such as the city's Master Plan, are routinely translated.

4　Bonnie Crombie dominated the mayoral race, and only 17 CMES respondents reported voting for a racialized mayoral candidate. Thus, we focus this discussion on council contests.

REFERENCES

Aflaki, K. (2018). Kevin Johnston denied entry into candidates forum. *The Medium.* 15 October. https://themedium.ca/news/kevin-johnston
-denied-entry-into-candidates-forum

Association of Municipalities of Ontario. (2018). *2018 municipal election – fast facts.* https://elections.amo.on.ca/web/en/stats

Bhatia, M, Poynting, S., & Tufail, W. (Eds.). (2018). *Media, crime and racism.* Palgrave.

City of Mississauga. (2019). *Diversity and inclusion advisory committee.* http://www.mississauga.ca/portal/cityhall/diversityandinclusioncommittee

Douglas, P. (2019). Brampton, Mississauga homicides spike 62 per cent in 2018. *Brampton Guardian.* 1 January. https://www.bramptonguardian.com/news-story/9100649-brampton-mississauga-homicides-spike-62-per-cent-in-2018

Fiorina, M. (1981). *Retrospective voting in American national elections.* Yale University Press.

Garreau, J. (1991). *Edge city: Life on the new frontier.* Anchor Books.

Good, K. (2009). *Municipalities and multiculturalism: The politics of immigration in Toronto and Vancouver.* University of Toronto Press.

Gordon, G. (2017). What happens when an anti-Muslim internet personality begins to face consequences. *Canadaland.* 11 August. https://www.canadalandshow.com/we-need-to-talk-about-kevin-johnston

Grewal, S. (2015). Can Mississauga's diversity committee temper legacy of all white councils? *Toronto Star.* 2 January. https://www.thestar.com/news/gta/2015/01/02/can_mississaugas_diversity_committee_temper_legacy_of_all_white_councils.html

Hajnal, Z., Lewis, P. G., & Louch, H. (2002). *Municipal elections in California.* Public Policy Institute of California.

Healy, A., & Malhotra, N. (2013). Retrospective voting reconsidered. *Annual Review of Political Science, 16,* 285–306. https://dx.doi.org/10.1146/annurev-polisci-032211-212920

Kan, A. (2018a). Mississauga councillor docked pay following racially-insensitive comments. *Insauga.* 17 July. https://www.insauga.com/mississauga-councillor-docked-pay-following-racially-insensitive-comments

Kan, A. (2018b). "Over Scrutinized," says Mississauga candidate on how she got kicked off ballot for municipal election. *Insauga.* 2 August. https://www.insauga.com/over-scrutinized-says-mississauga-candidate-on-how-she-got-kicked-off-ballot-for-municipal-election

Kan, A. (2018c). Who is running in Mississauga's municipal elections? *Insauga.* 5 August. https://www.insauga.com/who-is-running-in-mississaugas-municipal-elections

Kan, A. (2019). This is where Mississauga ranks on the list of Canada's most dangerous cities. *Insauga.* 18 April. https://www.insauga.com/this-is-where-mississauga-ranks-on-the-list-of-canadas-most-dangerous-cities

Knope, J. (2018). Mississauga, Brampton mayoral candidates lay out key challenges for growing cities. *CBC News.* https://www.cbc.ca/news/canada/toronto/election-905-local-peel-region-mayor-1.4857030

Krebs, T.B. (1998). The determinants of candidates' vote share and the advantages of incumbency in City Council elections. *American Journal of Political Science, 42*, 921–935.

Mississauga News. (2018). Meet your mayoral candidate for Mississauga: Kevin J. Johnston. https://www.mississauga.com/community-story/8899205-meet -your-mayoral-candidate-for-mississauga-kevin-j-johnston

Rosella, L. (2010). Voter turnout surpasses 30 percent. *Mississauga News.* 26 October. https://www.mississauga.com/news-story/3159456-voter -turnout-surpasses-30-per-cent

Schaffner, B., Streb, M., & Wright, G. (2001). Tearns without uniforms: The nonpartisan ballot in state and local elections. *Political Research Quarterly, 54*(7–30).

Spicer, Z., McGregor, M., & Alcantara, C. (2017). Political opportunity structures and the representation of women and visible minorities in municipal elections. *Electoral Studies, 48*, 10–18.

Statistics Canada. (2016). *Census profile, 2016 census.* Cat. no. 98–316-X2016001. Ottawa. http://www12.statcan.ca/census-recensement/2016/dp-pd/prof /index.cfm?Lang=E

Stewart, J. (2018). Dearth of all-candidates' meetings is death on democracy. *Mississauga News.* 11 October. https://www.mississauga.com/opinion -story/8946278-dearth-of-all-candidates-meetings-is-death-on-democracy

Trounstine, J. (2011). Evidence of a local incumbency advantage. *Legislative Studies Quarterly, 36*(2), 255–280. https://doi.org/10.1111/j.1939-9162 .2011.00013.x

Tulloch, M. H. (2018). Report of the independent street checks review. Queen's Printer for Ontario. http://www.mcscs.jus.gov.on.ca/sites/default /files/content/mcscs/docs/StreetChecks.pdf

Urbaniak, T. (2009). *Her worship: Hazel McCallion and the development of Mississauga.* University of Toronto Press.

Vincent, D. (2016). Hazel who? It's Bonnie Crombie's Mississauga. *Toronto Star.* 18 December. https://www.thestar.com/news/insight/2016/12/18/hazel -who-its-bonnie-crombies-mississauga.html

Wallace, R., McGregor, M., Tolley, E., & Chow, O. (2019). *Immigrants and turnout in Canadian local elections: A mixed-methods study.* Paper presented at annual meeting of the Canadian Political Science Association. Vancouver, 3 June.

8 Toronto

R. MICHAEL McGREGOR AND SCOTT PRUYSERS

At first glance, the 2018 Toronto municipal election may appear quite ordinary. Voter turnout was just over 40% (a figure typical of local elections in Canada), the sitting mayor was comfortably re-elected, and 80% of those elected to City Council were incumbents. Upon closer examination, however, the election was anything but ordinary. Indeed, the 2018 Toronto municipal election had a number of rather extraordinary features: a heated battle between former rivals John Tory and Doug Ford, now the Mayor of Toronto and the Premier of Ontario respectively; unilateral provincial intervention into the municipal election just hours before the campaign was to officially begin; a media firestorm surrounding Bill 5 (*The Better Local Government Act*); judicial rulings of unconstitutionality; and even threats to invoke the Notwithstanding Clause (Section 33 of the Charter). How did we get here? To understand the extraordinary nature of this election, some background is necessary.

In 1997 the *City of Toronto Act* amalgamated East York, Etobicoke, North York, Scarborough, York, and "Old Toronto" into a single municipality (doing so against the wishes of many politicians and residents in the affected areas). In 2005, the province revised that act, granting the city additional authority, including the ability to establish its own electoral boundaries. The city's last five elections (2000 to 2014), were all conducted with the same 44-ward system. In light of the fact that Toronto's population had changed considerably (and in a geographically uneven manner) over the previous decade and a half, in 2014, the city established the Toronto Ward Boundary Review Commission, which had a mandate to recommend the redrawing of ward boundaries. After a two-year process involving a number of consultations, surveys, and meetings with stakeholders, the commission recommended increasing the council's size to 47 to reflect population growth, with modest boundary changes to even out ward populations. Among the options considered and eventually rejected by the commission was a 25-ward system whereby ward boundaries would match those of federal and provincial ridings. The commission's report noted of the 25-ward system: "There was little support for this option at the public meetings and from Members of Council" (Toronto Ward Boundary Review, 2016, p. 5). In 2016, Toronto City Council voted 28 to 13 to accept the commission's recommendation that the 2018 election be conducted under a 47-ward system (Pagliaro, 2016).[1]

In a controversial move that sparked a widespread outcry, Premier Doug Ford (brother of former mayor Rob Ford, and himself a former mayoral candidate and Toronto city councillor), unveiled the *Better Local Government Act* (Bill 5), announcing that the size of Toronto City Council would be reduced from 47 to 25 seats (the system explicitly rejected by the Ward Boundary Review Commission) for the 2018 election. The move reportedly stunned Toronto's politicians, who largely opposed the change, and did so in a vocal manner (Rieti, 2018).[2] The decision itself was unprecedented, and so too was its timing. Ford made the announcement on 26 June 2018, *the day before* the official candidate nomination deadline and only four months before the election. The change was largely opposed on the grounds that changing the boundaries so close to the election, after candidates had already been campaigning for quite some time, was needlessly disruptive – opponents describe the change as having caused "widespread disruption and confusion" (Pagliaro, 2019). A series of legal challenges to the act emerged. On 10 September 2018, a Superior Court judge in one of those cases ruled that Bill 5 was unconstitutional, dictating that the election move forward with 47 wards:

> The enactment of provincial legislation radically changing the number and size of a city's electoral districts in the middle of the city's election is without parallel in Canadian history ... I find that the Province's enactment of Bill 5 in the middle of the City's election substantially interfered with the municipal candidate's freedom of expression that is guaranteed under s. 2(b) of the Charter of Rights ... I find that the reduction from 47 to 25 in the number of City wards and the corresponding increase in ward-size population from an average of about 61,000 to 111,000 substantially interfered with the municipal voter's freedom of expression under s. 2(b) of the Charter of Rights, and in particular her right to cast a vote that can result in effective representation ... The October 22 election shall proceed as scheduled but on the basis of 47 wards, not 25. (*City of Toronto et al v. Ontario (Attorney General)*, 2018)

This ruling, however, was not the end to the saga. In response to the court's decision, the Ford government made yet another shocking declaration, threatening to make use of the Notwithstanding Clause (Section 33 of the Charter) in order to bypass the judge's decision and move forward with the reduction of Toronto City Council to 25 wards: "Our first order of business will be to reintroduce the *Better Local Government Act*, and with it invoke Section 33 of the Constitution" (Russell, 2018). In the end, however, this unprecedented threat proved to be unnecessary. While Ford appeared ready to utilize s. 33 for what would have been the first time in the province's history, on 19 September, an Ontario Court of Appeal stayed the original judicial ruling. Ford had won, and the election went forward under the 25-ward system.[3]

Despite the excitement provided by these dramatic events, the campaign itself was relatively uneventful and unmemorable at both the council and mayoral levels. As with most municipal elections, incumbency proved paramount. John Tory, first elected in 2014, sailed to an easy victory in a crowded mayoral campaign that only had one credible challenger (Jennifer Keesmaat). He captured nearly two thirds of the vote and won in every ward. At the council level, the story was much the same: 20 of the 25 seats were filled by incumbents (though many sitting councillors lost their bids for re-election, as they were forced to run against other incumbents in the new 25-ward system).

After providing a more detailed overview of the important features of the 2018 Toronto mayoral and council elections, this chapter digs into the apparent dominance of the incumbent mayor. As in the other chapters in this volume, we consider the bases of the mayor's support. Building on this, we then consider *changes* in Tory's support over time (drawing upon data on vote choice from 2014). We find that the mayor's dominance at the aggregate level masked substantial changes at the individual level. A comparison with data on federal voting behaviour reveals that the mayor's supporters were considerably less loyal to the incumbent than tends to be the case in federal elections. Incumbents are famously successful in Canadian local elections, yet even a popular incumbent like Mayor Tory had to work to build a new coalition of voters in 2018.

Election Overview

The Mayoral Campaign

While John Tory won in both 2014 and 2018, the two elections were sharply different. The 2014 mayoral contest lacked an incumbent, for controversial mayor Rob Ford had dropped out of the race for medical reasons (though it has been argued that Doug Ford amounted to a pseudo-incumbent; see Stephenson et al., 2018). In the 2014 election there had been three credible candidates (in a field of 65 registered contenders), which resulted in a relatively competitive race. John Tory (40.3%), Doug Ford (33.7%), and Olivia Chow (23.2%) provided voters with an ideologically diverse slate of candidates (Chow being on the left, Tory the centre-right, and Ford on the right; see McGregor et al., 2016), and each won a substantial share of the popular vote. Combined, these three accounted for 97% of the vote. Tory ultimately won, but not by a particularly large margin (less than 7%).

The 2018 election was far less competitive: 30 fewer candidates registered than in 2014; there were only two main candidates (a number of high-profile potential candidates, including Mel Lastman's son Blayne, and former mayoral candidate Olivia Chow, declined to enter the race); and Tory's margin of victory grew by nearly 25 percentage points. In fact, for much of the lead-up to the election, it looked like incumbent "scare-off" effects would result in Tory running (virtually) unopposed as no strong challengers were willing to step forward. On the last day of registration, however, Jennifer Keesmaat entered the race. Keesmaat, a former chief planner for the City of Toronto, proved to be Tory's only credible challenger, and she credited her decision to enter the race to Doug Ford's *Better Local Government Act* (Gray, 2018).

In terms of the campaign, Tory began the election period with considerable support (70%) and maintained a commanding lead in the polls through to Election Day. The campaign proved to be of little help to Keesmaat – a series of polls conducted by Forum Research Inc. reveal remarkably little movement in support for the mayor's chief rival (see Figure 8.1). She began the campaign with around 30% support, and the final polls put her at 29%. These numbers turned out to be fairly accurate: Tory won with 63% to Keesmaat's distant 23.6%. There were 33 other candidates, but none were particularly popular. The third-place finisher, Faith Goldy, received just 3.4% of the vote.

We suggest one possible reason for this lack of movement in mayoral vote intentions during the campaign: the fact that the ward-redistricting scandal, and the subsequent court cases and threats of invoking the Notwithstanding Clause, dominated news coverage of the election for most of the campaign period (recall that the issue first arose in July and that the final court case was not until 19 September, just a month before Election Day). Torontonians are fairly attentive to municipal politics compared to people in other cities, and this was particularly true with respect to the 2018 campaign for City Council. CMES respondents in all eight cities included in the study were asked after the election how much attention they had paid to (a) the mayoral campaign and (b) the council campaign (both on a scale from 0 to 10).[4] The average level of attention

Figure 8.1. Mayoral polls – Toronto

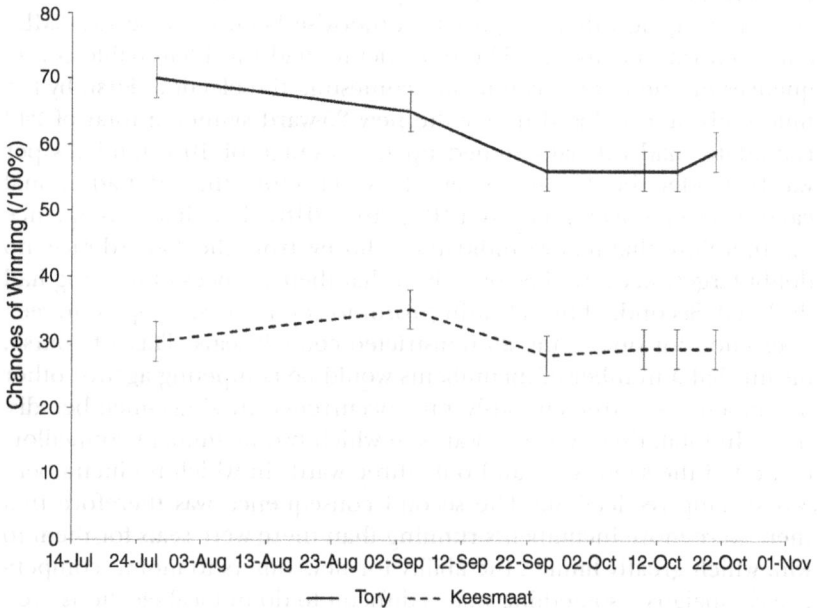

Chances of Winning (/100%)

14-Jul 24-Jul 03-Aug 13-Aug 23-Aug 02-Sep 12-Sep 22-Sep 02-Oct 12-Oct 22-Oct 01-Nov

—— Tory --- Keesmaat

paid by Torontonians to the mayoral race (7.65) was higher than in other cities (7.32) – a difference of 0.33 points, which is significant at $p < 0.05$. When it came to the council elections, however, this gap was significantly larger: Torontonians had an average score of 6.5, compared to a mere 5.2 for the other cities (this difference of 1.33 points is significant at $p < 0.01$). Though Torontonians did assign a higher score to the mayoral race than to the council elections, this gap (1.1 points) was half of that observed for the seven other cities (2.2 points). When voters focus a comparatively large share of their attention on the council elections rather than on the mayoral race, it stands to reason that mayoral vote intentions will be fairly constant. Furthermore, both Keesmaat and Tory were publicly opposed to ward redistricting, so the public's focus on the issue could do little to change the minds of voters.[5] At least at the aggregate level, the 2018 campaign seemed to have little effect on voters.

Council Races

Council races are often overshadowed by the parallel campaign for mayor. However, the Ontario government's last-minute change to the city's ward boundaries and the subsequent court challenges meant there was considerably more attention, especially in the news media, on the council campaign than might have otherwise been the case (as CMES data confirm; see above). The redistricting had two identifiable consequences on the pool of candidates contesting the election. First, by the time registration closed under the new 25-ward system, a total of 242 candidates had officially signed up (an average of 10 candidates per ward). Under the 47-ward system, however, more than 100 additional candidates had been registered (Pagliaro, 2018). The first consequence was therefore that many candidates withdrew from the 25-ward race, no doubt largely because they perceived that their chances of winning had declined. Second, of the 44 sitting Toronto councillors, 33 opted to seek re-election for one of the 25 redistricted council seats. This, of course, meant that a number of incumbents would be competing against other incumbents – a tremendously rare occurrence in single-member districts. In total, there were 11 wards in which two incumbent councillors contested the same seat[6] and only three wards in which no incumbent was seeking re-election.[7] The second consequence was therefore that there were more incumbents running than there were seats for them to win, which greatly limited the ability for newcomers to mount competitive campaigns – something that is difficult to do in local elections even under normal circumstances.

Issues and Events

When the campaign began, it seemed as though the question of ward boundaries, or at very least municipal autonomy from provincial interference, could be a central issue. After all, there had been a lot of drama around that issue: the province had cut the size of council nearly in half, there had been a series of court battles, and the premier had even threatened to invoke the Notwithstanding Clause. The intense news coverage devoted to the redistricting saga did not, however, accurately reflect voters' issue priorities. Figure 8.2 shows the mean importance of seven issues included in our CMES data (ranging from 0 to 10, where 10 is extremely important).

Immediately clear is that the least relevant issue among those presented to voters was ward boundaries. This is likely because there was very little debate or disagreement during the campaign among the leading candidates. A majority of councillors had voted in favour of the 47-ward system and of challenging Bill 5 in court, and both Tory and Keesmaat agreed on the issue during the campaign. In other words, there was a strong consensus among the candidates – almost all of them

Figure 8.2. Issue importance in the 2018 Toronto election

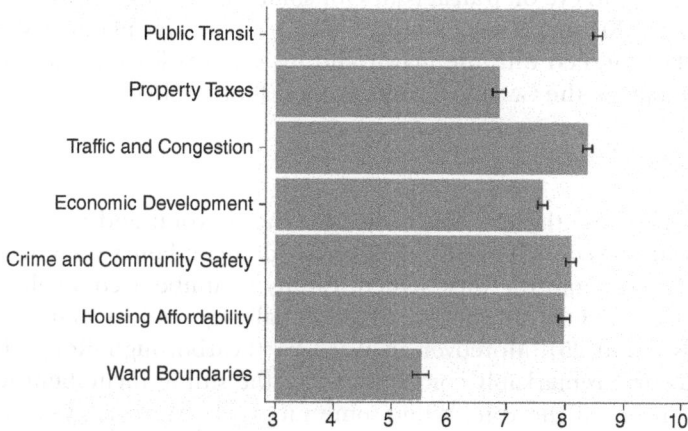

opposed redistricting – so the question did not differentiate them. This, of course, is not to say that Torontonians themselves were completely united. Though a majority of them (52.6%) did oppose the redistricting, a noteworthy minority (39.0%) supported it (8.5% had no opinion).[8] Had the candidates decided to take different positions, the issue might have played a more significant role in the campaign.

Transit and traffic/congestion were far more salient concerns for voters; these ranked as the top issues for Torontonians. This is not surprising, for these have long been central issues in Toronto (McGregor et al., 2016; McGregor et al., forthcoming). In contrast to the ward boundaries debate, there was meaningful debate on these matters. Keesmaat unveiled her transit platform, "A Real Plan for Transit," a month into the campaign. Among other things, that platform promised to build the downtown relief line three years ahead of schedule, add five new GO stations, and integrate service to the airport into the transit network; it also made a commitment to proceed with the Scarborough subway extension. Tory's plan was more modest, relying on existing infrastructure and emphasizing "SmartTrack," which had been part of Tory's 2014 election platform and continued to be front and centre in 2018. That plan called for six new transit stations and eight refurbished stations to be added to the existing regional GO transit network. There was, of course, more to Tory's transit plan, but SmartTrack was its centrepiece. Keesmaat was particularly critical of Tory's plan: "John Tory got elected by promising 'SmartTrack' as the solution to all our transit problems. As mayor, he focused on trying to get this plan approved. Almost nothing has come of it. It will never be built" (Keesmaat, 2018). Tory and Keesmaat had not seen eye to eye on transit issues for some time. Long before the election, when Keesmaat was employed as the city's chief planner, she had publicly disagreed with the mayor and his support for maintaining the eastern part of the Gardiner Expressway (Elliott, 2018).

The Election Result

Table 8.1 shows the election results for the mayoral and council campaigns. In the council results, the primacy of incumbency is immediately clear. By the time the dust settled, twenty incumbent councillors had been re-elected. In only two wards did a challenger defeat an incumbent (Wards 8 and 25). Moreover, in Ward 25 (Scarborough–Rouge Park), the race was remarkably competitive and the sitting incumbent lost by less than 1% of the vote. While some races, like Ward 25, were highly competitive, others were anything but. Ana Bailão, the incumbent in Ward 4, won her seat by 75 points. The average margin of victory across the 25 wards was 21 points. Clearly, then, the winning candidates enjoyed comfortable levels of support.

Table 8.1 also shows that the mayoral race was anything but competitive. City-wide, Tory won 63% of the vote, nearly 40 points more than Keesmaat (24%). He also received the most votes in all of the city's 25 wards. His margin of victory was slim in some places (less than 1 point in Ward 9, for instance) but was considerably higher in others (just over 58 points in Wards 2, 6, and 15). There was therefore noteworthy geographic variation in voter preferences. Figure 8.3 shows the geographic distribution of Tory's support, with darker areas indicating a higher vote share.

The implications of Figure 8.3 are clear: Tory performed much better on the periphery of the city than in Toronto's downtown core. This pattern matches what has previously been observed in Toronto: left-leaning candidates tend to perform well downtown, while their right-leaning opponents are stronger in the inner suburbs (Walks 2004, 2005, 2013). As has been observed elsewhere, this pattern corresponds largely with voting results from other orders of government, which show that the NDP is strongest downtown (McGregor et al., forthcoming). Tory's dominance in 2018 stood in stark contrast to 2014, which saw a more competitive, three-way race between Tory, Doug Ford, and Olivia Chow, in which the mayor won only 40.3% of the vote. Voters themselves were well aware of the uncompetitive nature of the mayoral campaign. On average, CMES respondents gave Tory a 76.2% chance of winning; the anticipated likelihood of a Keesmaat victory was 38.3% (N = 2,085, $p < 0.01$).

Table 8.1. Toronto election results, by ward

Ward	Number of candidates	Number of incumbents	Council winner	Margin (council)	Mayoral winner	Margin (mayoral)
1	9	2	Michael Ford*	7.9	John Tory*	50.6
2	5	2	Stephen Holyday*	3.1	John Tory*	59.0
3	10	1	Mark Grimes*	13.7	John Tory*	47.1
4	10	1	Gord Perks*	23.0	John Tory*	9.7
5	10	2	Frances Nunziata*	10.5	John Tory*	47.6
6	4	2	James Pasternak*	9.6	John Tory*	58.8
7	8	2	Anthony Perruzza*	12.0	John Tory*	49.0
8	10	1	Mike Colle	19.7	John Tory*	54.8
9	4	1	Ana Bailão*	74.7	John Tory*	0.5
10	14	1	Joe Cressy*	43.5	John Tory*	15.4
11	7	1	Mike Layton*	56.4	John Tory*	10.3
12	6	2	Josh Matlow*	9.5	John Tory*	32.8
13	19	2	Kristyn Wong-Tam*	35.1	John Tory*	14.7
14	10	2	Paula Fletcher*	16.1	John Tory*	16.6
15	5	2	Jaye Robinson*	5.4	John Tory*	58.5
16	8	1	Denzil Minnan-Wong*	16.0	John Tory*	55.9
17	9	0	Shelley Carroll	11.5	John Tory*	54.0
18	18	1	John Filion*	11.3	John Tory*	52.2
19	16	0	Brad Bradford	0.8	John Tory*	31.8
20	10	2	Gary Crawford*	1.4	John Tory*	48.7
21	11	1	Michael Thompson*	62.2	John Tory*	53.7
22	7	2	Jim Karygiannis*	9.8	John Tory*	54.5
23	11	0	Cynthia Lai	7.0	John Tory*	52.8
24	10	1	Paul Ainslie*	58.3	John Tory*	55.6
25	11	1	Jennifer McKelvie	0.5	John Tory*	57.3

Source: compiled by authors.

* = incumbent.

A final noteworthy feature of the election outcome is that the turnout rate of 40.9% represented a significant drop from 2014 (54.7%). This decline may be partly attributable to the aforementioned uncompetitiveness of the 2018 election. Note, however, that 2018's turnout figure represents a regression to the mean; 2014 was, in fact, a high-water mark for turnout in Toronto. Excluding 2014, average turnout in Toronto's post-amalgamation history has been 41.8%. By this comparison, 2018 is more norm than outlier.

Vote Choice

We turn discuss the correlates of vote choice in the mayoral election. Figure 8.4 shows the marginal effects plots, with the vote for the winner

Figure 8.3. Vote share for Tory, by ward

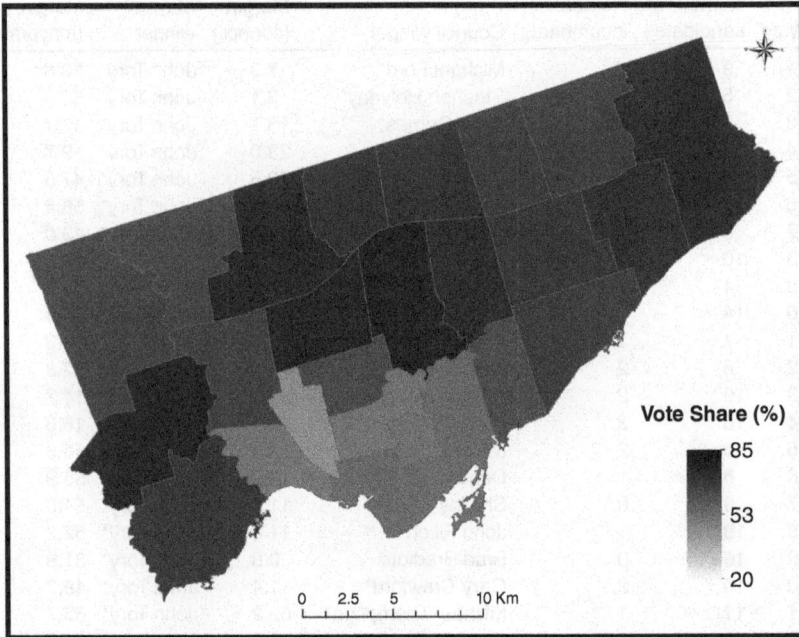

(Tory) serving as the outcome variable. The four models introduce a series of explanatory variables in step-wise fashion, according to the funnel of causality and the proximity to vote choice (Campbell et al., 1960).[9]

Both socio-demographically and attitudinally, Tory's supporters differed from those of his opponents in many ways. As one would expect for a right-wing incumbent, the mayor performed well among older, less educated, more ideologically conservative voters, as well as those who were pleased with the city's economy. A closer look at Figure 8.4 points to two themes in particular that were central to vote choice: housing and economic indicators.

In terms of housing, Tory performed well among those for whom property taxes were an important issue but extremely poorly among those who cared about housing affordability (the latter variable had the largest effect of any in Model D). Tory's position has always been to freeze property taxes at the rate of inflation, which no doubt appealed to many constituents. As a result, the city has come to rely heavily on its real-estate transfer tax, which effectively increases the cost of purchasing housing in the city by 5%. Tory has made no moves to reduce or eliminate this tax. At the same time, the issue of housing affordability was a

Figure 8.4. Vote choice for Tory – marginal effects

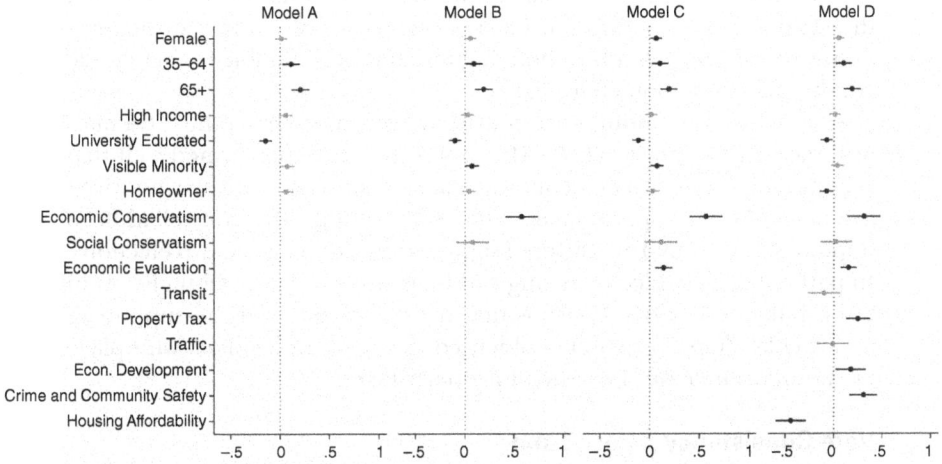

Notes: Entries report marginal effects and 95% confidence intervals. Coefficients in black are statistically significant at p < 0.1.

major theme of Jennifer Keesmaat's campaign, which no doubt drew to her many individuals who sought a remedy for the city's increasingly expensive housing market.

Related to both these factors is homeownership. This variable is not associated with vote choice in Models A, B, or C, but in Model D, it shows a negative relationship with support for Tory. This is no doubt a result of the addition of the "property tax" and "housing affordability" variables. Homeowners are more likely than renters to place high importance on the issue of property taxes (p < 0.001) and a low value on housing affordability (p < 0.001). Accordingly, we suggest that the observed relationship between homeownership and vote choice (which is itself only significant at the p < 0.10 level) is an artefact of the inclusion of these other variables. The key takeaway here is that Tory did well among those for whom property taxes were an important issue, but very poorly among those who cared most about housing affordability.

The second important theme revealed in Figure 8.4 is that the economy matters. Setting aside housing issues (which themselves have obvious financial implications), a variety of factors suggest a clear divide between Tory supporters and other voters on this dimension. The mayor performed well among economically conservative voters, those who believed that the economy had performed well in the previous year, and those who placed a high priority on economic development. Municipal governments arguably have much less capacity to shape the economy than their federal or provincial counterparts, yet it has been established that Toronto voters view their local government as having a strong economic impact, and that they hold incumbents accountable for economic conditions (Anderson et al., 2017).

Several of these findings are consistent with those from the 2014 mayoral race. McGregor et al. (2016) found that Tory performed well that year among older voters, economic conservatives, and those who cared the most about property taxes. This, even though the constellation of opponents faced by Tory differed significantly between the two elections. In particular, Tory faced a strong candidate on the right (Doug Ford) in 2014, but not in 2018. It seems that the mayor enjoyed the support of a particular "type" of voter – older, conservative individuals who place great importance on the issue of property taxes.

Vote Consistency across Time

Incumbency is known to be a significant advantage in municipal elections (Kushner et al., 1997; Krebs, 1998; Moore et al., 2017). This is particularly true at the council level, but it also applies in mayoral elections. Incumbents have name recognition, an established track record, and existing fundraising apparatuses, and their mere presence may be enough to "scare off" high-quality challengers, who may well be wary of taking on a candidate with such formidable advantages (King, 1991; Levitt and Wolfram, 1997; Moore et al., 2017). Of the six mayors discussed in this volume who sought re-election, only one (Montreal's Denis Coderre) was unsuccessful. Since the creation of the "Mega-City" in Toronto in 1997, no incumbent mayor who has sought re-election has lost. John Tory's landslide victory in 2018 fits this trend; in fact, the mayor saw his vote share increase from 40.3% in 2014 to 63.5% in 2018 (an increase in raw votes from 394,775 to 479,659).

It seems that such results point to consistency, at least on the surface. Municipal voters are generally deciding whether to reward the incumbent mayor with another term in office, and they generally do. In contrast, at the time of writing, in seven of the ten most recent provincial elections in each of Canada's provinces, the incumbent party won fewer seats than a challenger.[10] The country also saw a change in government after the most recent federal election prior to the Toronto election (2015). On the basis of these results, municipal electorates would appear to be relatively stable.

We end this chapter by considering two questions. First, while mayoral elections where an incumbent is present would seem to be relatively stable in the aggregate, can the same be said at the individual level? Tory won in both 2014 and 2018, but did he attract or lose many supporters between elections? In answering this question, we compare individual-level consistency of vote choice in Toronto to the five most recent federal elections. Second, what are the correlates of individual-level volatility? Using the same battery of factors considered in the vote choice model above, we identify the voter-level factors associated with changes in support for the mayor between 2014 and 2018. We find that, in the case of Toronto, there was a great deal of individual-level volatility between elections. Despite surface-level consistency, Tory lost many of his 2014 supporters, even attracting many who had not previously supported him.

Consistency of Vote Choice

We begin by examining the consistency of John Tory's support between 2014 and 2018. The fact that Tory won both elections (and by an increased margin in 2018) might suggest that those who backed him when first elected remained loyal in 2018. At the individual level, however, there are reasons to expect there was inter-election stability *and* change.

Why might we expect that many voters chose to support Tory in 2014 but not 2018 (or vice versa)? As in most municipal elections, the constellation of candidates was quite different between the two contests. In 2014, Tory faced off against noteworthy challengers from both the right (Doug Ford) and the left (Olivia Chow) (McGregor et al., 2016). In 2018, Jennifer Keesmaat was viewed by Torontonians as being on the left of the ideological spectrum, and there was no serious challenger from the right.[11] Add to this that there were fewer viable candidates in 2018 – the "effective number of candidates" (Laakso and Taagepera, 1979) had dropped from 3.03 in 2014 to 2.17 in 2018. The decrease in the number of competitive options, coupled with the fact that there was no serious candidate on the right in 2018, suggests there was a great deal of potential for Tory to attract new voters.

The election's non-partisan nature is another good reason to expect inter-election instability. Partisanship (commonly conceptualized as a long-standing psychological attachment to a party – Campbell et al., 1960) is a major determinant of vote choice in Canadian politics (Blais et al., 2002; Anderson and Stephenson, 2011). Over the course of multiple elections, voters gather information about a party's ideology and issue positions, and that information can be factored into future vote decisions. If a party system remains stable over time, voters can develop long-term partisan orientations (positive or negative), which can dampen the likelihood of changing one's vote between elections (LeDuc et al., 1984). No such long-term effects exist in non-partisan elections, and thus changing one's vote between elections (particularly if the slate of candidates is different) may be comparatively likely.

What, then, are the reasons to expect individual-level consistency in Toronto from 2014 to 2018? First, as noted earlier, incumbents perform exceptionally well in Canadian local elections, and this was certainly the case here. This aggregate-level consistency provides perhaps the best reason to expect the same at the individual level. Though ecological observations of this nature are admittedly dubious, if the same candidate is easily winning multiple elections, it seems plausible that this is due to consistent support from individual voters. The aforementioned decrease in number of viable candidates provides a second reason to expect voter consistency. The absence of a major candidate to the right of Tory in 2018 (the role filled by Doug Ford in 2014) means that the most ideologically conservative of Tory's supporters had no viable alternative, even if they were dissatisfied with the mayor's performance. Finally, Tory's former partisan ties may have led to cross-level partisan "contamination" effects (see Stephenson et al., 2018, as well as chapter 2 of this volume). Torontonians largely associated Tory with the Progressive Conservative Party (which is not surprising, given that he led the provincial party from 2004 to 2009) (McGregor et al., 2016). These perceptions had the potential to dampen vote switching in the manner described above as applying to partisan elections. The circumstances of the 2018 Toronto election provide several reasons to expect that inter-election vote consistency would have been high.[12]

Theorizing aside, how consistent were Torontonians between 2014 and 2018? We answer this question by way of a cross-tabulation of vote choice in 2014 and 2018 (both measured in 2018). The results of this analysis are provided in Table 8.2. The table allows us to consider the consistency of Tory's support at an individual level and to map out how voters shifted among other candidates over time. Recall that in 2014, Tory won 40.3% of the vote, Doug Ford 33.7%, and Olivia Chow 23.2%. In 2018, Tory won 63.5% of the popular vote, followed by Jennifer Keesmaat (23.6%). Entries in the table report column percentages.

Table 8.2 shows several findings of note. It suggests, perhaps unsurprisingly, that most voters who supported Tory in 2014 also supported him in 2018; more than two-thirds (69.2%) of those who backed the mayor when he was first elected also voted for him in the most recent election. Interestingly, this value is not the largest in the table: 72.1% of Chow's voters from 2014 backed Tory's rival in 2018, Keesmaat. Such a finding suggests that voters clearly saw the two candidates as ideologically similar.

Table 8.2. Consistency of mayoral vote choice (%)

Vote in 2018	Vote in 2014			
	Tory	Ford	Chow	Other
Tory	69.2	41.7	19.4	37.4
Keesmaat	28.8	26.9	72.1	37.8
Goldy	0.9	25.8	0.8	11.1
Other	1.2	4.9	7.1	13.7
N	378	83	305	14

Doug Ford's former 2014 support was divided much less consistently in 2018. Though Tory was the recipient in 2018 of a plurality of this support, Keesmaat received a noteworthy share.[13]

The fact that Tory increased his vote share between elections, coupled with the finding that nearly one third of his 2014 supporters abandoned him for another candidate in 2018, suggests that he must have secured many new voters in the most recent election. This is, in fact, the case: nearly one quarter (24.7%) of individuals who voted for another candidate in 2014 backed the mayor in 2018. Thus while Tory lost many old voters, he also gained many (more) new ones. Though the same candidate won both elections, there was a great deal of change at the individual level.[14]

To put these findings in context, it is useful to compare them with results from other elections. To that end, we employ data from the Canadian Election Study (CES) to consider the consistency of support for incumbent parties in federal elections from 2004 to 2015.[15] For each election, we calculate the share of those who voted for the incumbent party in the previous election (T1) who also did so in the present election (T2) – recall that the analogous value was 69.2% for Tory. We also consider the share of voters who supported another party in the previous election, but the incumbent currently (again, this value is 24.7% for Toronto 2018). For instance, for the 2015 federal election, we calculate the share of Conservative voters from 2011 who voted for that party again in 2015, as well as the share of non-Conservative 2011 voters who voted for the party in 2015. We performed these calculations for the five most recent national elections, including those in which both the Liberals (2004 and 2006) and the Conservatives (2008, 2011, and 2015) were incumbents, and those in which there was a change of government (2006 and 2015) and where there was not (2004, 2008, and 2011).[16] We show the results of this analysis for federal results, along with the results for Toronto, in Figure 8.5.[17]

Figure 8.5. Consistency of vote choice across time

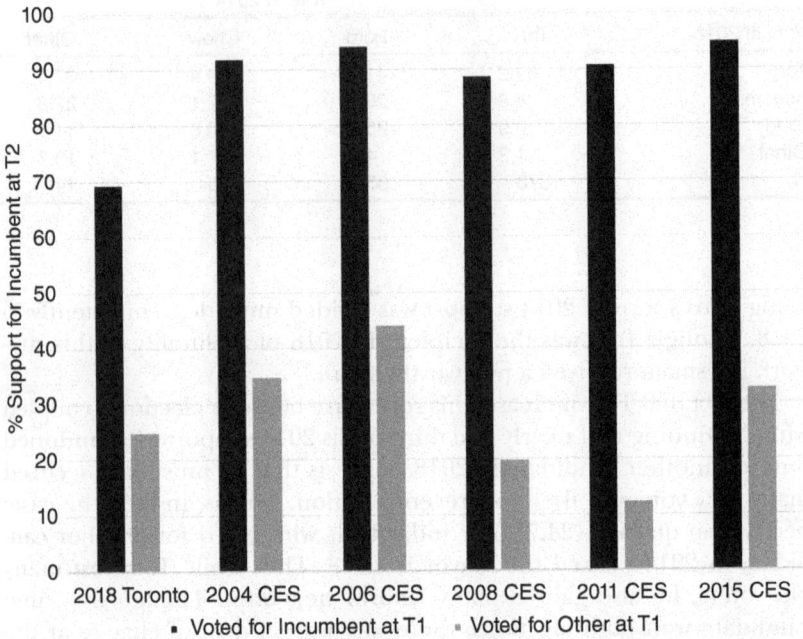

Figure 8.5 shows unequivocally that, compared what happens at the federal level, John Tory was unsuccessful at retaining his supporters. On average, federal incumbent parties were able to retain the support of 91.9% of their voters from the previous election – John Tory lost more than *three times* as much of his support between 2014 and 2018. In terms of attracting new supporters, the 2018 Toronto election result sits near the middle of the federal results. In 2006, the Conservatives were able to steal away 43.9% of voters who previously supported their opponents, but in 2011, they were much less successful at doing so (the figure was 12.2% that year). Thus while Tory did fairly well at attracting new supporters, he did a poor job at retaining old ones.

Further highlighting Tory's comparatively weak performance in this respect is the fact that his vote share increased so significantly (from 40.3% to 63.5%). In many of the national elections considered in Figure 8.5, the incumbent party *lost* vote share – the Conservatives dropped 7.7 percentage points from 2011 to 2015, and the Liberals saw a decrease of 6.5 points in 2006. In both these elections, the incumbent parties nevertheless maintained the support of more than 90% of their voters from the previous election.

Despite his re-election, and apparent consistency at the aggregate, an individual-level analysis reveals that John Tory's bases of support shifted significantly between 2014 and 2018. He retained a much smaller share of his support than do incumbent parties in federal elections, all the while winning many new voters. We expect that such a result is largely due to the non-partisan nature of local elections. Torontonians were offered an almost entirely new slate of options in 2018, while federal elections are generally contested by exactly the same constellation of parties. In such an environment, individuals may form (long-term) partisan ties to parties, leading to consistent support for their party of choice. When voters are presented with new options in each election, the incumbent cannot rely so heavily on past supporters, for partisan ties are lacking. Municipal elections have a reputation for being dominated by incumbents; even so, as the 2018 Toronto election suggests, mayors can hardly rest on their laurels.

The Correlates of Vote-Switching

We have thus far shown that there was a great deal of volatility in vote choice in Toronto between 2014 and 2018. Though John Tory won both elections, he did so with the backing of very different voters. He was able to attract a great deal of new support in 2018 from individuals who formerly backed his opponents. Yet at the same time, he lost a large share of his 2014 voters, particularly when compared to the losses experienced by incumbent parties at the federal level. High levels of incumbent success in local elections seemingly occur despite a relatively high level of individual-level volatility.

We conclude with an exploratory analysis of the sources of this volatility. That is, we consider the correlates of either abandoning or beginning to support Tory between 2014 to 2018. The explanatory variables considered are the same as those in Figure 8.6 (socio-demographic factors, ideology, economic evaluations, and issue importance variables). We run models for two binary outcome variables. The subsample used for the first model includes only those voters who supported Tory in 2014, and the model is meant to identify the correlates of defecting from Tory between elections – the outcome variable compares those individuals who supported Tory in both elections to those who did so in only 2014 (values for this variable are 1 if voters were loyal to Tory in 2018, and 0 if they abandoned him). The subsample for the second variable includes only those respondents who did not vote for Tory in

Figure 8.6. The dynamics of support for Tory, 2014–2018

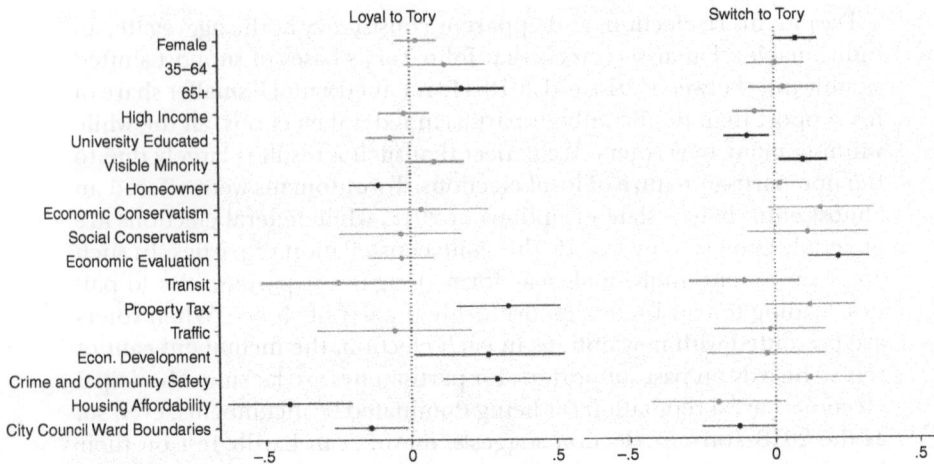

Notes: Entries report marginal effects and standard errors. Coefficients in black are statistically significant at p < 0.1.

2014, and this model is meant to provide insight into the correlates of switching *to* the mayor between elections. The outcome variable here is coded as 1 if they voted for Tory in 2018, and 0 if they once again decided not to back the mayor. High values for both variables therefore indicate support for Tory.

The results of these models are found in Figure 8.6, which shows the marginal effect of each explanatory factor on either abandoning or beginning to support Tory between 2014 and 2018.[18] Effects to the right of the vertical axis indicate that a factor is positively associated with support for Tory (either continuing to support him across elections, or beginning to support him). Identifying the correlates of these "loyal to Tory" and "come to Tory" variables provides insight into the sources of the significant inter-election volatility observed earlier and the reasons why voters changed their position (or not) toward the incumbent mayor.

Figure 8.6 reveals that a very different set of factors are associated with the two outcome variables; those factors that caused Tory 2014 voters to stay with him in 2018 differ from those that led new voters to back him. The issue variables are largely driving the retention/defection of Tory's 2014 voters – five of the seven issue importance indicators are significant. Those individuals who placed a great deal of emphasis on housing affordability or ward redistricting were likely to abandon the mayor. On the other hand, those voters who placed emphasis on property taxes, economic development, and crime and community safety tended to vote for the mayor again. Two other factors were associated with abandoning the mayor: age and homeownership – younger voters and owners were comparatively likely to defect.

As for attracting new voters, quite a different story emerges. Of note, only one issue (ward redistricting) is a factor; those who prioritized this were relatively unlikely to switch to Tory. Instead, socio-demographic characteristics and retrospective economic evaluations determined whether those individuals who did not support Tory in 2014 decided to do so in 2018. Tory was comparatively likely to win new support from women and visible minorities, while university-educated voters did not embrace him. He was able to attract new support from respondents who had positive retrospective evaluations of the city's economy – such a finding is not at all surprising for an incumbent. It is these groups of individuals who helped Tory win in 2018, even though he lost so many of his voters from 2014.

There is very little overlap between the two models. Issues were a significant factor in Tory's ability to retain support, but not in attracting it. Women, visible minorities, voters without a university education, and those who had a positive assessment of the economy were relatively likely to vote for Tory for the first time in 2018, while homeowners and young voters were comparatively likely to abandon him. These data suggest that there were clear patterns to individual-level changes in vote choice between elections. Though Tory won both elections in a convincing fashion, his bases of support in 2018 were, in fact, quite different from those that existed in 2018.

Conclusion

In some ways, the 2018 Toronto municipal election was typical of Canadian local contests. Despite the tumult caused by the stunning provincially imposed reduction in the size of City Council, 80% of council seats were won by incumbents. Voter turnout was just over 40%, and the sitting mayor won by a comfortable margin. The mayoral election appears particularly ordinary when contrasted to the exceptionally high-profile 2014 contest.

CMES data provide novel insights into Tory's seemingly conventional victory, in terms of both the sources of his support and how the bases of his support shifted between elections. In 2018, the mayor received the backing of segments of the population that were largely to be expected to support him, given his status as a right-of-centre incumbent. He performed well among older and less educated voters, as well as those with economically conservative attitudes and those who had positive retrospective economic evaluations. Voters who placed a high priority on property taxes, economic development, and crime and community safety, and a low priority on housing affordability and the ward redistricting scandal, tended to back him.

Though Tory's success in multiple elections is fairly conventional, we find that his repeated success at the aggregate level masks a great deal of volatility at the individual level – a striking result given that municipal incumbents are famously dominant. Tory lost a much greater share of his support from the previous election than incumbent parties tend to do at the federal level. He only increased his vote share because he was able to attract the support of a sizable share of voters who backed his opponents in 2014. Importantly, there are clear patterns in the correlates of abandoning, or newly supporting, the mayor; of particular note, given Tory's comparatively weak ability to retain support, is the finding that issues seemed to drive patterns of defection. All of this points to a very clear conclusion: the high levels of success that municipal incumbents enjoy cannot be attributed to a consistent set of supporters. When a new set of opponents emerges, bases of elector support shift and new coalitions of support must be created.

NOTES

1 There was some opposition to changing the number of wards from 44 to 47, and this led to a hearing by the Ontario Municipal Board. Supporters of the shift to 47 seats claimed that the change was needed to ensure proper representation in the downtown core, where population growth had been particularly high in recent years (Beattie, 2018). Coincidentally, downtown happens to be a particularly progressive part of the city. Recent research on Ford's decision to adopt the 25-ward scheme has shown that attitudes toward redistricting in Toronto are strongly shaped by partisan and ideological considerations (McGregor et al., forthcoming).

2 A small group of seven incumbent councillors did publicly support the move. Among them, three did not run in 2018 (David Shiner, Justin Di Ciano, and Cesar Palacio), two lost against another incumbent (Giorgio Mammolitti and Vince Cristani), and two were re-elected (Michael Ford and Stephen Holyday)

3 The matter remains unresolved, however, as in early 2020 the Supreme Court agreed to hear the city's appeal to the change (Pagliaro, 2020).

4 N = 9.251 for all values reported in this paragraph.

5 Keesmaat did arguably oppose the redistricting more strongly than Tory. She attributed her last-minute entry into the mayoral race as a result of Tory's "tepid" response to Premier Ford (Gray, 2018). Though she later backtracked, she even hinted at Toronto secession as a potential solution to provincial interference (Elliott, 2018).

6 Wards 1, 2, 5, 6, 7, 12, 13, 14, 15, 20, and 22.

7 Wards 17, 19, and 23.

8 N = 2,281.

9 N = 974 for all models. Pseudo R-squared for Model D is 0.1657.

10 As of July 2019, of the most recent elections in each province, only in Saskatchewan, Nova Scotia, and Newfoundland did the incumbent party win.

11 On a scale of 0 (left) to 10 (right), CMES respondents placed Tory at an average of 6.4 and Keesmaat at 3.7 (N = 877, difference significant at $p < 0.001$). In 2014, McGregor et al. found that Tory was placed at 6.5, Chow at 3.0, and Ford at 7.4.

12 Toronto is the only city in the CMES where changes in vote choice across elections can be considered (the questions necessary to do so were not asked in any other city).

13 The share of Ford voters is lower in the sample than should be expected given the 2014 election outcome. Among other things, this may be due to self-selection into (or out of) the survey by these voters, or a reluctance of such individuals to "admit" to having voted for Ford – i.e., a municipal "shy-Tory" effect (we suspect the latter option to be particularly likely, given Ford's intrusion into the election regarding the council ward boundaries). Both of these factors might conceivably have some biasing effect upon values in the "Ford" column of the table. However, the most important value in the table is that of the top-left corner, which indicates consistency among Tory supporters. This value is unaffected by any potential issues with sampling former Ford voters.

14 If participation is related to vote choice, turnout can be an important factor in shaping election outcomes. CMES data show no difference, however, in the 2018 turnout rates of individuals who supported Tory versus other candidates in 2014 (though non-voters are underrepresented in the sample, as is the case in most election surveys). We therefore limit our analysis to those individuals who voted in both elections.

15 See https://ces-eec.arts.ubc.ca.

16 All results are weighted to the population.

17 For both the CES and CMES, vote choice for T1 was asked in the pre-election survey, while T2 vote choice was asked in the post-election questionnaire.

18 N = 455 and Pseudo R2 = 0.2004 for the "leave Tory" model. N = 402 and
    Pseudo R2 = 0.1639 for the "come to Tory" model.

REFERENCES

Anderson, C., McGregor, R. M., Moore, A., & Stephenson, L. (2017).
    Economic voting and multi-level governance: The case of Toronto. *Urban
    Affairs Review, 53*(1), 71–101. https://doi.org/10.1177%2F1078087415617302
Anderson, C., & Stephenson, L. (2011). *Voting behaviour in Canada.* UBC Press.
Beattie, S. (2018). Toronto councillor to fight OMB decision to boost the
    number of wards. *Toronto Star.* https://www.thestar.com/news/city_hall
    /2018/01/01/toronto-councillor-to-fight-omb-decision-to-boost-the
    -number-of-wards.html
Blais, A., Gidengil, E., Nadeau, R., & Nevitte, N. (2002). *Anatomy of a Liberal
    victory: Making sense of the vote in the 2000 Canadian election.* Broadview Press.
Campbell, A., Converse, P., Miller, W., & Stokes, D. (1960). *The American voter.*
    John Wiley & Sons.
Canadian election study (datasets). https://ces-eec.arts.ubc.ca/english
    -section/surveys
City of Toronto v. Ontario (Attorney General). (2018). ONSC 5151. http://
    www.ontariocourts.ca/scj/decisions
Elliott, M. (2018). Jennifer Keesmaat's mayoral bid already a small win for
    Toronto's progressive voters. *CBC News.* https://www.cbc.ca/news/canada
    /toronto/keesmaat-mayor-progressive-toronto-tory-1.4765726
Gray, J. (2018). Why Toronto mayoral candidate Jennifer Keesmaat feels she
    has to keep running. *The Globe & Mail.* https://www.theglobeandmail.com
    /canada/toronto/article-why-toronto-mayoral-candidate-jennifer-keesmaat
    -feels-she-has-to-keep
Keesmaat, J. (2018). My network transit plan. phttps://www.jenniferkeesmaat
    .com/keesmaat_network_transit_plan
King, G. (1991). Constituency service and incumbency advantage. *British
    Journal of Political Science, 21*(1), 119–128.
Krebs, T. B. (1998). The determinants of candidates' vote share and the
    advantage of incumbency in City Council elections. *American Journal of
    Political Science, 42*(3), 921–935. https://doi.org/10.2307/2991735
Kushner, J., Siegel, S., & Stanwick, H. (1997). Ontario municipal elections:
    Voting trends and determinants of electoral success in a Canadian
    province. *Canadian Journal of Political Science, 30*(3), 539–553.
Laakso, M., & Taagepera, R. (1979). Effective number of parties: A measure
    with application to West Europe. *Comparative Political Studies, 12,* 3–27.
    https://doi.org/10.1177/001041407901200101

LeDuc, L., Clarke, H., Jenson, J, & Pammett, J. (1984). Partisan instability in Canada: Evidence from a new panel study. *American Political Science Review, 78*(2), 470–484. https://doi.org/10.2307/1963376

Levitt, S. D., & Wolfram, C. D. (1997). Decomposing the sources of incumbency advantage in the U.S. House. *Legislative Studies Quarterly, 22*(1), 45–60.

McGregor, R. M., Anderson, C., & Pruysers, S. (Forthcoming). Partisanship, motivated reasoning and the notwithstanding clause: The case of provincially imposed redistricting in the City of Toronto. *Commonwealth and Comparative Politics.*

McGregor, R. M., Moore, A., & Stephenson, L. (2016). Political attitudes and behaviour in a non-partisan environment: Toronto 2014. *Canadian Journal of Political Science, 49*(2), 311–333. doi:10.1017/S0008423916000573

McGregor, R. M., Moore, A., & Stephenson, L. (2021). *Electing a mega-mayor: Toronto 2014.* University of Toronto Press.

Moore, A., McGregor, R. M., & Stephenson, L. (2017). Paying attention and the incumbency effect: Voting behaviour in the 2014 Toronto municipal election. *International Political Science Review, 38*, 85–98. https://doi.org/10.1177%2F0192512115616268

Pagliaro, J. (2016). Toronto City Council approves addition of three new members. *Toronto Star.* https://www.thestar.com/news/city_hall/2016/11/09/council-to-add-three-new-members-with-ward-boundary-change.html

Pagliaro, J. (2018). Toronto City Council candidates re-file paperwork for 25-ward election. *Toronto Star.* https://www.thestar.com/news/toronto-election/2018/09/20/city-council-candidates-re-file-paperwork-for-25-ward-election.html

Pagliaro, J. (2019). Toronto asks Supreme Court of Canada to overturn Doug Ford government's council cut. *Toronto Star.* https://www.thestar.com/news/city_hall/2019/11/15/toronto-asks-supreme-court-to-overturn-doug-ford-governments-council-cut.html

Pagliaro, J. (2020). Supreme Court of Canada agrees to hear Toronto's appeal of cuts to City Council. *Toronto Star.* https://www.thestar.com/news/city_hall/2020/03/26/supreme-court-of-canada-agrees-to-hear-torontos-appeal-of-cut-to-city-council.html

Rieti, J. (2018). Councillors, Ontario opposition attack Premier Doug Ford's Toronto council cuts. *CBC News.* 30 July. https://www.cbc.ca/news/canada/toronto/toronto-city-council-ford-horwath-1.4766834

Russell, A. (2018). Ontario premier Doug Ford plans to invoke notwithstanding clause. *Global News.* https://globalnews.ca/news/4438198/notwithstanding-clause-doug-ford-bill-5-toronto-city-council

Stephenson L., McGregor, R. M., & Moore, A. (2018) Sins of the brother: Partisanship and accountability in Toronto 2014. In S. Breux and J. Couture

(Eds.), *Accountability and responsiveness at the local level: Views from Canada.* McGill–Queen's University Press.

Toronto Ward Boundary Review. (2016). Supplementary report. https://static1.squarespace.com/static/53bc0914e4b0eb57996e4dee/t/5807a5ef20099ecb24249b07/1476 896247228/TWBR.SupplementaryReport.161014.pdf

Walks, R. A. (2004). Place of residence, party preferences and political attitudes in Canadian cities and suburbs. *Journal of Urban Affairs, 26*(3), 269–295. https://doi.org/10.1111/j.0735-2166.2004.00200.x

Walks, R. A. (2005). The city–suburban cleavage in Canadian federal politics. *Canadian Journal of Political Science, 38*(2), 383–413.

Walks, R. A. (2013). Metropolitan political ecology and contextual effects in Canada. In J. M. Sellers, D. Kübler, M. Walter-Rogg, & R. A. Walks (Eds.), *The political ecology of the metropolis.* ECPR Press.

9 Winnipeg

AARON A. MOORE

In 2014, voter turnout in the Winnipeg municipal election hit 50%, a recent high for turnout in that city. The electorate had been galvanized by an opportunity to elect a new mayor – the highly unpopular incumbent, Sam Katz, had chosen not to run – and to shake up City Council. What's more, the candidates for mayor included former NDP MLA and MP Judy Wasylycia-Leis as well as two dynamic newcomers to the political realm, Robert-Falcon Ouellette, an Indigenous candidate later elected to the House of Commons, and the eventual victor, Brian Bowman, who would become the city's first Métis mayor. Much of the Bowman's dazzle had worn off by the time he announced his bid for re-election in 2018, but there were no high-profile challengers for his position – in particular, there was no strong candidate on the left to oppose him. From its onset, the 2018 Winnipeg municipal election looked likely to be a snooze-fest; the incumbent mayor appeared poised to win re-election easily. The only outstanding question early on in the campaign was whether the mayor would retain a majority of support on council, for a number of his strongest supporters had chosen not to seek re-election or faced stiff competition in their own races.

The perception that the 2018 election was a *fait accompli* was evident in early news stories that focused on the mayor's refusal to campaign throughout the first two thirds of the nearly six-month campaign period. Journalists chafed at the lack of major stories and often had to focus on the outlandish proposals of some of the fringe mayoral candidates, such as the one for a "reverse toll-road" to the city's North End (Sanders and Thorpe, 2018). For much of the early campaign, the media focused on the mayor's main challenger, Jenny Motkaluk, and her repeated attacks on the mayor. This changed, however, when Bowman decided to support the inclusion of a non-binding plebiscite on the ballot to decide the future of the Portage and Main intersection. Bowman had promised to open the intersection to pedestrian traffic during his 2014 campaign. During the 2018 campaign, his opponents on council, in an apparent attempt to undermine support for the mayor in the city's suburbs, pushed for a binding plebiscite on the issue. Ultimately, to prevent the issue from driving a wedge through his support, Bowman gave in to the pressure from the councillors. The plebiscite on whether or not to open Portage and Main to pedestrians became the main focus of the news media, and a major point of division between the mayor and his main rival.

In the end, however, voters did not rush to the polls for the opportunity to vote in the city's first plebiscite in more than three decades (contrary to the positive effect of plebiscites on turnout in many other elections) (CBC News, 2018). Voter turnout dropped by 7 points from 2014, and the mayor easily won re-election. Furthermore, the mayor's majority on council remained intact: his main supporters all won re-election, while those who had chosen not to run again were replaced by new mayoral allies. This chapter examines the campaign, issues, and election results for the 2018 Winnipeg municipal election as well as the correlates of mayoral vote choice that year. The final section focuses on the growing issue of crime and safety and its effect on voters, as well as the Portage and Main plebiscite and what it tells us about the importance of plebiscites in elections. The case of Portage and Main suggests that plebiscites may influence turnout only when the issue is important to most voters.

Election Overview

The Mayoral Campaign

In 2014, Brian Bowman turned politics in Winnipeg on its head, first by breaking away from a packed field to become the leading right-wing candidate, despite the presence of a number of higher-profile conservatives, and then by handily defeating early front-runner Judy Wasylycia-Leis, in the process becoming the city's first Métis mayor. Bowman, the former chair of the Winnipeg Chamber of Commerce, entered the campaign as a political neophyte, in contrast to the early front-runner, Wasylycia-Leis, a former provincial minister, federal MP, and past mayoral candidate. Bowman, along with fellow newcomer Robert-Falcon Ouellette, managed to flip the script of the campaign – which in the early going focused on good stewardship and fiscal responsibility – by proposing a bold new vision for the city and galvanizing voter interest in that vision.

Early in his tenure as mayor, Bowman was often compared to other high-profile visionary mayors, such as Calgary's Naheed Nenshi. He acquired this reputation based in part on his 2014 campaign promises. Among others things, he had promised to complete six new BRT lines by 2030, attract new high-rise development and residents to the city's downtown, rejuvenate the city's famous Portage and Main intersection by opening it up to pedestrians, and keep property tax increases at or below inflation (Brodbeck, 2014). By the start of the 2018 campaign, however, much of the lustre of his grand vision had worn off as the reality of the city's shaky finances set in during his first term. During the 2018 campaign, the mayor championed himself as a fiscally responsible builder of roads rather than the visionary he once was (Kives, 2018c). Early promises to govern differently by allowing council to choose the chairs of different standing committees and elect the members of the mayor's Executive Policy Committee (EPC) also fell to the side, as Bowman flexed his authority to appoint the EPC and committee chairs so as to maintain a majority of support on council (Moore, 2014). His use of the "EPC+2" (members of the EPC plus the deputy and assistant deputy mayors) as a pseudo-caucus resulted in the emergence of an unofficial opposition comprised of councillors who either had been cast out of his inner circle or had never been part of it. These councillors would prove to be his biggest opponents during the election, as they used perceived slights against different areas of the city to rile up their constituents.

The mayor's popularity had dropped significantly since 2014. Between the fall of 2015 and the summer of 2018, his approval rating declined from a high of 77% to just over 50%, suggesting some vulnerability going into the 2018 election (Kives, 2018b). However, the 2018 mayoral campaign was marked by the absence of any high-profile candidate to oppose him. Jenny Motkaluk, a lawyer, would eventually become his main challenger – backed, by some accounts, by housing developers opposed to the mayor's introduction of impact fees (such fees are a form of development charge – municipalities apply development charges on each new building in their jurisdiction in order to pay for the necessary infrastructure to service the new development). Motkaluk entered the race as a complete unknown and spent the majority of her campaign attempting to raise her profile among the electorate. Thus, she began the campaign at a serious disadvantage, exacerbated by the fact that she was running to the right of a centre-right mayor, which further limited her appeal among Winnipeggers.

In some respects, Winnipeg's 2018 mayoral election mirrored those in many other cities included in this volume (such as Calgary, Montreal, and Toronto), in that only two competitive candidates were running for mayor. Winnipeg is unique among these cities, however, as no noteworthy candidate ran on the left of the political spectrum. According to news media and pundits, the absence of a prominent left-leaning mayoral candidate likely reflected the potential candidates' assessment of their chances. Bowman's support had dropped, but he was still the incumbent mayor and still enjoyed 50% support (Santin, 2018b). Winnipeggers perceived both the incumbent and his main challenger as being to the right of centre; respondents to our survey assigned Bowman a value of 5.3 on a left–right scale – where 1 is the far left and 10 is the far right – while assigning Motkaluk a 6.3.

Initially, Bowman's major Achilles heel appeared to be his support for the opening of Portage and Main to pedestrians, a stance that was deeply unpopular outside the city's downtown (Kives, 2018a) and among the suburbanite base that had elected him mayor in 2014. Jenny Motkaluk and the mayor's opponents on council attempted to use his pledge to open the intersection as a wedge issue early on in the campaign. Two of the mayor's strongest opponents on City Council began to push him to hold a plebiscite on the issue, hoping to further alienate voters from him (Santin, 2018a). The mayor, however, unexpectedly agreed to hold the plebiscite; apparently, he hoped to mitigate the issue's effect on his re-election (Sanders, 2018).

Motkaluk offered voters few new policies, focusing instead on those of the present mayor that she would terminate if she was elected. Her promises included an end to property tax increases earmarked for infrastructure, cancellation of the expansion of the city's fledgling bus rapid transit (BRT) system, and an end to impact fees. She portrayed herself as the better option between two fiscally conservative candidates. Once it became clear that these promises would not be enough to defeat Bowman, and as the effect of the methamphetamine crisis in the city became more apparent, she began to attack the mayor on issues of crime and safety.

Council Races

From the start of the 2018 campaign, a Bowman victory looked to be a foregone conclusion. However, changes in ward boundaries and the higher than typical number of wards with no incumbents meant that council would have a new look again – only four years after Winnipeggers elected 7 new councillors to the 15-member City Council, unseating three incumbents in the process. Beyond the potential to add new blood to council, and the usual competitiveness of open races, the elections had the potential to substantially shift the balance of power in favour of the mayor's opponents. Of the four councillors who chose not to run for re-election in 2018, three had been regular members of the mayor's EPC and among his closest allies. Meanwhile, changes to ward boundaries meant that another of his inner circle was facing off against a fellow incumbent. Scott Gillingham, chair of council's budget committee, was running against Shawn Dobson, one of the mayor's fiercest critics, in the new St James Ward. In the wake of the boundary changes, Dobson's old ward of St Charles, on the far western edge of the city, had ceased to exist, having been replaced by a new ward, St Norbert, in the rapidly growing south.

When the Province of Manitoba dismantled Winnipeg's commissioner system in 1998, it had created the EPC in order to strengthen the city's mayoral office. The Province of Manitoba created the EPC in 1998 in order to strengthen the mayor of Winnipeg as it dismantled the city's commissioner system. The EPC comprises six councillors and the mayor. The mayor appoints council members to the committee, and each member serves as the chair of one of six standing committees. The mayor's authority to appoint councillors to these plum positions, which include additional pay, provides him or her with the sticks and carrots necessary to regularly secure 43.8% of the council vote (the mayor plus the other six members of the EPC). Over the course of his first term in office, Bowman further cemented his hold on council by including two other councillors, the deputy mayor and acting deputy, in discussions with the EPC, much to the chagrin of the seven remaining councillors, who were barred from these meetings. Of course, the mayor's ability to reward and punish councillors by including or excluding them from his inner circle only works so long as there are enough councillors willing to work with the mayor and accept the positions proffered to them. With one strong ally facing another incumbent, and five open races, there was a strong possibility that the mayor would face a much more hostile council in 2018.

Despite the importance of the council elections, however, there was limited media coverage of the individual races. In most of the city's wards, there was an absence of clear ideological divides, so voters had little to go on except name recognition. Most of the incumbents running in the election focused on their support for or opposition to the mayor and their own track records. Their main contribution to the 2018 election campaign was largely to the mayoral race, where many either attacked or supported the mayor on issues such as the opening of Portage and Main, infrastructure funding, and crime and safety.

Issues and Events

At the start of the campaign, the election looked like it would largely be a referendum on Brian Bowman. The mayor chose to forgo campaigning until the very end of the election period and offered few new policies, likely in hope of limiting his exposure to attack from his political opponents. Despite his efforts to steer clear of divisive topics, however, two issues eventually came to dominate media coverage of the election – if not the minds of all voters. Early in the campaign, Jenny Motkaluk and two of the mayor's most vociferous opponents on council, Janice Lukes and Jeff Browaty, focused their attention on the mayor's controversial call to reopen Portage and Main to pedestrians.

In the 1970s, under pressure from local property owners, the city installed barriers around the iconic intersection to prevent pedestrians from crossing, as well as to push pedestrian traffic into the underground shops and paths linking the office buildings in the downtown core. In proposing to reopen the intersection to pedestrians, Bowman hoped to jump-start revitalization in the area by making it more accessible and inviting for people working, living, and visiting the downtown. The mayor was backed in part by the same property owners who had championed the closing of the intersection in the first place, as they sought to address limited accessibility in the underground walkways and the need for substantial repairs to the underground, as well as to bring life back to the ground floors of their buildings.

While the proposal seemed popular among urbanists, planners, downtown residents, and the city's newspaper of record, the *Winnipeg Free Press*, many commuters who regularly drove through the intersection on their way to work vehemently opposed it, citing fears of "safety" and increased gridlock. Many other critics balked at the millions of dollars that it would cost to reopen the intersection. Bowman's opponents seemed intent on using the issue to increase their own support and weaken that of the mayor. In the absence of any other stories during the early days of the campaign, the city's news media jumped on the issue, identifying it as the key one in the election. When the mayor relented to pressure from councillors Lukes and Browaty by supporting a non-binding plebiscite on the issue – and promising to abide by the result – the media coverage surrounding it grew exponentially. A campaign supporting the reopening of the intersection began in earnest and continued throughout the election. By contrast, no organized campaign emerged for the No side.

Up until the last two months of the campaign, the 2018 Winnipeg election looked poised to be the Portage and Main election, as few other issues appeared to animate the media or the electorate – even as many voters expressed dismay over the ongoing debate about the intersection. This changed as the rise in crime related to methamphetamine use in the city came to the fore in the lead-up to Election Day. The end of the campaign period coincided with growing awareness that an epidemic had gripped the city. As Figure 9.1 demonstrates, in

Figure 9.1. Issue importance in the 2018 Winnipeg election

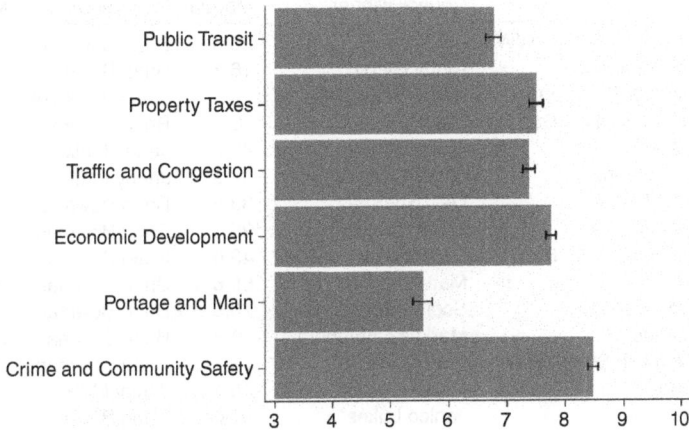

the weeks leading up to election, voters responding to our survey identified crime and community safety as the most important issue in the city – while relegating the opening of Portage and Main to sixth out of six issues available to them. Jenny Motkaluk, so far unable to make any gains on the mayor in the polls, grasped at the issue, vehemently attacking the mayor for his failure to address the growing prevalence of crime and meth use.

Despite the attacks, however, candidates offered few ideas about addressing either issue. Media coverage placed little blame for the problem on the city's government. Most articles noted the need for provincial and federal funding and direction to combat the meth crisis. Nevertheless, crime and community safety was a growing concern as the election neared.

The Election Results

Table 9.1 breaks down the results of the mayoral and council races in the city. Come election day, Brian Bowman was quickly declared the winner by news media outlets, handily beating Jenny Motkaluk by a margin of 17.6 points and with 53.3% of the popular vote, 6 points higher than his support in 2014. The 2018 mayoral election in Winnipeg is a testament to the power of incumbency and the importance of competitive races for turnout. Bowman's re-election was never really in doubt, and his choice to not campaign through much of the campaign period and to offer few new policies shows he was largely focused on not rocking the boat in

Table 9.1. Election results, by ward

Ward	Council winner	Margin	Mayoral winner	Margin
1. Charleswood–Tux.–WW	Kevin Klein	26.6	Brian Bowman	27.0
2. Daniel McIntyre	Cindy Gilroy*	16.1	Brian Bowman	38.4
3. Elmwood–E. Kildonan	Jason Schreyer*	9.6	Jenny Motkaluk	5.6
4. Fort-Rouge–Fort Garry	Sherri Rollins	3.9	Brian Bowman	48.0
5. Mynarski	Ross Eadie*	48.7	Jenny Motkaluk	4.5
6. North Kildonan	Jeff Browaty*	54.3	Jenny Motkaluk	0.8
7. Old Kildonan	Devi Sharma*	33.5	Brian Bowman	0.3
8. Point Douglas	Vivian Santos	25.8	Brian Bowman	4.5
9. River Heights–E. Ft.	John Orlikow*	43.6	Brian Bowman	42.7
Garry	Matt Allard*	65.6	Brian Bowman	25.9
10. St Boniface	Scott Gillingham*	20.6	Brian Bowman	6.4
11. St James	Markus Chambers	3.6	Brian Bowman	22.8
12. St Norbert–Seine River	Brian Mayes*	78.7	Brian Bowman	21.0
13. St Vital	Shawn Nason	20.4	Jenny Motkaluk	8.4
14. Transcona	Janice Lukes*	ACC	Brian Bowman	26.2
15. Waverly West		Overall	Brian Bowman*	17.6

Note: An asterisk signifies an incumbent.

2018. This tactic, and his weak opposition, likely accounted for a steep drop in voter turnout from 50% in 2014 to 42% in 2018.

Yet there was a clear geographical divide in support for the mayor, as evidenced in Figure 9.2, suggesting a shift in support from the 2014 election. Despite his victory, there was a clear geographical divide in support for the mayor, as evidenced in Figure 9.2, suggesting a shift in support from the 2014 election. In that year, Bowman won the popular vote throughout the city's far-flung suburbs, losing only in the North End and the city centre. By contrast, in 2018, Bowman's strongest support came from the city centre, and while he led in the suburban regions to the south and west, Jenny Motkaluk outperformed him in the city's northern and eastern suburbs, areas that had strongly supported him in 2014.

There are likely a number of reasons for this shift in Bowman's support. First, absent a strong candidate to his left, most voters in the city centre who typically supported left-of-centre candidates had the option of voting for Bowman, a candidate viewed as just slightly right of centre, or Motkaluk, who was further to the right. Second, the opening of Portage and Main was popular with most voters in the city's downtown and the surrounding neighbourhood, possibly driving more voters his way. By contrast, voters in the north and east of the city appeared to be punishing the mayor based on the perception that he was not delivering the same infrastructure investment in those areas that he had delivered in the south and west. Commuters in the city's north were also the most likely to be negatively affected by the reopening of Portage and Main.

Figure 9.2. Vote share for Bowman, by ward

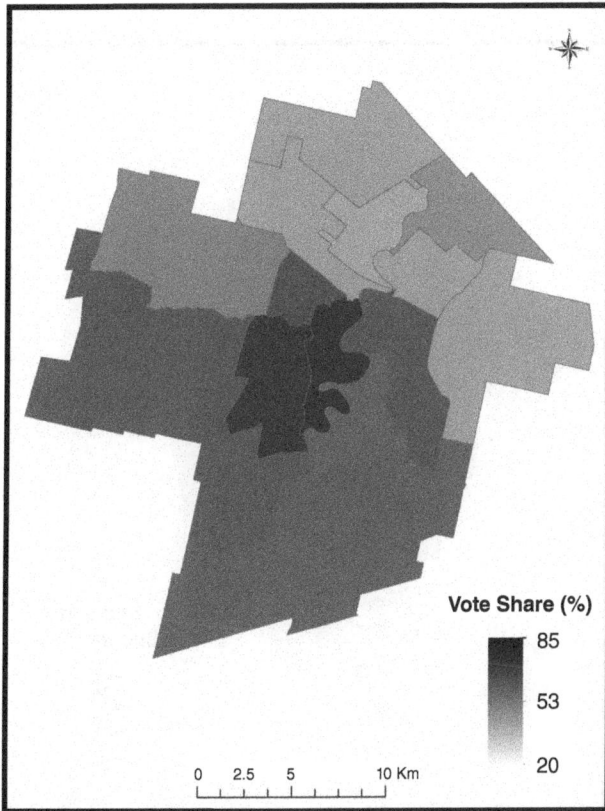

As with the mayor, nine of the ten incumbent councillors who ran for re-election won by double-digit margins. The outcome of the council campaigns, again, points to the incumbency advantage in municipal elections. St Vital's Brian Mayes led the way, winning by a margin of 78.7 points. Only incumbent Jason Schreyer faced any real competition, even though Scott Gillingham was competing against a fellow incumbent in Shaun Dobson, the councillor orphaned after the change in ward boundaries.

A number of the open races also resulted in blowouts. Kevin Klein, Vivian Santos, and Shawn Nason won their wards by 20 or more points. For Klein and Santos, name recognition and endorsements likely paved the way to victory. Klein was the former publisher and CEO of the *Winnipeg Sun* and had been endorseed by the city's strong Firefighters Union. Vivian

Figure 9.3. Percentage of electorate in favour of opening Portage and Main to pedestrians, by ward

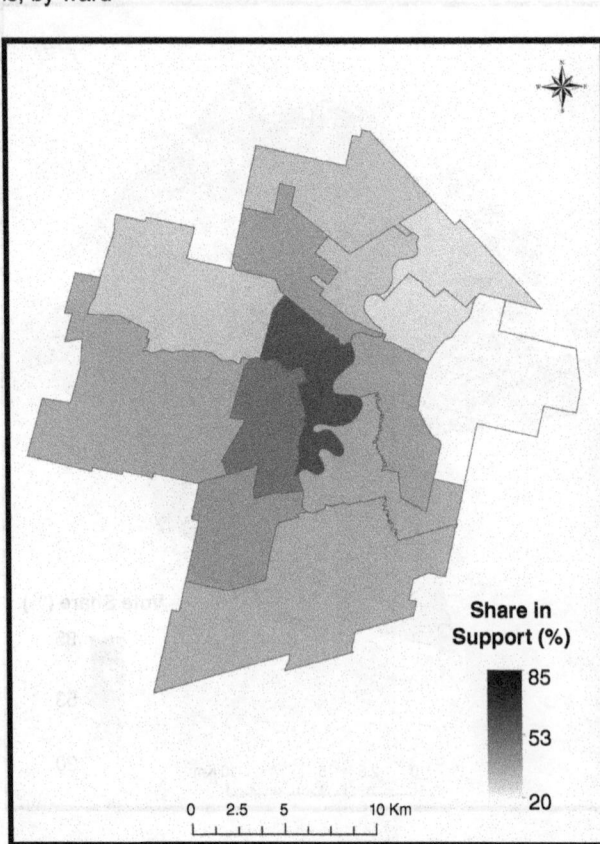

Santos, who had worked for Mayor Bowman and served as former Point Douglas councillor Mike Pagtakhan's chief of staff, likely benefited from her ties to and endorsement by the popular outgoing councillor. The other two open races were the only ones that were truly competitive: Sherri Rollins and Markus Chambers squeaked out their victories by less than 4 points.

After the election, the mayor's dominance of council appeared intact. Most of the mayor's EPC+2 remained, with Rollins replacing the outgoing councillor for Fort-Rouge, Jenny Gerbasi, on the EPC, and Chambers and Santos filling the roles of deputy and assistant deputy mayor, respectively. The final results of the Winnipeg 2018 municipal election suggested that the political dynamics on council would remain little changed despite five new councillors.

Lastly, the proposal to reopen Portage and Main to pedestrians was soundly defeated, with 65% of voters voting no. As demonstrated in Figure 9.3, there was a very clear geographic divide, with a majority of voters in the city centre voting yes, and a majority in the suburbs voting no.

Vote Choice

This section takes a more in-depth look at the determinants of voting for or against Brian Bowman in the mayoral election by examining the marginal effects of different variables on vote choice. Figure 9.4 breaks down the findings for each model. Model A focuses solely on demographic variables; B adds ideology in the form of social and economic conservatism; C adds economic evaluation; and, finally, Model D adds policy issues. Model A shows which demographic variables influenced votes for or against Bowman. The outcome of this model is very different from the same model for many of the other cities, perhaps signifying that some factor was present in Winnipeg that was absent elsewhere. Winnipeg is the only city where there was a significant and positive relationship between being female and voting for the victor (Bowman). It is also the only city, aside from Calgary, where university education factored into vote choice. Beyond these two variables, voters in the 35–64 age range were less likely to vote for the incumbent mayor. Income, homeownership, and being a visible minority did not matter.

In Model B, which includes two measures of conservatism, Winnipeg is again an outlier: age ceases to matter, but the effects of gender and education remain. The mayor did poorly among economically conservative voters, which is consistent with other cities where the more left-wing candidate won. However, Winnipeg is one of only two cities where social conservatism mattered in the election. As in Calgary, socially conservative voters were less likely to vote for the winner. Given that voters in Calgary perceived Mayor Nenshi as left-wing, such a result was not entirely surprising in that city. However, Winnipeg voters perceived Bowman and Motkaluk as fairly close ideologically (relative to the margins in many of the other cities).

Model C adds economic evaluation to the analysis. As with a number of other cities in which an incumbent was running, a positive outlook on the economy – which had performed well during Bowman's first term in office – made voters more likely to vote for him again, which supports Anderson et al.'s (2017) findings. As with the addition of the conservatism variables, the inclusion of the economic factor did not erase the influence of gender and education. In fact, the importance of gender *increases* in this model. The effect of social conservatism remains.

Figure 9.4. Vote choice for Bowman – marginal effects

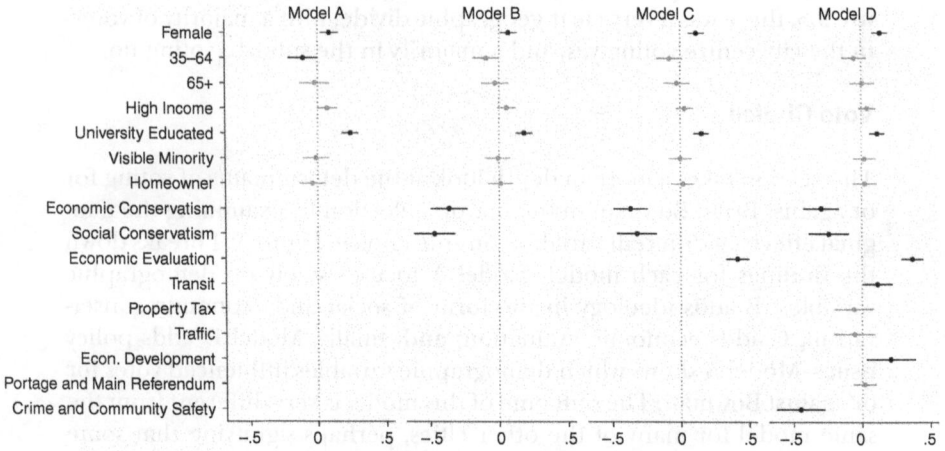

Notes: Entries report marginal effects and 95% confidence intervals. Coefficients in black are statistically significant at p < 0.1.

Finally, Model D adds issue importance to the analysis. The mayor fared well among voters who identified transit and economic development as important and very poorly among voters who identified crime and community safety as an important issue. The issue of property taxes and traffic had no appreciable effect on vote choice in Winnipeg. More importantly, the inclusion of these additional variables did not erase the importance of gender, university education, or social conservatism.

There is no obvious or easy explanation for these outcomes. Given that Bowman's main opponent was a woman, affinity voting clearly had little effect on the race's outcome and cannot account for the observed role of gender. Women and university-educated voters were more likely to vote for left-wing candidates, and while respondents did not perceive Bowman as left-wing, he was further to the left than his main adversary. However, the addition of two ideological variables (economic and social conservatism) did not erode the importance of either gender or education. In addition, issue importance did not significantly affect the importance of gender, education, or social conservatism. So we can conclude that the importance of different issues cannot account for these findings. That leaves one possibility: voters' assessment of the candidates themselves.

Toward the end of the campaign, many media accounts of Jenny Motkaluk suggested that she was being too negative and focusing too much on attacking the mayor rather than presenting her own policy ideas. Motkaluk's behaviour may have negatively affected university-educated and female voters' perceptions of her as a candidate, thus driving support to Bowman, who largely avoided similar mudslinging and focused on the positives of his first term in office. Research into both of these possibilities is very limited. One study by Brooks (2010) has found that gender affects how voters respond to negative campaigning. However, her findings also suggest that negative campaigning is more likely to motivate men to vote. Brooks found little evidence that women are more likely to punish candidates for negative campaigning. Regardless, both educated voters and woman were more likely to vote for Bowman in this election after all other variables were considered, a significant deviation from outcomes in the other eight cities.

Social conservatives' tendency to vote against the mayor may be easier to explain. While Motkaluk and Bowman agreed that the city needed more safe consumption sites, during the election they differed in their support for the construction of a rehab centre in a middle-class suburb. Bowman supported the plan, which was highly unpopular with some local residents, while Motkaluk opposed it, though mainly due to the location and lack of community consultation, not out of opposition to rehabilitation programs *per se*. Bowman also championed policies throughout his first term in office that encouraged diversity and inclusion, and he marched in the city's Gay Pride Parade. Motkaluk did not attack such policies, but neither did she focus on them in her campaign. Though few of these issues resonated in the campaign, social-conservative voters may have felt that Bowman was too different ideologically during his tenure as mayor to gain their support.

Crime, Safety, and Pedestrian Crossings

By the summer of 2018, the news media in Winnipeg and Mayor Bowman's opponents had zeroed in on the opening of Portage and Main to pedestrians as the election's defining issue. We too identified the issue as a key one when composing our survey questions for the city. However, as Figure 9.1 shows, by the time we began collecting data in the last months of the election, voters had relegated Portage and Main to sixth out of six issues, while placing crime and community safety at the top. Clearly, by election time, this issue was not defining the election.

In fact, polls conducted by CBC News and Probe Research before and during the election suggest that for the vast majority of voters in the city,

Table 9.2. Most important issues to Winnipeggers, by percentage of respondents

December 2017		August 2018	
1. Infrastructure/roads/potholes	17%	1. Crime/violence/vandalism	24%
2. Health care/Medicare	16%	2. Infrastructure/roads/ potholes	17%
3. Crime/violence/vandalism	11%	3. Poverty/homelessness	10%
4. Poverty/homelessness	9%	4. Morality issues	9%
5. Morality issues (pornography, drugs, prostitution)	3%	5. Health care/Medicare	3%

Source: Probe Research 2018, https://www.cbc.ca/news/canada/manitoba/crime
-winnipeg-civic-election-poll-1.4821219.

opening Portage and Main to pedestrians was never a pressing issue. Table 9.2 compares the top five results of CBC News/Probe Research polls carried out in December 2017 and August 2018. The two polls asked Winnipeggers to identify the most important issues in their city. The differences between the two polls are quite striking. In December 2017, infrastructure repair was the leading issue, with 17% of respondents identifying it as a top concern, while health care, an issue largely within the purview of the province, came second. Crime and poverty were third and fourth, respectively, and "morality issues" was a distant fifth. The question of opening Portage and Main did not even register with voters.

By contrast, by August 2018, close to one quarter of respondents were identifying crime/violence/vandalism as a top concern, a 13-point jump in eight months, and references to morality issues, including drug use, had tripled. If any issue dominated the mayoral campaign in Winnipeg, our own findings and that of the polls conducted leading up to election suggest that crime and safety was it. Meanwhile, after months of media coverage and the promise of a plebiscite on the issue, Portage and Main still failed to crack the top five most important issues – although the pollsters noted in a footnote that 2% of respondents had identified it as important.

This section addresses the failure of the Portage and Main plebiscite to generate voter interest, contrary to what one would expect from the inclusion of a referendum in an election, and whether it ultimately mattered in the mayoral and council races. It then examines the issue of crime and community safety, investigating why it became such an important issue as well as whether and how it affected voting behaviour.

Portage and Main, or the Referendum That Wasn't

While voter fatigue resulting from the overuse of direct democracy (plebiscites and referendums) does exist – the most notable examples coming from Switzerland, where constant use of direct democracy has resulted in abysmally low turnout – the limited research on the impact of referendums and plebiscites on voter turnout in municipal elections suggests that they tend to increase voter participation. Hajnal and Lewis's (2003) analysis of voter turnout at the local level in California, where the use of direct democracy is common, found that municipal elections with local ballot questions typically led to increases in turnout 4% higher than in elections where such questions were absent. In a recent Canadian example, a stand-alone referendum on transit taxes held throughout Metro Vancouver in 2015, turnout in the City of Vancouver was just over 50%. In comparison, turnout in the 2014 and 2018 Vancouver municipal elections was 43% and 39% respectively, providing some evidence that Hajnal and Lewis's findings may have applicability in Canadian municipalities.

Given all this, the 7-point drop in voter turnout in Winnipeg between 2014 and 2018 is perhaps surprising. It is possible that the inclusion of the question on the ballot did raise turnout there, suggesting that it would have been even lower had there been no referendum. However, as noted earlier, the issue of Portage and Main did not appear to resonate with most voters, so it is equally possible that the Portage and Main referendum was an outlier when compared to ballot initiatives in other local elections. Model D in Figure 9.4 also suggests that the issue had little effect, overall, on support for the mayor. Perhaps the Portage and Main referendum is evidence that the inclusion of plebiscite on a municipal election ballot only influences turnout when the issue is salient to voters.

To examine what, if any, influence the plebiscite had on turnout, we first consider the determinants of turnout for the referendum, the mayoral race, and the council races. These votes were all held on the same day and were included on the same ballot, but due to voter roll-off, the number of voters for each race varied slightly, allowing for comparison. The modest ballot roll-off between the vote for mayor and the referendum – 212,303 voted for mayor, compared to 206,503 who voted in the plebiscite – itself suggests that the opportunity to vote on the question of opening Portage and Main was unable to lift voter turnout to the levels seen in 2014. Figure 9.5 includes the findings for three models. Each model includes the same demographic, ideological, economic, and issue variables we included in Model D in Figure 9.4 (only the results for the issues are shown), with the addition of a variable for voters supporting the opening of Portage and Main. We added this variable to determine whether supporting the reopening of Portage and Main had a positive effect on turnout – the supposition being that proponents of opening the intersection might have been more motivated to vote.

Figure 9.5. Correlates of voter turnout in the 2018 Winnipeg municipal election, by race

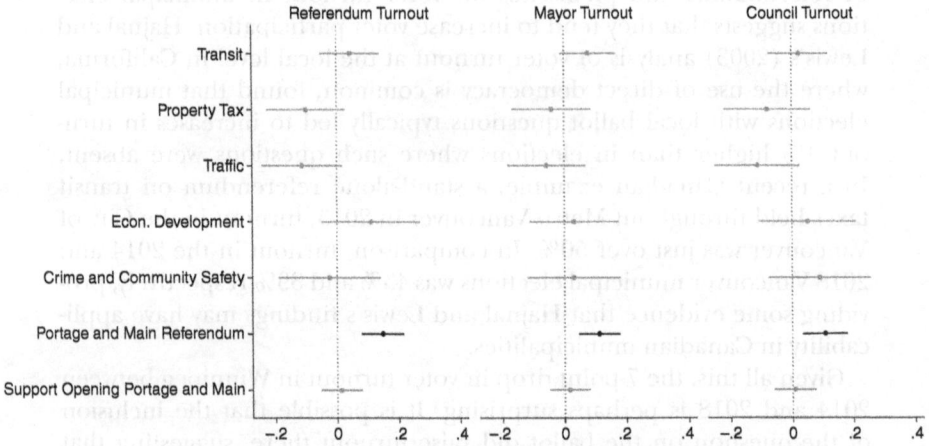

Notes: Entries report marginal effects and 95% confidence intervals. All models include socio-demographic, ideological, and retrospection controls. Coefficients in black are statistically significant at p < 0.1.

The purpose of this analysis is to examine whether voters' attitudes regarding the importance of the plebiscite or their position on Portage and Main had an effect on turnout. If either had a positive relationship with turnout, it might suggest that, even though turnout decreased in 2018, the inclusion of the plebiscite dampened this decline. In other words, had the vote on Portage and Main not been on the ballot, turnout might have dropped even further.

Naturally, we would expect the importance of the plebiscite to influence turnout *in* the plebiscite. However, if the importance of the plebiscite influenced turnout in the mayoral and council elections, this would be evidence that that plebiscite influenced *overall* turnout. As Figure 9.5 reveals, opinions on the importance of the plebiscite did have a positive relationship with voter turnout in the council and mayoral races. In fact, it was the only issue that had any relationship with turnout. However, *support* for the opening of Portage and Main had no effect on turnout in any of the three votes. This finding suggests that supporters were no more or less motivated than opponents to vote on the issue or in the council and mayoral races. Given how few respondents mentioned Portage and Main as an important issue in the CBC News and Probe Research polls, this finding is not that surprising.

For the few voters who did care, the inclusion of the question did increase turnout, as the results in Figure 9.5 demonstrate. This finding calls into question the argument, best articulated by Hajnal and Lewis (2003), that direct democracy in and of itself has a positive influence on turnout. The case of Portage and Main suggests that a plebiscite may only influence turnout when the issue is important to most voters. The chance to vote directly on an issue of importance may well increase turnout, but the salience of the issue itself is key.

Crime and Community Safety in Winnipeg

Although Winnipeg has historically had a much higher crime rate than most other large cities in Canada – it has held the dubious title of Canada's murder capital on a number of occasions – crime there, as in much of the rest of Canada, was in decline for decades until the mid-2010s. The first noticeable change in this trend occurred in 2015, as the number of violent crimes and crime severity began to increase (CBC News, 2017). However, the issue did not seem to resonate with many Winnipeggers until crime stats for 2017 were released in July 2018, in the middle of the municipal election.

Purportedly fuelled by the growth in methamphetamine use, violent crime in 2017 increased by 7% over the previous year, while property crime went up by 9% and drug crimes by 15% (Keele, 2018). Following the release of these numbers, the news media in Winnipeg launched a sustained discussion on the issue that continued throughout the election. Eventually, Jenny Motkaluk, and some council candidates, adopted the issue as a means to attack the mayor – a tactic that may have worked, given the results in Figure 9.4. Voters who identified crime and community safety as a major issue in the election were far less likely to vote for Brian Bowman. This finding is interesting, as it is not clear what the mayor, or the council for that matter, could have done to prevent or address the problem, nor was it clear how other candidates would better tackle the issue.

Winnipeg has a Police Board comprised of appointees from the City of Winnipeg and the Province of Manitoba. This board, which relies heavily on the advice and direction of the Chief of Police, directs policing in the city – not City Council or the mayor. City Council sets the budget for the police, and history suggests it is loath to make cuts to that budget. Nevertheless, some voters clearly held the incumbent mayor responsible for the level of crime in the city.

In many ways, this finding parallels research findings on economic voting in cities, where voters hold mayors or councils responsible for the economic direction of the city despite the limited influence municipal governments have on economic growth. In fact, there is evidence of economic voting in Winnipeg: voters who viewed economic development as a major issue in the election were more likely to vote for the mayor. There are two possible explanations for the converse effect in the matter of crime and community safety in Winnipeg.

There is little reason to believe that voters preferred the policies on crime and safety proffered by other candidates to that of the mayor, as there was little difference between the candidates, who offered very few substantive proposals to address the issue. Motkaluk and third-place mayoral candidate Tim Diack did promote the use of detox facilities similar to drunk tanks to address meth use in the city, and Motkaluk promised a police task force on meth distribution. However, the latter policy is beyond the authority of the mayor to implement, and in any case, such a task force already existed in the city. Thus some voters were either unaware of the restraints on the municipality's ability to tackle the issue of crime and drug use, and/or they held the mayor accountable for the increase in crime in the city because it occurred during his tenure as mayor – a form of retrospective voting. Fortunately for Bowman, crime and community safety was not a salient enough issue to lead to his defeat in the election.

Conclusion

The 2018 Winnipeg municipal election was an outlier on many fronts when compared to the other seven elections discussed in this volume. It was the only election that included a plebiscite. It was the only election where gender and university education were factors in the mayoral contest in all circumstances, and while social conservatism also influenced the mayoral vote in Calgary, in Winnipeg it mattered despite the ideological proximity of the two leading candidates. Despite the uniqueness of the election, however, the 2018 Winnipeg municipal election also demonstrates why voters often lack interest in municipal races.

Despite declining approval ratings, Bowman appeared destined to win re-election from the onset of the election. As an incumbent facing no high-profile challengers, lukewarm support among the electorate was all Bowman needed to win. These symptoms all point towards a low-turnout election and offer clear evidence of an incumbency advantage. Although crime and community safety was the dominant issue for voters by the end of the campaign, and did affect vote choice, ultimately, the news media and the leading mayoral candidates repeatedly stressed that the city could do little to address the meth epidemic without the aid of more senior governments. As an issue, crime and community safety had no apparent impact on voter turnout, despite its importance to voters. By contrast, evaluations of the importance of the Portage and Main issue had no effect on vote choice, though it did have a relationship with turnout. The plebiscite's effect on turnout was limited, however, by the fact that the issue was of relatively little importance to Winnipeggers. Given the limited options in the mayoral election, a referendum on a topic few voters cared about, and candidates' inability to offer substantive solutions to the most important issue of the day, it is no surprise that turnout in Winnipeg in 2018 was lower than in the past.

REFERENCES

Anderson C., McGregor R. M, Moore A. A., & Stephenson L. B. (2017). Economic voting and multilevel governance: The case of Toronto. *Urban Affairs Review, 53*(1), 71–101.

Brodbeck, R. (2014). Bowman's got 96 promises. *Winnipeg Sun.* 8 November. https://winnipegsun.com/2014/11/08/so-many-promises-can-bowman -deliver-on-them/wcm/dde64ca7–3844–496f-805d-241c5414b3da

Brooks, D. J. (2010). A negativity gap? Voter gender, attack politics, and participation in American elections. *Politics and Gender, 6,* 319–341. https://doi.org/10.1017/S1743923X10000218

CBC News. (2017). "Continuing and worrying trend": Violent crime in Winnipeg rises, reports say. [Video File]. *CBC News Manitoba.* 24 July. https://www.cbc.ca/news/canada/manitoba/continuing-and-worrying -trend-violent-crime-in-winnipeg-rises-reports-say-1.4219982

CBC News. (2018). 42% voter turnout lowest for Winnipeg since 2006 election. *CBC News Manitoba.* 24 October. https://www.cbc.ca/news/canada /manitoba/winnipeg-election-2018-voter-turnout-1.4877474

Hajnal, Z. L., & Lewis, P. G. (2003). Municipal institutions and voter turnout in local elections. *Urban Affairs Review, 38*(5), 645–668. https://doi.org/10 .1177%2F1078087403038005002

Keele, J. (2018). Annual crime stats show substantial jump in 2017 for Winnipeg, Manitoba. *CTV News Winnipeg.* 23 July. https://winnipeg.ctvnews .ca/annual-crime-stats-show-substantial-jump-in-2017-for-winnipeg -manitoba-1.4023944

Kives, B. (2018a). "Deep, intense dislike for this idea" of opening Portage and Main, poll finds. *CBC News Manitoba.* 11 September. https://www.cbc.ca /news/canada/manitoba/portage-main-probe-poll-1.4818959

Kives, B. (2018b). Bowman leads Motkaluk 2-to-1 in mayoral poll, but majority of voters still undecided. *CBC News Manitoba.* 14 September. https://www.cbc .ca/news/canada/manitoba/winnipeg-mayor-poll-1.4822896

Kives, B. (2018c). Greying hair isn't the only change in candidate Brian Bowman. *CBC News Manitoba*. 16 October. https://www.cbc.ca/news /canada/manitoba/brian-bowman-feature-election-1.4862595

Moore, A. A. (2014). The tale of two mayors. [Op-ed]. *Winnipeg Free Press*. 17 September, A9.

Sanders, C. (2018). Mayor throws support behind proposed referendum on reopening Portage and Main." *Winnipeg Free Press*. 18 July. https:// www.winnipegfreepress.com/local/mayor-throws-support-behind-proposed -referendum-on-reopening-portage-and-main-488556851.html

Sanders, C., & Thorpe, R. (2018). Everything you need to know before you vote. *Winnipeg Free Press*. 24 October. https://www.winnipegfreepress.com /civicelection2018/voter-toolkit-498361801.html

Santin, A. (2018a). Councillors push for public vote on Portage–Main reopening. *Winnipeg Free Press*. 21 June. https://www.winnipegfreepress .com/local/councillors-push-for-public-vote-on-portage-main -reopening-486213631.html

Santin, A. (2018b). Whither the left? For the first time in years, there is no mayoral candidate endorsed by the Winnipeg Labour Council. *Winnipeg Free Press*. 10 May. https://www.winnipegfreepress.com/civicelection2018 /whither-the-left-495299051.html

10 Conclusion

JACK LUCAS AND R. MICHAEL McGREGOR

Each of the chapters in this book has provided a data-driven narrative of the fascinating elections that took place in eight of Canada's largest cities in 2017 and 2018: the surprising defeat of Montreal's incumbent mayor, Denis Coderre; the ongoing saga of John Tory versus "Ford Nation" in Toronto; the record-breaking turnout in Calgary; and much more. Each city's election helps us understand a particular corner of the urban political landscape, revealing many of the issues that matter to urban residents, the factors that shape municipal vote choice, and the variety of ways that big city elections play out in Canada.

The preceding chapters also illustrate the academic value of comparative urban election surveys like the Canadian Municipal Election Study. Taken together, the chapters reveal the range of questions that can now be tackled with individual-level survey data: the applicability of Pinard's theory of third-party emergence at the municipal level (chapter 3), the effects of affordability considerations and social pressure on local attitudes (chapter 5), the effects of electoral reform on municipal voting behaviour (chapter 6), how coalitions of local candidate support can change dramatically between elections (chapter 8), and the role of referendums in local elections (chapter 9). These analyses also speak to questions that could well be applied to other settings, such as how partisan perceptions influence decisions in non-partisan races (chapter 2), how competitive expectations affect vote choice (chapter 4), and how particularly diverse settings affect voter support for minority candidates (chapter 7). As a whole, the chapters speak to the two central questions in the field of voting behaviour: Why do electors vote (or not) (chapter 9)? And why do they vote the way they do (chapters 2, 3, 4, and 8)? They also speak to a third group of topics that these specific cities offer particular insights into, including pressure from peers (chapter 5), ballot structure (chapter 6), and population diversity (chapter 7). In all instances, local data enrich our understanding of these phenomena. Clearly, there is much that we can learn from the Canadian municipal voter.

In this concluding chapter, we will not try to provide a "nutshell" summary of the arguments in each chapter. Instead, we offer something slightly different: a synthesis of the evidence provided in the vote choice analyses in each of the eight cities. Each chapter contains material that is meant to allow for easy comparison across cities – issue importance plots, mayoral vote share maps, vote choice models – as well as material that is distinctive to each city and of special interest to the political scientists who authored the chapter. In this conclusion, we seek to synthesize the comparative materials to engage with a set of questions whose importance among urban political scientists continues to grow: What really shapes elections in Canada's big cities? For all their diversity, can we speak in general terms about voting behaviour in city elections? And how *distinctive* are city elections compared with elections at other scales? In these closing pages, we identify patterns in the correlates of vote choice in the eight cities considered in this volume and offer the beginnings of a made-in-Canada answer to these important questions.

What Shapes Elections? Three Urban Political Science Traditions

Scholars of urban politics and policy have long debated the distinctiveness of urban politics.[1] A first phase of postwar urban scholarship treated municipal politics as a microcosm of politics in general, a laboratory in which to explore fundamental questions about power and policy-making (Dahl, 1961). The debate between "elitists" and "pluralists" focused primarily on power and agenda-setting rather than electoral politics; it also rested on the assumption that lessons learned in the urban setting could be usefully generalized to other scales.

Since the 1980s, this foundational assumption has come under sustained attack from two distinct angles. The first line of attack, originating in the work of Paul Peterson (1981), argued that the political-economic context in which American cities are situated, combined with the constrained policy jurisdiction resulting from that context, makes local politics totally different from state or national politics. Unlike national politics, which is structured by political parties and buffeted by well-organized interest groups, cities "are generally a quiet arena of decision making where political leaders can give reasoned attention to the longer range interests of the city, taken as a whole" (Peterson, 1981, p. 109). Others have followed this reasoning, arguing that municipal elections tend to be non-ideological and are dominated by property owners who have the most at stake in the politics of urban growth – particularly because of local governments' reliance on property tax revenues (Fischel, 2005). Local elections are often little more than retrospective referendums on the managerial competence of the mayor and council (Oliver, 2012).

A second tradition of urban political science has been equally insistent on the distinctiveness of local politics, not so much as a result of the political-economic context but rather because of the distinctive role played by ethnic and racial groups in city elections. In low-turnout, low-information local elections, and in cities in which racial segregation is salient (Enos, 2017), many scholars expect ethno-racial appeals and racial affinity voting to be particularly important for election outcomes (Barreto, 2007; Collet, 2005; Doering, 2019; Kaufmann, 2004; Liu, 2003). In the most systematic study of this hypothesis to date, Hajnal and Trounstine (2014) draw on data from hundreds of American elections to argue that "it is race more than anything else that tends to dominate voter decision making in city elections" (86).

While these two attacks on the "cities as microcosm" approach are very different from each other, both articulate a "localist" view that cities are in important respects worlds unto themselves and that arguments developed to explain national voting behaviour may not be especially helpful for understanding local elections (Kaufmann, 2004). Recently, however, this localist argument has itself come under increasing criticism.[2] Drawing on a variety of data sources, a new generation of scholars has argued that local elections may in fact be more like national elections than the localists have suggested. In the United States, recent research has suggested that ideology is powerfully related to vote choice in local elections, both in big cities and in smaller municipalities (Sances, 2018), and that the importance of racial and gender cues fades when local voters are aware of candidates' partisanship, as they often are even in formally non-partisan races (Crowder-Meyer et al., 2019). In Canada, past research has similarly shown that partisanship and ideology shape municipal vote choice in ways that resemble their effects in provincial and federal elections (Cutler and Matthews, 2005; McGregor et al., 2016; Stephenson et al., 2018). Even Hajnal and Trounstine's (2014) analysis, while clearly demonstrating the importance of racial cleavages in many urban elections, also revealed that partisanship and ideology are often equally important for understanding local voting behaviour. This new body of research findings, Christopher Warshaw has recently concluded, "show[s] that local politics in the modern, polarized era is much more similar to other areas of American politics than previously believed" (2019, p. 1).

In this chapter, we contribute to this debate by synthesizing the vote choice analyses presented in each of the preceding chapters. Building on those analyses, we offer an interpretation of mayoral vote choice in big-city Canadian elections that seeks to assess each of the main traditions described above: the *retrospective managerial* tradition, the *urban identities* tradition, and the *national voting writ small* tradition. Unsurprisingly, given the success that each argument has enjoyed in urban political science, we find evidence to support all three traditions. But we also argue that in the Canadian context, evidence from the CMES ultimately supports a suitably modified version of the third approach – the "national voting writ small" argument.

Mayoral Vote Choice in City Elections: An Overview

To provide a basis for our analysis in this chapter, we begin with two summary tables. The first, Table 10.1, is inspired by a similar table in Hajnal and Trounstine (2014) and summarizes the average gap in support for the winning mayoral candidate between members of different groups. These values allow us to compare the magnitude of the effect of each variable on vote choice. This gap is simply the difference between the winning candidate's estimated vote share within the different groups, averaged across the eight cities. For example, if 60% of men supported the winning mayoral candidate and 50% of women supported the same candidate, this would be a gap of 10% between the two. We perform this calculation on many dimensions, including socio-demographic indicators, ideology, retrospective economic evaluations, and indicators of issue importance for the issues common to all cities.[3] In the table, we report the *average* gap across all eight cities. By comparing values across variables, we can use this table to compare the magnitude of the gap in vote choice between members of different groups of urban residents.

A cursory scan of the results in Table 10.1 provides readers with a "sneak preview" of the arguments we will soon be making about the determinants of vote choice in Canadian city elections, suggesting that the effects of ideology (economic conservatism, in particular) and retrospective economic perceptions outstrip those of any other factors included in the table. Socio-demographic indicators appear to have a weak relationship with vote choice. Issues appear to be somewhere between the two extremes.

Before we move on to the more detailed analysis, we need to introduce a second table, Table 10.2, which summarizes the results in the vote choice models in each of the preceding chapters. For each city, the table provides the direction – symbolized by plus (+) or minus (–) symbols – and the significance of the effects observed in the full vote choice models, symbolized by one, two, or three signs for the 90%, 95%, and 99%

Table 10.1. Average gaps in support for the winning mayoral candidate, by group

	Average difference (%)
Demographics	
Age (young, middle, old)	11
Income	4
Gender	6
Education	8
Visible minority	9
Homeowner	7
Ideology	
Social conservatism	14
Economic conservatism	23
Retrospection	
Economic retrospection	22
Issue importance	
Transit	13
Property taxes	19
Traffic and congestion	9
Economic development	10

confidence level, respectively. Note that these results are simply a distilled version of the final vote choice models in each chapter; the model includes socio-demographic characteristics, ideology, retrospective economic evaluations, and perceived issue importance.[4] We also include a summary column indicating how often each variable was significant as well as a summary row that shows the share of the model's variables that was significant in each city.

Whereas Table 10.1 provides information on the relative impact of each variable on vote choice, Table 10.2 clarifies which variables had a statistically significant relationship with vote choice across the eight cities. It also allows for easy comparison across cities in terms of both the number and type of variables associated with vote choice. Together, the tables help us adjudicate between the three theories of municipal voting that we described above.

Table 10.2 reveals several important findings. The first finding, drawn from the final column in the table, is that some variables are more consistently related to vote choice than others. In general, socio-demographic factors appear to be relatively unimportant for mayoral vote choice after adjusting for ideology, retrospection, and issue importance. The only socio-demographic variable that is significant in even half of the elections is visible minority status. By contrast, ideological indicators are much more consistently significant. Economic conservatism is significant in all cities but Mississauga (which is unique among our case

Table 10.2. Simplified vote choice models – correlates of support for the winning candidate

	Calgary	Montreal	Quebec	Vancouver	London	Mississauga	Toronto	Winnipeg	Significant in % of cities
Demographics									
Gender	+++							+++	12.50
Middle age					+		++		25.00
Old					++		+++		25.00
Income									0.00
Education	+++							+++	37.50
Visible minority	++		+++			−	−−		50.00
Homeowner	+						−		12.50
Ideology									
Economic conservatism	---	−	·	---	+		+++	---	87.50
Social Conservatism	---	---						---	37.50
Economic evaluations									
Retrospective evaluation	+++	---	+++			+++	+++	+++	75.00
Issue importance									
Transit	+++	+			+	++	+++	+	50.00
Property tax	---							+	50.00
Traffic									0.00
Economic development	---		+++		++		+++	+	37.50
City issue 1	---	---			---		+++	---	62.50
City issue 2	++			++					37.50
Variables significant (%)	63.00	37.50	37.50	12.50	37.50	18.80	56.30	50.00	
Pseudo-R2	0.3761	0.2063	0.1097	0.174	0.1449	0.2019	0.1657	0.262	
N	881	553	860	473	623	388	974	713	

cities in that it had only one viable candidate). Social conservatism is less consistently significant; combined, however, 62.5% of the ideology variables are statistically significant. Retrospective economic evaluations are significant in every single election in which an incumbent was contesting the election (75% of cities in total). Finally, issues tend to be more important than socio-demographic indicators but less important than ideology and economic evaluations.

The table also reveals important variation between cities. This is partly a function of sample size: the cities with the most respondents (Calgary and Toronto) have the highest number of significant coefficients, while those at the other end (Mississauga and Vancouver) have the lowest. Still, even in cities with comparable sample sizes, we see considerable variation. For instance, different socio-demographic variables are significant in Calgary when compared to Toronto, social conservatism matters in only one of the two cities, and different issues are important. Similarly, Mississauga and Vancouver do not share a single significant factor. Pseudo-R2 values also vary a great deal by city, ranging from 0.15 in London to 0.38 in Calgary.

Without belabouring the point, these findings suggest great variability in the correlates of vote choice across cities. That is, this standard, bloc-recursive approach to studying vote choice explains the choices of voters in some of Canada's big city elections better than in others. Nevertheless, the patterns that do turn up in Tables 10.1 and 10.2 help us understand which of the theories of mayoral vote choice best fits the eight cities in our analysis. Are mayoral elections in Canada shaped by retrospective evaluations of performance, local cleavages, or ideology and partisanship?

Which "Tradition" Applies to Canada's Big Cities?

Having identified the most important factors in vote choice in our eight cities, we are now in a position to adjudicate among the three theories of urban vote choice outlined earlier: managerial retrospection, cleavages specific to the local level, or ideology and partisanship.

Theory 1: Managerial Retrospection – Is It All about Performance?

As we noted earlier, some urban political scientists have argued that city elections, being non-partisan affairs, are shaped primarily by voters' assessment of the managerial competence and administrative performance of local politicians (Peterson, 1981; Oliver, 2012). We see at least three clear empirical implications of the managerial retrospective

Figure 10.1. Satisfaction and incumbent support

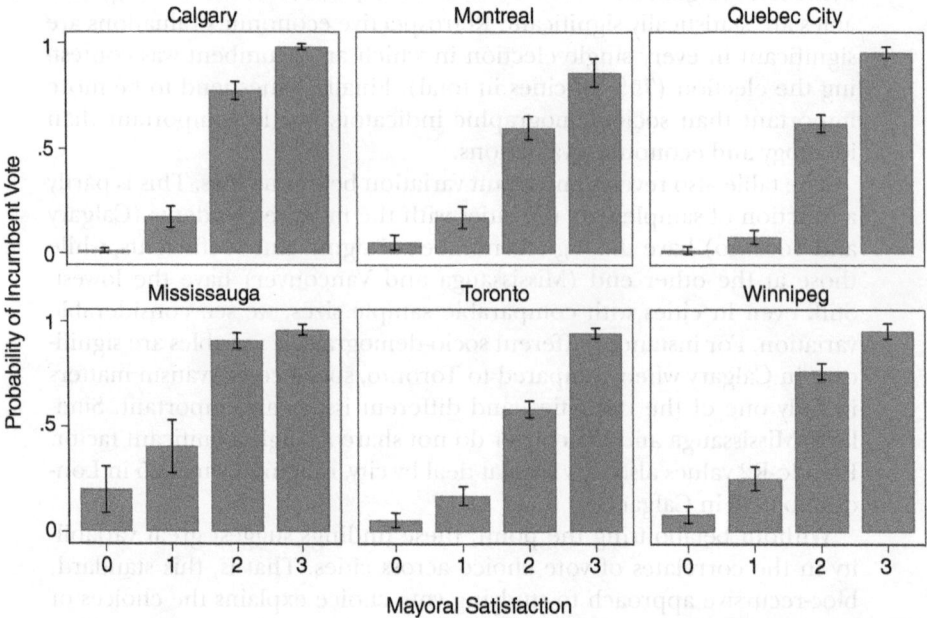

argument. First, in mayoral elections, we should find that an individual's general satisfaction with the mayor's performance is strongly related to mayoral vote choice. Second, because this retrospective assessment is ostensibly based on non-ideological considerations, we should also find that mayoral satisfaction scores are at least partly independent of individual ideology. Finally, in open races without incumbents, we should find that ideology is a relatively unimportant factor in mayoral vote choice.

To test these implications, we begin with Figure 10.1, which summarizes, for each incumbent mayoral race in the CMES data, the predicted probability of voting for the incumbent across four values of mayoral satisfaction: very unsatisfied, somewhat unsatisfied, somewhat satisfied, and very satisfied. The figure reveals that satisfaction is strongly related to vote choice in all instances (at $p < 0.01$); notice especially how the probability of a vote for the incumbent leaps upward in each city as we move from the two unsatisfied categories to the satisfied categories. Given these results, it would not be misleading to characterize many mayoral elections as referendums on the incumbent mayor. Thus far, the data are compatible with the managerial retrospection theory.

But where do these satisfaction scores come from? Is this mayoral "performance assessment" an unbiased, non-ideological assessment of the

Figure 10.2. Left–right ideology and mayoral satisfaction

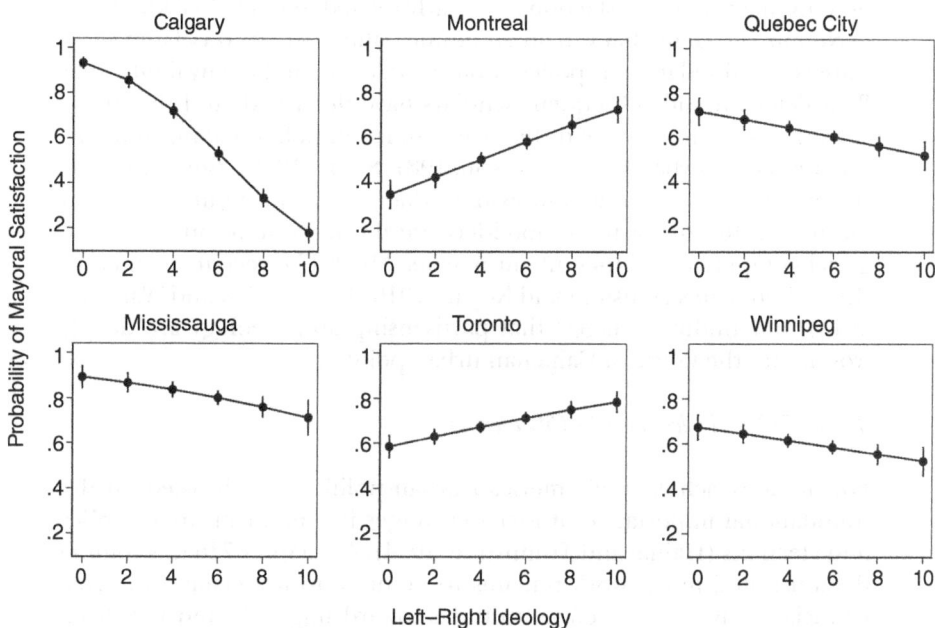

managerial competence of the incumbent mayor? Figure 10.2 provides the beginning of an answer to these questions, reporting the predicted probability of mayoral satisfaction (that is, the probability of selecting either "somewhat" or "very" satisfied), broken down by the respondent's self-reported ideology on a scale ranging from 0 (left) to 10 (right). If municipal vote choices are based on retrospective assessments of managerial performance, rather than ideology, we should see no relationship between ideology and satisfaction: that is, the lines in the graphs should be flat. Each of these predicted probabilities in Figure 10.2 is drawn from a larger model containing socio-demographic variables (age, gender, income, university education, visible minority) along with the respondent's assessment of the performance of the local economy in the past year.

Even when we compare respondents who are otherwise similar across a variety of socio-economic and retrospection variables, Figure 10.2 reveals substantial differences in mayoral satisfaction among individuals with different ideological positions. These differences are not what a managerial retrospection account of city elections would lead us to expect; on this account, we should find that an individual's ideology has little to no relationship to satisfaction with the mayor, especially in a model that controls for socio-demographic characteristics and economic retrospection. Evaluations of satisfaction are clearly related to individual ideology.[5]

No one can deny that Canadian municipalities – even very large cities – are constrained in their policy choices as a result of the "city limits" that Paul Peterson and subsequent scholars have described, and that these constraints often produce distinctive patterns of policy-making and governance at the urban scale (Peterson, 1981; Stone, 1989). But our results suggest that it is a mistake to assume that these constraints turn local elections into non-partisan, non-ideological referendums on the managerial competence of incumbent mayors. Much like recent research in the United States (Einstein and Kogan, 2016; Tausanovich and Warshaw, 2014), our findings suggest that partisanship and ideology are deeply woven into the fabric of Canadian urban politics.

Theory 2: Local Cleavages in City Elections

For decades, scholars of American urban politics have insisted on the foundational importance of racial cleavages in American urban policy and elections (Hajnal and Trounstine, 2014). As chapter 7 in this volume demonstrates, much work remains to be done to understand the role of racial cleavages, as well as attitudes toward linguistic and racialized groups, in Canadian urban politics. This work connects in important ways with wider discussions of race as a concept in Canadian political science (Thompson, 2008).

At the same time, recent comparative research, using fine-grained aggregate electoral and census data in Canada, the United States, and the United Kingdom, has found that racial demographics are much less important for explaining variation in mayoral vote choice in Canadian and British cities relative to cities in the United States (Doering et al., 2020). Our findings in Tables 10.1 and 10.2 generally support this interpretation. Table 10.1 suggests that the average difference between visible minorities and non-visible minorities in mayoral support is 9 percentage points, and Table 10.2 shows that this difference is statistically significant in half of the cities in the analysis. It is important to acknowledge that this finding must be considered preliminary; it relies on a survey question that is better suited to the study of ethnicity and place of origin than to racial cleavages, and grouping "visible minorities" into a single category probably obscures as much as it reveals. Even so, our findings appear to align with previous aggregate research in suggesting that racial cleavages do not structure urban electoral politics in Canada in anything like the same way as in the United States.

Digging into the specific cases in which these cleavages *are* statistically significant also helps clarify this point. While the "visible minority"

variable is significant in half the cities in the CMES study, the gap in mayoral vote support is substantively large in only one city, Calgary, where
Naheed Nenshi, an incumbent mayor of Muslim faith and Indian ances-
try, faced off against Bill Smith, a white Christian. In the closing weeks of
Calgary's mayoral election, with accusations of racism and counter-accu-
sations of "playing the race card" filling the pages of local newspapers
and social media, the salience of race and religion in the election was
especially heightened. As past research in the United States has shown,
racial cleavages are likely to be especially important when candidates
with different racial identities face off against one another (Kaufmann,
2004; Hajnal and Trounstine, 2014; Lucas and McGregor, 2020). The
case of Calgary's election in 2017 suggests that this is likely to be true in
Canadian cities as well. However, our findings suggest that these cleavages have a much less important effect outside of those contests than
they do in the United States.

It is also possible that the socio-demographic cleavages that drive vote
choice in Canada are simply *different* than in the United States. CMES
data provide little evidence that social cleavages are the primary drivers of local electors in this country. Table 10.2 shows that many socio-
demographic indicators are significant, but that there is great variation
between cities and that no factor is significant in more than half the
cities. While socio-demographic factors undoubtedly have some relationship with vote choice, their role appears to be less consistent and less
substantial than that of other variables in the vote choice models.

Theory 3: Ideology

In contrast to the two theories discussed above, we find consistent and
unambiguous evidence for the role of ideology in mayoral vote choice
in Canadian cities. Notice the substantively large gaps in the "ideology"
categories in Table 10.1: an average gap of 14% for social ideology and
23% for economic ideology. These are enormous differences (among
the largest in the table), and they are present in the majority of cities
(the exception is Mississauga, where support for the incumbent mayor
was extremely high across nearly all groups). Coupled with the previous finding that ideology appears to influence retrospective evaluations
of mayoral performance, these data provide compelling evidence that
ideology is of paramount importance in the minds of municipal voters.[6]

Such a finding is hardly surprising given the importance of ideology
at the provincial and federal levels in Canada. However, the findings also
suggest that the *economic* dimension of ideology is especially important
at the municipal scale. Notice that social conservatism, unlike economic
conservatism, was statistically significant in just three elections in the

study. Returning to Table 10.2, notice that economic retrospection – the respondent's evaluation of the state of the local economy in the past year – was significant in six of the eight cities. Thus, while partisanship and ideology are clearly important for understanding mayoral vote choice in Canadian cities, it is the *economic* dimension of ideology that appears to be in the driver's seat in these models.

The Character of Urban Vote Choice in Canada

Our synthesis of the mayoral vote choice analyses in each of the chapters in this volume has uncovered little evidence to support the argument that Canadian city elections are driven by non-ideological assessments of managerial performance. Nor have we found strong support for the view that these elections are distinctively structured by racial (or other socio-demographic) cleavages. In contrast, we have found strong support for the argument that a core cleavage of provincial and federal politics in Canada, namely ideology, is also deeply important at the urban scale.

At first glance, these findings support a "nation-state writ small" interpretation of city elections – or perhaps, given the idiosyncrasies of Canadian federal politics, a "provincial elections writ small" argument. However, the subtleties in the vote choice analyses are as important as the marquee results. As we noted above, it is *economic* conservatism, rather than social conservatism, that is the most powerful variable across all of the models in Table 10.2. Economic retrospection is similarly powerful, second only to economic conservatism as the most consistently significant variable in the analysis. Thus it is the local economy – economic conservatism, economic retrospection, economic development – that appears to be especially salient in city elections.

This distinctive quality of Canadian city elections aligns with recent research outside Canada. In one recent study, for example, Einstein and Kogan (2016) found that a municipality's overall conservatism or liberalism clearly shapes municipal spending, but that more liberal cities do not spend more on redistribution than more conservative cities, nor do they have higher taxes (to fund their increased spending, more liberal cities appear to advocate more strenuously for intergovernmental transfers). Similarly, in a sophisticated study of local governments in the United States, Michael Sances (2021) has found that county-level ideology shapes local government spending, but not in the areas of education and welfare. These studies show that ideology and partisanship influence city politics, but they neither demonstrate nor argue that this makes city politics a mere "microcosm" of politics at other scales. The same is true in Canadian cities.

In each of these studies, and in our own analysis in this chapter, we see what might be called the *revenge of city limits:* the character of municipal policy-making, which plays out in an environment of intermunicipal competition and constrained policy jurisdiction, shapes not only policy-making but also how urban residents think about their mayoral vote choices. Cities are decidedly *not* the nation-state writ small. Yet the ideological attitudes and partisan identities that figure so prominently in voting behaviour at the provincial and federal levels also decisively shape voting behaviour in city politics. Voters do not switch off their ideology or partisanship in city elections. But in city elections, those attitudes and identities are channelled through the constraints of city limits.

What's Next?

The study of local elections is crucial to our development of a holistic understanding of Canadian electors. The arguments and analyses in this book are just the beginning of the many potential uses of the CMES data. Much work remains to be done. For starters, urban political scientists – along with students of political behaviour more generally – will benefit from analyses that divide CMES data not by city but by theme, leveraging both the sample size and the comparative potential of the data to explore issues such as turnout, partisanship, retrospective voting, and strategic voting at the municipal scale. Large-sample datasets such as the CMES also make it possible to explore attitudes and behaviour among important subgroups in the population, such as specific racial or ethnic communities. These thematic and subgroup analyses will reveal important features of urban elections and municipal political behaviour that are currently not well understood.

Urban political scientists also need to turn their attention to *council* elections. Nearly everything we know about municipal elections and voting in both Canada and the United States is about *mayoral* elections. But mayoral elections – high-profile, city-wide contests that often involve competing visions for the city as a whole – may prove to offer a misleading picture of municipal elections more generally, the overwhelming majority of which are for City Council positions. While the past focus on mayoral elections has been understandable for practical reasons, datasets such as the Toronto Election Study and the CMES make it possible to systematically explore patterns of council-level vote choice for the first time. Understanding these council elections is a vital task for scholars of urban electoral politics.

We are also excited about the potential for large individual-level datasets to contribute to an important emerging research agenda on urban political geography. The maps in each of the chapters in this volume provide a preliminary look at geographic variation in mayoral vote choice across each of our case cities, and even at the coarse-grained scale of city wards, we see consistent spatial variation. These findings align with recent comparative research on urban political geography that uses aggregate election results and census data to identify spatial cleavages in Canadian city elections (Doering et al., 2020). Combining individual-level data with aggregate patterns will provide new insights into the ways in which urban political attitudes and identities are spatially patterned. They may even help us understand the relative importance of "sorting" (similar individuals choosing to settle in particular neighbourhoods) and "neighbourhood effects" (attitudinal or identity change resulting from the qualities of our distinctive local environments) in producing the spatial patterning that is visible in the maps in this book and in other analyses.

Finally, we believe that explicit comparison across *levels* of government will provide deeper insights into the questions we have explored in this chapter about the distinctiveness of urban politics and political behaviour and the contexts in which individuals think differently about their municipal vote than they do about their provincial or federal decisions. The CMES contains a wide range of questions that are identical to questions in the Canadian Election Study, enabling municipal–federal comparison; future provincial election studies, to be carried out by the Consortium on Electoral Democracy in the coming years, will provide additional leverage for this multi-level work. Ultimately, a comparative research agenda on urban elections may lead to what might be called a multi-level panel study, in which scholars track the same individuals across elections at each scale of electoral politics – municipal, provincial, and federal. There would be much to be learned from this multi-level analysis about the distinctiveness of urban politics and the factors that shape individual political behaviour across scales.

NOTES

1 Some portions of this section are drawn from Lucas and McGregor (2019).
2 The "localist thesis" has also been challenged in urban political science more generally by public policy scholars (Sapotichne et al., 2007) and by political scientists who emphasize the ways that cities are structured by state and federal regulatory environments and embedded in regional, continental, and global flows of capital and ideas (Brenner, 2009). We focus here on the more specific issue of the localist thesis in urban *electoral* politics.

3 For any groups involving more than two categories, the gap is calculated as the absolute average difference between every group and every other group. For instance, the economic ideology gap is the average gap between conservatives/moderates, conservatives/liberals, and moderates/liberals across all eight cities. The groups are coded as follows. Age: 18–34, 45–64, above 65; Income: above and below $100K. Gender: men and women. Education: no university education, university education. Visible minority: visible minority or Caucasian. Homeowner: renter or homeowner. Social conservatism and economic conservatism: social/economic conservative vs social/economic moderate vs social/economic liberal. Retrospection: worse, same, better. Issue importance: low (0–3), medium (4–6), high (7–10).

4 Recall that two of the issue indicators are unique to each city. The city-specific issues are: Calgary: Calgary Flames arena and campaign finance; Montreal: environmental protection and family services; Quebec: immigration, management style of Labeaume; London: bus rapid transit and social services; Mississauga and Toronto: crime and community safety and housing affordability; Winnipeg: Portage and Main plebiscite and crime and community safety.

5 While this is not a causal claim, and without denying the importance of leadership cues, we think it is much more common that ideology affects performance evaluation than that performance evaluation affects respondents' ideology.

6 Though most local elections in Canada are non-partisan (and those that are partisan have party systems that do not match those that exist either provincial or federally), we know that individual partisanship influences mayoral vote choice. Using the same method employed to produce Table 10.1, we compared federal partisan groups to one another with respect to mayoral vote choice. The magnitude of these gaps is consistently large: 30 points for Liberal vs Conservative partisans, 23 points for Liberal vs NDP partisans, and 36 points for Conservative vs NDP partisans.

REFERENCES

Barreto, M. A. (2007). Sí se puede! Latino candidates and the mobilization of Latino voters. *American Political Science Review, 101*(3), 425–441. https://doi.org/10.1017/S0003055407070293

Brenner, N. (1999). Globalisation as reterritorialisation: The re-scaling of urban governance in the European Union. *Urban Studies, 36*(3), 431–451. https://doi.org/10.1080%2F0042098993466

Brenner, N. (2009). Is there a politics of "urban" development? Reflections on the US case. In *The city in American political development* (pp. 121–140). Routledge.

Collet, C. (2005). Bloc voting, polarization, and the panethnic hypothesis: The case of Little Saigon. *Journal of Politics, 67*(3), 907–933. https://doi.org/10.1111/j.1468-2508.2005.00345.x

Crowder-Meyer, M., Gadarian, S. K., & Trounstine, J. (2019). Voting can be hard, information helps. *Urban Affairs Review.* https://doi.org/10.1177/1078087419831074

Cutler, F., & Matthews, J. S. (2005). The challenge of municipal voting: Vancouver 2002. *Canadian Journal of Political Science, 38*(2), 359–382. https://doi.org/10.1017/s0008423905040151

Dahl, R. (1961). *Who governs? Democracy and power in an American city.* Yale University Press.

Doering, J. (2019). Ethno-racial appeals and the production of political capital: Evidence from Chicago and Toronto. *Urban Affairs Review.* https://doi.org/10.1177/1078087419833184

Doering, J., Silver, D., & Taylor, Z. (2020). The spatial articulation of urban political cleavages. *Urban Affairs Review.* https://doi.org/10.1177%2F1078087420940789

Einstein, K. L., & Kogan, V. (2016). Pushing the city limits: Policy responsiveness in municipal government. *Urban Affairs Review, 52*(1), 3–32. https://doi.org/10.1177/1078087414568027

Enos, R. (2017). *The space between us.* Cambridge University Press.

Fischel, W. A. (2005). *The homevoter hypothesis.* Harvard University Press.

Hajnal, Z., & Trounstine, J. (2014). What underlies urban politics? Race, class, ideology, partisanship, and the urban vote. *Urban Affairs Review, 50*(1), 63–99. https://doi.org/10.1177/1078087413485216

Kaufmann, K. M. (2004). *The urban voter.* University of Michigan Press.

Liu, B. (2003). Deracialization and urban racial contexts. *Urban Affairs Review, 38*(4), 572–591. https://doi.org/10.1177/1078087402250370

Liu, B., & Vanderleeuw, J. M. (2007). Race rules: Electoral politics in New Orleans, *1965–2006.* Lexington Books.

Lucas, J. (2016). Patterns of urban governance: A sequence analysis of long-term institutional change in six Canadian cities. *Journal of Urban Affairs, 39*(1), 68–90. https://doi.org/10.1111/juaf.12291

Lucas, J. & McGregor, R. M. (2020). Are city elections unique? Perceptions of electoral cleavages and social sorting across levels of government. *Electoral Studies.* https://doi.org/10.1016/j.electstud.2020.102165

McGregor, R. M., Moore, A. A., & Stephenson, L. B. (2016). Political attitudes and behaviour in a non-partisan environment: Toronto 2014. *Canadian Journal of Political Science, 49*(2), 311–333. https://doi.org/10.1017/S0008423916000573

Ogorzalek, T. (2018). *The cities on the hill: How urban institutions transform national politics.* Cambridge University Press.

Oliver, J. E. (2012). *Local elections and the politics of small-scale democracy.* University of Chicago Press.

Peterson, P. (1981). *City limits.* University of Chicago Press.

Sances, M. W. (2018). Ideology and vote choice in US mayoral elections: Evidence from Facebook surveys. *Political Behavior, 40*(3), 737–762. https://doi.org/10.1007/s11109-017-9420-x

Sances, M. W. (2021). When voters matter: The limits of local government responsiveness. *Urban Affairs Review, 57*(2), 402–427. https://doi.org/10.1177/1078087419878812

Sapotichne, J., Jones, B. D., & Wolfe, M. (2007). Is urban politics a black hole? Analyzing the boundary between political science and urban politics. *Urban Affairs Review, 43*(1), 76–106. https://doi.org/10.1177%2F1078087407302901

Stephenson, L. B., McGregor, R. M., and Moore, A. A. (2018). Sins of the brother: Partisanship and accountability in Toronto, 2014. In S. Breux & J. Couture (Eds.), *Accountability and responsiveness at the municipal level: Views from Canada* (pp. 23–48). McGill–Queen's University Press.

Stone, C. N. (1989). *Regime politics: Governing Atlanta 1946–1988.* University Press of Kansas.

Tausanovitch, C., & Warshaw, C. (2014). Representation in municipal government. *American Political Science Review, 108*(3), 605–641. https://doi.org/10.1017/S0003055414000318

Thompson, D. (2008). Is race political? *Canadian Journal of Political Science, 41*(3), 525–547. https://doi.org/10.1017/S0008423908080827

Warshaw, C. (2019). Local elections and representation in the United States. *Annual Review of Political Science, 22*(1), 1–19. https://doi.org/10.1146/annurev-polisci-050317-071108

Appendix I: CMES Codebook – Relevant Survey Questions

We present below the CMES survey questions used in the analyses contained in this volume. Questions are present in the order in which they were asked in the respective surveys (pre- and post-election).

Pre-election Survey

Age

In what year were you born?

Please enter your year of birth in the box below.

- ○ Box provided
- ○ Prefer not to say

Mayoral Vote Intention

Which mayoral candidate do you think you will vote for?

- ○ Names indicated
- ○ Don't know or haven't decided

Councillor Vote Intention

Which City Council candidate do you think you will vote for in your ward?

- ○ Names indicated
- ○ Don't know or haven't decided

Plebiscite Opinion (Winnipeg only)

Do you support the opening of Portage & Main to pedestrian crossings?

○ Yes
○ No
○ Don't know/prefer not to answer

Satisfaction with Elected Officials

How satisfied are you with the performance of:

	Very satisfied	Somewhat satisfied	Somewhat unsatisfied	Very unsatisfied	Don't know
The current Mayor	○	○	○	○	○
Your current City Councillor	○	○	○	○	○

Political Identity (Vancouver only)

When it comes to (municipal) politics, do you think of yourself as (choose the one that best applies):

○ Liberal
○ Left-wing
○ Progressive
○ Libertarian
○ Right-wing
○ Conservative
○ None of the above
○ Don't know

Group Expectations (Vancouver only)

How do you think other [insert response from previous, unless the response was "none of the above", in which case insert nothing] Vancouverites would approve if you said you opposed lowering rental and housing prices in your neighbourhood in order to combat housing affordability:

- ○   0 – They would strongly disapprove
- ○   ...
- ○   5 – They would neither approve nor disapprove
- ○   ...
- ○   10 – They would strongly approve

Donation Experiment (Vancouver only)

As part of this study we are going to give $500 to the campaign of one of the mayoral candidates. We will choose the candidate at random but you get to vote on whether or not we include the following statement with the donation: "With this contribution, we ask that if elected you enact policies to lower rental and housing prices in my neighbourhood." The statement will be included with the donation if a majority of 1000 survey respondents vote for it. Would you like this statement included or not?:

- ○   Yes
- ○   No
- ○   Don't know

Federal Partisanship

In FEDERAL politics, do you usually think of yourself as a:

- ○   Liberal
- ○   Conservative
- ○   NDP
- ○   Green
- ○   Bloc (cities in Quebec only)
- ○   Other
- ○   None of the above
- ○   Don't know

Strength of Federal Partisanship

[if selected a party in previous question]

How strongly do you identify with that party?

- ○   Very strongly
- ○   Fairly strongly

o   Not very strongly
o   Don't know

Provincial Partisanship

In PROVINCIAL politics, do you usually think of yourself as a:

o   List parties – varies by province
o   None of the above
o   Don't know

Strength of Provincial Partisanship

[if selected a party in previous question]

How strongly do you identify with that party?

o   Very strongly
o   Fairly strongly
o   Not very strongly
o   Don't know

Municipal Partisanship (Montreal, Quebec, and Vancouver only)

In MUNICIPAL politics, do you usually think of yourself as a:

o   List parties
o   None of the above
o   Don't know

Strength of Municipal Partisanship

[if selected a party in previous question]

How strongly do you identify with that party?

o   Very strongly (1)
o   Fairly strongly (2)
o   Not very strongly (3)
o   Don't know (9)

Feelings toward Groups

How do you feel about each of the following groups? Please use the sliders to indicate your feelings on a scale from 0 to 100, where zero means you REALLY DISLIKE the group and one hundred means you REALLY LIKE the group.

Racial Minorities

○ 0 ... 100
○ Don't know

Immigrants

○ 0 ... 100
○ Don't know

Muslims

○ 0 ... 100
○ Don't know

Government Impact

Governments at all levels make decisions that have the potential to impact the lives of citizens. Please indicate how much impact each level of government has upon your quality of life.

	A lot	Some	Not very much	None	Don't know
Municipal	○	○	○	○	○
Provincial	○	○	○	○	○
Federal	○	○	○	○	○

Federal Partisanship Association

Which FEDERAL political party, if any, would you associate with each of the following mayoral candidates?

	For each candidate
None	○
Conservative Party of Canada	○
Green Party of Canada	○
Liberal Party of Canada	○
New Democratic Party of Canada	○
Other federal party	○
Don't know	○

Candidate Ratings

How do you feel about each of the following mayoral candidates? Please use the sliders to indicate your feelings on a scale from 0 to 100, where zero means you REALLY DISLIKE the candidate and one hundred means you REALLY LIKE the candidate. [0 and 100 should be on opposite sides of the sliders; only allow 1 answer]

Technical note: Separate variables have been created for each city.

For each candidate

o   0 … 100
o   Don't know

Candidate "Likes"

We would like to know if there is anything in particular that you LIKE about the candidates.

For each of the candidates below, please indicate up to three things that you LIKE about them, if anything.

For each candidate:

o   There is nothing I LIKE about this candidate
o   Open ended box
o   Don't know

Candidate "Dislikes"

We would like to know if there is anything in particular that you DISLIKE about the candidates.

For each of the candidates below, please indicate up to three things that you DISLIKE about them, if anything.

For each candidate:

o   There is nothing I DISLIKE about this candidate
o   Open ended box
o   Don't know

Chances of Winning

What are the following candidates' chances of winning the mayoral race? Please use the sliders to indicate your expectations on a scale from 0 to 100, where zero means the candidate has NO CHANCE of winning, and one hundred means the candidate is CERTAIN TO WIN. [0 and 100 should be on opposite sides of the sliders; only allow one answer]

Technical note: Separate variables have been created for each city.

For each candidate:

○ 0 … 100
○ Don't know

Respondent Ideology

In politics people sometimes talk of left and right. Where would you place yourself on a scale from 0 to 10, where 0 means left and 10 means right?

Left					Centre					Right	
0	1	2	3	4	5	6	7	8	9	10	Don't know
○	○	○	○	○	○	○	○	○	○	○	○

Candidate Ideology

Using the same scale, where would you place the following mayoral candidates?

	Left					Centre					Right	
	0	1	2	3	4	5	6	7	8	9	10	Don't know
Candidates listed	○	○	○	○	○	○	○	○	○	○	○	○

Issue Importance

How important are each of the following issues to you in this election? Please indicate each issue's importance on a 0–10 scale, where 0 means not at all important and 10 means extremely important.

	Not at all important (0)	1	2	3	4	5	6	7	8	9	Extremely important (10)	Don't know
A: Public Transit	O	O	O	O	O	O	O	O	O	O	O	O
B: Property Taxes	O	O	O	O	O	O	O	O	O	O	O	O
C: Traffic and Congestion	O	O	O	O	O	O	O	O	O	O	O	O
D: Economic Development	O		O	O	O	O	O	O	O	O	O	O
E: City specific #1	O		O	O	O	O	O	O	O	O	O	O
F: City specific #2	O		O	O	O	O	O	O	O	O	O	O

Opinion of Ranked Ballots

London is the first city in Ontario to use ranked ballots for its election. In your opinion, is this a good change, a bad change, or will it not matter?

- O A good change
- O A bad change
- O It won't matter
- O Don't know

Retrospective Economic Evaluations

Over the past year has the economy in the following places gotten better, gotten worse, or stayed about the same?

	Better	Worse	Stayed about the same	Don't know
[City Name]	O	O	O	O

2014 Mayoral Vote Choice (Toronto only)

For which mayoral candidate did you vote for in the 2014 Toronto mayoral election?

- O Olivia Chow
- O Doug Ford
- O John Tory
- O Other
- O Don't know/Don't remember

Interest in Politics

How interested are you ...

	Not at all interested (0)	1	2	3	4	5	6	7	8	9	Very interested (10)	Don't know
in Municipal politics?	O	O	O	O	O	O	O	O	O	O	O	O
in Provincial politics?	O	O	O	O	O	O	O	O	O	O	O	O
in Federal politics?	O	O	O	O	O	O	O	O	O	O	O	O

Voting a Duty or Choice

People have different views about voting. For some, voting is a DUTY. They feel that they should vote in every election. For others, voting is a CHOICE. They only vote when they feel strongly about that election.

For you personally, is voting FIRST AND FOREMOST a DUTY or a CHOICE at the Municipal, Provincial and Federal levels?

	Duty	Choice	Don't know
Municipal	O	O	O
Provincial	O	O	O
Federal	O	O	O

Opinions of Reduction in Size of City Council (Toronto only)

Do you strongly agree, somewhat agree, somewhat disagree, or strongly disagree with each of the following statements?

	Strongly agree	Somewhat agree	Somewhat disagree	Strongly disagree	Don't know
It is a good thing that Toronto City Council has been reduced from 47 to 25 councillors.	O	O	O	O	O

Education

What is the highest level of education that you have completed?

- No schooling
- Some elementary school
- Completed elementary school
- Some secondary/high school
- Completed secondary/high school
- Some technical, community college
- Completed technical, community college
- Some university
- Bachelor's degree
- Master's degree
- Professional degree or doctorate
- Prefer not to say/Don't know

Immigrant Status

Were you born in Canada?

- Yes
- No
- Prefer not to say/Don't know

Visible Minority Status

To which ethnic or cultural group or groups do you belong? Please select up to two options.

- Canadian
- American
- Mexican
- Caribbean (for example, Jamaican, Haitian, etc.)
- Aboriginal (for example, Cree, Métis, etc.)
- Other North American
- Central American (for example, Nicaraguan, Panamanian, etc.)
- Brazilian
- Argentinian
- Other South American (for example, Chilean)

- ○ Northern African (for example, Egyptian, Algerian, etc.)
- ○ Central African (for example, Chadian, Congolese, etc.)
- ○ Eastern African (for example, Somali, Kenyan, etc.)
- ○ Western African (for example, Nigerian, Ghanaian, etc.)
- ○ Southern African (for example, South African, Namibian, etc.)
- ○ Mainland Chinese
- ○ Hong Kong Chinese
- ○ Korean
- ○ Other East Asian (for example, Japanese, Taiwanese, etc.)
- ○ Indian
- ○ Tamil
- ○ Pakistani
- ○ Other South Asian (for example, Nepalese, Bangladeshi, etc.)
- ○ Filipino
- ○ Other South East Asian (for example, Vietnamese, Cambodian, etc.)
- ○ Persian/Iranian
- ○ Other Middle-eastern/Southwest Asian (for example, Arabian, Israeli, Afghani, etc.)
- ○ British (English, Irish, Scottish, Welsh)
- ○ French
- ○ Other Northern European (for example, German, Dutch, etc.)
- ○ Italian
- ○ Portuguese
- ○ Other Southern European (for example, Spanish, Greek, etc.)
- ○ Polish
- ○ Russian
- ○ Ukrainian
- ○ Other Eastern European (for example, Czech, Romanian, etc.)
- ○ Australian/New Zealander
- ○ Other Oceanian (for example, Papua New Guinean)
- ○ Other ethnic or cultural group [OPEN ENDED]
- ○ Prefer not to say/Don't know

Home Ownership

Do you or someone else in your household own your home?

- ○ Yes
- ○ No
- ○ Prefer not to say

Gender

Are you:

○ Male
○ Female
○ Other/gender non-binary
○ Prefer not to say

Income

The confidentiality of your responses to this survey is guaranteed, and knowing the approximate income of respondents helps researchers to identify important patterns and trends.

Which of the following best indicates your annual household income before taxes?

○ Less than $25,000
○ $25,000–$49,999
○ $50,000–$74,999
○ $75,000–$99,999
○ $100,000–$124,999
○ $125,000–$149,999
○ $150,000–$174,999
○ $175,000–$199,999
○ $200,000 or more
○ Prefer not to say/Don't know

Post-Election Survey

Voter Turnout

In each election we find that a lot of people were not able to vote because they were not registered, they were sick, or they did not have time. Others do not want to vote.

Did you vote in the recent municipal election? Please select the statement that best describes you.

○ I did not vote in the election
○ I thought about voting but didn't
○ I usually vote but didn't in that election
○ I am sure I voted in the election
○ Don't remember/Don't know

Vote Choice

All cities but London:

Which mayoral candidate did you vote for?

○ Candidates listed
○ Don't know/Don't remember

London:

How did you rank the mayoral candidates on your ballot? Recall that you had the option to choose up to 3 candidates.

○ Candidates listed
○ Don't know/Don't remember

Vote Choice under First Past the Post

If the voting method was the same as in 2014, and you were asked to vote for ONE mayoral candidate, who would that have been? (London only)

○ Candidates listed
○ Don't know/Don't remember

Council Vote Choice

Which City Council candidate did you vote for in your ward?

○ Names indicated
○ Don't know/Don't remember

Voter Turnout in Federal Election

Thinking back, did you vote in the 2015 Canadian FEDERAL election?

○ I did not vote in the election
○ I thought about voting but didn't
○ I usually vote but didn't in that election
○ I am sure I voted in the election
○ I could not vote/I was not eligible
○ Don't remember/Don't know

Attention to Politics

On a scale of 0–10, how much attention did you pay to ...

	None (0)	1	2	3	4	5	6	7	8	9	A lot (10)	Don't know
The mayoral election campaign	O	O	O	O	O	O	O	O	O	O	O	O
The campaign for City Council in your ward	O	O	O	O	O	O	O	O	O	O	O	O

Political Views Battery 1

For each statement below, please indicate if you strongly agree, somewhat agree, somewhat disagree, or strongly disagree.

	Strongly agree	Somewhat agree	Somewhat disagree	Strongly disagree	Don't know
Government should leave it entirely up to the private sector to create jobs.	O	O	O	O	O
Government should see to it that everyone has a decent standard of living.	O	O	O	O	O
More should be done to reduce the gap between the rich and poor in Canada.	O	O	O	O	O
Society would be better off if more women stayed home with their children.	O	O	O	O	O

Political Views Battery 2

For each statement below, please indicate if you strongly agree, agree, disagree, or strongly disagree.

	Strongly agree	Somewhat agree	Somewhat disagree	Strongly disagree	Don't know
The gender composition of City Council should reflect the gender composition of the population. (i.e. roughly 50% of the population is female, so 50% of councillors should also be female).	O	O	O	O	O
The racial composition of City Council should reflect the racial composition of the population.	O	O	O	O	O

Mandate to Govern? (London only)

Group 1: London's new mayor, Ed Holder, won 34.2% of support on the first round of ballots. Do you think he has a mandate to govern London?

Group 2: London's new mayor, Ed Holder, received 58.8% of support on the final round of counting ballots, after lower placed candidates were eliminated. Do you think he has a mandate to govern London?

O Yes
O No
O Don't know

Donations and Lawn Signs

In the past five years, have you engaged in any of the following activities?

	Yes	No	Prefer not to say
Made a donation to a FEDERAL political party or candidate?	O	O	O
Made a donation to a PROVINCIAL political party or candidate?	O	O	O
Made a donation to a MUNICIPAL party or candidate?	O	O	O
Displayed an election campaign sign for a FEDERAL party or candidate?	O	O	O
Displayed an election campaign sign for a PROVINCIAL party or candidate?	O	O	O
Displayed an election campaign sign for a MUNICIPAL party or candidate?	O	O	O

Appendix II: Full Model Results – Vote Choice Models

In each chapter, we provided a visual summary of our mayoral vote choice models by plotting the estimated marginal effects in a coefficient plot. In this appendix we provide complete tables of results. Each table reports marginal effects drawn from logit models of vote choice, where the dependent variable = 1 if the respondent voted for the winning mayoral candidate, and the dependent variable = 0 if the respondent voted for another mayoral candidate.

Calgary

	Model A		Model B		Model C		Model D	
Female	2.4	(3.6)	−5.1	(3.2)	−4.5	(3.2)	−0.7	(3.0)
35–64	−17.3***	(4.9)	−10.5**	(4.1)	−8.1**	(3.9)	−5.5	(3.8)
65+	−23.7***	(5.1)	−14.1***	(4.4)	−9.5**	(4.3)	−6.6	(4.1)
High income	0.5	(4.1)	0.6	(3.5)	0.3	(3.5)	−0.2	(3.2)
University educated	15.5***	(3.6)	13.5***	(3.2)	12.4***	(3.1)	9.8***	(3.0)
Visible minority	6.3	(5.6)	6.2	(5.2)	7.4	(4.8)	9.2**	(4.3)
Homeowner	−12.1**	(5.0)	−1.4	(4.3)	−1.9	(4.2)	7.9*	(4.1)
Economic conservatism	–	–	−67.0***	(6.2)	−60.2***	(6.2)	−36.7***	(6.3)
Social conservatism	–	–	−48.2***	(7.2)	−41.5***	(7.0)	−33.0***	(6.6)
Economic evaluation	–	–	–	–	22.4***	(3.7)	17.4***	(3.5)
Transit	–	–	–	–	–	–	20.0***	(6.0)
Property tax	–	–	–	–	–	–	−54.9***	(10.4)
Traffic	–	–	–	–	–	–	11.7	(7.7)
Econ. development	–	–	–	–	–	–	−14.4	(8.8)
Arena	–	–	–	–	–	–	−17.7***	(4.4)
Campaign finance	–	–	–	–	–	–	10.9**	(5.4)
Observations	881	–	881	–	881	–	881	–

Standard errors in parentheses.

* $p < 0.10$

** $p < 0.05$

*** $p < 0.01$

Montreal

	Model A		Model B		Model C		Model D	
Female	−0.3	(4.8)	−4.7	(4.7)	−6.4	(4.3)	−6.1	(4.4)
35–64	10.4	(6.5)	7.1	(6.4)	5.4	(6.1)	4.7	(6.0)
65+	−7.5	(7.4)	−11.6	(7.3)	−6.9	(6.8)	−6.3	(6.7)
High income	−16.4***	(4.9)	−11.2**	(4.9)	−6.8	(4.8)	−6.2	(4.8)
University educated	6.3	(4.8)	2.2	(4.7)	6.7	(4.5)	5.5	(4.4)
Visible minority	−10.7	(6.9)	−9.5	(6.7)	−13.9**	(6.7)	−11.9*	(6.6)
Homeowner	−2.8	(5.6)	0.4	(5.4)	−1.7	(5.3)	0.5	(5.6)
Economic conservatism	–	–	−58.5***	(12.5)	−54.4***	(12.6)	−43.7***	(12.7)
Social conservatism	–	–	−19.8	(12.5)	−35.9***	(11.3)	−33.4***	(11.1)
Economic evaluation	–	–	–	–	−45.6***	(5.9)	−46.1***	(5.6)
Transit	–	–	–	–	–	–	20.8*	(11.2)
Property tax	–	–	–	–	–	–	−7.4	(11.1)
Traffic	–	–	–	–	–	–	10.7	(11.1)
Econ. development	–	–	–	–	–	–	−31.7**	(14.9)
Environmental protection	–	–	–	–	–	–	15.7	(13.5)
Family services	–	–	–	–	–	–	9.1	(11.7)
Observations	553	–	553	–	553	–	553	–

Standard errors in parentheses.

* $p < 0.10$

** $p < 0.05$

*** $p < 0.01$

Quebec City

	Model A		Model B		Model C		Model D	
Female	4.1	(3.6)	1.3	(3.7)	2.4	(3.6)	3.5	(3.5)
35–64	−3.2	(5.3)	−4.5	(5.2)	−4.1	(5.2)	−4.0	(5.3)
65+	9.1	(5.9)	5.7	(6.0)	1.8	(5.8)	1.2	(5.9)
High income	3.4	(4.0)	5.5	(4.0)	3.8	(3.9)	2.2	(3.9)
University educated	2.2	(3.7)	−0.2	(3.8)	−0.9	(3.7)	−0.9	(3.7)
Visible minority	34.2***	(12.9)	33.7***	(12.4)	31.9***	(11.6)	33.1***	(11.2)
Homeowner	−5.5	(4.6)	−3.0	(4.6)	−2.8	(4.4)	0.1	(4.4)
Economic conservatism	–	–	−37.0***	(8.5)	−21.4**	(8.9)	−16.3*	(9.4)
Social conservatism	–	–	7.5	(9.7)	9.3	(9.5)	9.6	(9.9)
Economic evaluation	–	–	–	–	44.3***	(5.2)	41.1***	(5.3)
Transit	–	–	–	–	–	–	7.5	(6.6)
Property tax	–	–	–	–	–	–	−20.3**	(9.7)
Traffic	–	–	–	–	–	–	−9.8	(8.8)
Econ. development	–	–	–	–	–	–	36.7***	(12.3)
Immigration	–	–	–	–	–	–	−15.1*	(8.4)
Management style of Labeaume	–	–	–	–	–	–	5.4	(6.3)
Observations	860	–	860	–	860	–	860	–

Standard errors in parentheses.

* $p < 0.10$

** $p < 0.05$

*** $p < 0.01$

Vancouver

	Model A		Model B		Model C		Model D	
Female	5.9	(4.8)	0.5	(4.4)	1.3	(4.4)	−0.1	(4.4)
35–64	1.6	(6.4)	2.4	(5.9)	3.0	(6.0)	1.0	(6.3)
65+	−3.2	(7.3)	−0.5	(6.5)	0.4	(6.6)	−2.4	(6.8)
High income	−5.6	(5.2)	−2.7	(5.0)	−2.5	(5.0)	−2.6	(5.0)
University educated	8.2	(5.0)	6.9	(4.8)	6.1	(4.9)	5.9	(4.9)
Visible minority	−1.2	(5.7)	3.1	(5.6)	3.5	(5.6)	7.0	(5.7)
Homeowner	−13.4***	(5.2)	−3.4	(5.1)	−4.6	(5.1)	−4.0	(5.3)
Economic conservatism	–	–	−89.2***	(11.6)	−88.1***	(11.7)	−79.6***	(14.1)
Social conservatism	–	–	−13.0	(10.8)	−11.4	(10.8)	−14.5	(11.1)
Economic evaluation	–	–	–	–	6.7	(5.9)	5.7	(5.9)
Transit	–	–	–	–	–	–	−16.2	(12.5)
Property tax	–	–	–	–	–	–	−8.5	(9.2)
Traffic	–	–	–	–	–	–	12.1	(11.9)
Econ. development	–	–	–	–	–	–	−10.5	(13.6)
Homelessness	–	–	–	–	–	–	31.4***	(12.1)
Affordability	–	–	–	–	–	–	−14.7	(13.1)
Observations	473	–	473	–	473	–	473	–

Standard errors in parentheses.

* $p < 0.10$

** $p < 0.05$

*** $p < 0.01$

London

	Model A		Model B		Model C		Model D	
Female	−5.8*	(3.1)	−1.8	(3.1)	−1.9	(3.1)	−3.6	(3.2)
35–64	9.4	(6.7)	10.9*	(6.4)	10.8*	(6.4)	10.9*	(6.2)
65+	21.5***	(6.2)	21.4***	(5.9)	21.4***	(5.9)	21.8***	(5.8)
High income	1.4	(3.9)	0.8	(3.9)	0.9	(3.9)	0.1	(3.7)
University educated	−6.6*	(3.6)	−3.1	(3.6)	−3.1	(3.6)	−0.2	(3.5)
Visible minority	−5.6	(6.6)	−4.9	(6.3)	−4.8	(6.2)	−6.4	(6.0)
Homeowner	12.3**	(5.2)	10.7**	(5.1)	10.7**	(5.1)	6.7	(5.0)
Economic conservatism	–	–	27.0***	(7.2)	27.0***	(7.2)	15.2*	(8.2)
Social conservatism	–	–	9.9	(8.8)	9.3	(8.9)	−2.3	(9.0)
Economic evaluation	–	–	–	–	−1.5	(4.9)	−1.7	(4.4)
Transit	–	–	–	–	–	–	−1.9	(5.8)
Property tax	–	–	–	–	–	–	15.0*	(8.0)
Traffic	–	–	–	–	–	–	−5.5	(7.7)
Econ. Development	–	–	–	–	–	–	20.4**	(10.1)
Bus rapid transit	–	–	–	–	–	–	−12.5***	(4.6)
Social services	–	–	–	–	–	–	−13.5	(8.2)
Observations	623	–	623	–	623	–	623	–

Standard errors in parentheses.

* $p < 0.10$

** $p < 0.05$

*** $p < 0.01$

Mississauga

	Model A		Model B		Model C		Model D	
Female	−0.7	(4.4)	−2.4	(4.4)	1.0	(4.0)	0.3	(3.9)
35–64	−12.7*	(7.7)	−11.7	(7.3)	−12.4*	(6.5)	−9.6	(6.6)
65+	−4.1	(7.9)	−4.0	(7.5)	−6.9	(6.7)	−4.5	(6.6)
High income	−1.0	(4.6)	−1.3	(4.5)	−1.6	(4.3)	−0.3	(4.1)
University educated	2.3	(4.1)	2.6	(4.2)	−0.3	(3.8)	0.0	(3.7)
Racialized	−11.9***	(4.4)	−11.6***	(4.4)	−9.7**	(4.3)	−10.0**	(4.2)
Homeowner	−2.3	(7.7)	1.3	(8.0)	2.3	(6.9)	3.8	(7.0)
Economic conservatism	–	–	−18.0*	(9.9)	−9.4	(8.3)	−4.2	(9.1)
Social conservatism	–	–	−14.4	(9.4)	−4.7	(9.6)	−2.7	(9.1)
Economic evaluation	–	–	–	–	39.4***	(6.7)	38.3***	(6.9)
Transit	–	–	–	–	–	–	14.5**	(6.9)
Property tax	–	–	–	–	–	–	−1.5	(12.5)
Traffic	–	–	–	–	–	–	−1.2	(11.7)
Econ. development	–	–	–	–	–	–	−8.4	(15.1)
Crime and community safety	–	–	–	–	–	–	2.7	(16.5)
Housing affordability	–	–	–	–	–	–	1.9	(9.3)
Observations	388	–	388	–	388	–	388	–

Standard errors in parentheses.

* $p < 0.10$

** $p < 0.05$

*** $p < 0.01$

Toronto

	Model A		Model B		Model C		Model D	
Female	1.3	(3.6)	5.5	(3.5)	6.9**	(3.5)	5.3	(3.4)
35–64	11.3**	(5.3)	9.0*	(5.0)	10.7**	(5.0)	10.7**	(5.1)
65+	20.8***	(5.4)	18.9***	(5.2)	19.7***	(5.2)	19.9***	(5.4)
High income	6.0	(4.0)	2.7	(3.9)	2.1	(3.8)	0.8	(3.7)
University educated	−14.5***	(3.8)	−10.0***	(3.8)	−11.3***	(3.7)	−7.8**	(3.7)
Visible minority	7.2	(4.4)	7.0*	(4.2)	7.6*	(4.1)	3.4	(4.0)
Homeowner	6.1	(4.3)	4.0	(4.1)	3.1	(4.1)	−7.4*	(4.2)
Economic conservatism	–	–	58.0***	(10.1)	56.9***	(9.9)	25.1**	(10.6)
Social conservatism	–	–	7.8	(10.0)	11.7	(10.1)	−0.9	(10.0)
Economic vealuation	–	–	–	–	14.2***	(5.2)	15.9***	(5.1)
Transit	–	–	–	–	–	–	−10.6	(10.3)
Property tax	–	–	–	–	–	–	25.4***	(7.2)
Traffic	–	–	–	–	–	–	−0.7	(9.9)
Econ. development	–	–	–	–	–	–	19.0**	(9.5)
Crime and community safety	–	–	–	–	–	–	27.6***	(8.6)
Housing affordability	–	–	–	–	–	–	−41.8***	(9.8)
Ward redistricting	–	–	–	–	–	–	−11.7**	(5.6)
Observations	974	–	974	–	974	–	952	–

Standard errors in parentheses.

* $p < 0.10$

** $p < 0.05$

*** $p < 0.01$

Winnipeg

	Model A		Model B		Model C		Model D	
Female	8.6**	(4.0)	6.7*	(3.7)	11.7***	(3.5)	13.9***	(3.4)
35–64	−10.7*	(6.4)	−9.2	(5.8)	−7.7	(5.6)	−5.2	(5.4)
65+	−2.2	(6.6)	−3.0	(5.9)	−2.4	(5.7)	0.7	(5.5)
High income	6.9	(4.4)	5.2	(4.0)	3.4	(3.8)	4.1	(3.8)
University educated	23.9***	(3.6)	18.0***	(3.5)	15.4***	(3.4)	11.6***	(3.3)
Visible minority	−1.4	(5.7)	−0.7	(5.6)	−0.0	(5.1)	2.1	(5.1)
Homeowner	−3.8	(5.6)	1.0	(5.4)	1.8	(5.2)	2.3	(5.4)
Economic conservatism	–	–	−36.5***	(8.1)	−36.6***	(7.5)	−29.7***	(7.9)
Social conservatism	–	–	−47.2***	(9.0)	−31.9***	(8.8)	−24.2***	(8.9)
Economic evaluation	–	–	–	–	41.5***	(5.1)	37.0***	(4.9)
Transit	–	–	–	–	–	–	11.4*	(6.6)
Property tax	–	–	–	–	–	–	−5.9	(8.7)
Traffic	–	–	–	–	–	–	−5.5	(9.1)
Econ. development	–	–	–	–	–	–	20.8*	(10.9)
Crime and community safety	–	–	–	–	–	–	−44.9***	(10.6)
Portage and main referendum	–	–	–	–	–	–	1.8	(5.0)
Observations	713	–	713	–	713	–	713	–

Standard errors in parentheses.

* $p < 0.10$

** $p < 0.05$

*** $p < 0.01$

Contributors

Cameron D. Anderson is an associate professor in the Department of Political Science at the University of Western Ontario. His research interests lie in public opinion, voting behaviour, and Canadian politics.

Éric Bélanger is a professor in the Department of Political Science at McGill University. His research interests include political parties, public opinion, and voting behaviour, as well as Quebec and Canadian politics.

Sandra Breux is an associate professor at the Centre Culture Urbanisation Société of the INRS (Institut national de la recherche scientifique). Her research interests focus on municipal representative democracy and the role of territory on individual behaviour.

Jérôme Couture has a background in political science. His thesis is about municipal elections in Quebec. He is also a specialist in quantitative methods, which he has been teaching for four years at Laval University.

Jean-François Daoust is a lecturer (assistant professor) at the University of Edinburgh. His research interests include political behaviour, public opinion, and comparative and Canadian politics.

Eline A. de Rooij is an associate professor of political science at Simon Fraser University with an interest in individual political behaviour, specifically voting and non-electoral forms of participation. Much of her work uses (field) experimental methods.

Jack Lucas is an associate professor in the Department of Political Science at the University of Calgary. His research is focused on democracy and representation in Canadian cities.

J. Scott Matthews is an associate professor of Political Science at Memorial University of Newfoundland. He studies voting behaviour and public opinion across established democracies, with a particular interest in the impact of information on political decision-making.

R. Michael McGregor is an associate professor in the Department of Politics and Public Administration at Ryerson University. His research interests include political behaviour, local democracy, Canadian politics, and political psychology.

Aaron A. Moore is an associate professor in Political Science at the University of Winnipeg. His interests include the politics and governance of urban development and planning, municipal governance and finance, the governance and finance of infrastructure, municipal elections, and urban public administration.

Mark Pickup is an associate professor in the Department of Political Science at Simon Fraser University. Mark is a specialist in political behaviour, political psychology, and political methodology.

Scott Pruysers is an assistant professor in the Department of Political Science at Dalhousie University. His research focuses on how political parties organize and operate as well as how ordinary individuals participate and engage in electoral politics.

Erica Rayment is an instructor in the Department of Political Science at the University of Calgary. Her research focuses on Canadian parliamentary institutions and women's political representation.

John Santos is a PhD student in the Department of Political Science at the University of Western Ontario. His research interests are voter behaviour and public opinion.

Laura B. Stephenson is a professor in the Department of Political Science at Western University. She specializes in political behaviour, elections, and voting and is co-director of the Consortium on Electoral Democracy.

Erin Tolley is the Canada Research Chair in Gender, Race, and Inclusive Politics and an associate professor of political science at Carleton University. Her research focuses on socio-demographic diversity and representation in Canadian politics.

Index of Issue Importance Variables by City

Index